THE ARMED PEACE

For Val, Ruairi, Elle, PJ and Moya.

THE
ARMED
PEACE

Life and Death After the Ceasefires

BRIAN ROWAN

MAINSTREAM
PUBLISHING

EDINBURGH AND LONDON

First published in Great Britain in 2003 by
MAINSTREAM PUBLISHING (EDINBURGH) LTD
7 Albany Street
Edinburgh EH1 3UG

ISBN 1 84018 754 9

A catalogue record for this book is available from the British Library

Typeset in Gill Sans and Janson Text

Printed in Great Britain by
CPD Wales, Ebbw Vale

Acknowledgements

It was in the week leading up to the historic Good Friday Agreement that I made the mistake of asking my friend and colleague at the BBC Mervyn Jess for his assessment of the negotiations and the prospects for a political breakthrough. I'd decided to ask because my own vision was being blurred by the bombs and the bullets of this period, and I got a typical Jess response – the response of the practical joker – but an assessment that was absolutely spot on in terms of its prediction.

He started to tell me the story of the Comber woman he knew – a Protestant with varicose veins. He was making it up, of course, and that was obvious, but I decided to listen anyway.

The last time she'd had trouble with them, he told me, was in 1974 – the year of the last power-sharing experiment in Northern Ireland. But all these years later, in the run-up to Easter 1998, the woman's veins had 'twitched' again. 'Something's going down,' he told me.

It was an analysis that you would never hear from him on radio or television, and he delivered it with such a typically straight Jess face. A few days later he was boasting of his political insight, and he came back to tell me, 'I told you so', and so he had.

Jess has been one of my touchstones, whose sense of humour has kept me – and others – sane during many moments of pressure. He is one of a number of colleagues whose judgement I value and whom I've come to rely on.

I have been fortunate that I have been able to lift the telephone and seek the advice of journalists such as David McKittrick, Eamonn Mallie, Deric Henderson and Peter Taylor; and fortunate, too, to have the trust of my senior colleagues inside the BBC – the editors Andrew Colman, Kathleen Carragher, Michael Cairns, Angelina Fusco, Lena Ferguson, Eddie Fleming and Jeremy Adams. In my job as the BBC's security editor in Belfast, there are times when I walk a thin line, and there've been occasions when I've needed them to stand up with me and for me, and so they have.

Reporting the 'war', and now the 'peace', is something that just seemed to happen – happen when the BBC's then head of news, John Conway, offered me a three-month contract way back in 1989. It has been a long 14 years since, and very different from my days of sports reporting on the *Sunday News* – the Belfast newspaper on which Jim McDowell gave me my first job in journalism way back in the early 1980s.

Reporting the transition from conflict towards some sort of peace has meant speaking to all sides in Northern Ireland and I want to thank the many sources who assist me in my work each and every day and who've helped me with this book. There are many of them I cannot name – sources inside the IRA, the loyalist organisations, political sources and contacts inside the security forces. I also want to thank those who've given their time to be interviewed for *The Armed Peace*: Gerry Adams, David Ervine, Archbishop Robin Eames, General John de Chastelain, Sir Ronnie Flanagan, Gary McMichael, David Trimble, Michael McGimpsey, Jeffrey Donaldson, Denis Bradley and all the others. This book has been years in the making, and it is a stock-taking exercise – a look at how far we've come since 1994 and the original republican and loyalist ceasefires. It is a story told through many voices and the story of much change – a changing political landscape, change within the various paramilitary organisations and change to the day-to-day life of a place that has been to war and is now looking for peace.

I want to thank Ailsa Bathgate at Mainstream for all her help, and my cousin Marie Therese Hurson – the photographer for *The Armed Peace* – for her help and support. There are also others to thank for many different reasons: Damien Magee, Neal Sutherland, Marinda Hamill, Seamus Kelters, Stephen Grimason, Mark Simpson, Gareth Gordon, Martina Purdy, Mark Devenport, Gwyneth Jones, Robin Walsh, Pat Loughrey, Anna Carragher, Tim Cooke, Tony Maddox, Keith Baker, and so the list goes on. But more than anyone else, I want to thank my family – my wife Val, and my children Ruairi, Elle and PJ who have worried with me and for me. They, more than anyone else, know the pressure of reporting Northern Ireland and of trying to do so by talking to all sides. There have been stand-offs with the 'Provos', the 'Prods' and the 'Peelers' – moments of silence and periods of disagreement. In this place this is something that is bound to happen – something I've come to accept – but we speak again and there is a working relationship. I know how this place is changing. I've seen it happen, seen it with my own eyes, and those who can't aren't looking.

Contents

Introduction

Northern Ireland, Ulster, the North, the Six Counties – May 2003. In this place of many names, the battles are continuing and people are still dying. This is Northern Ireland after the ceasefires, and this is the story of its struggle for peace.

The 'Long War' may well be over. There is no longer the daily routine of death and destruction, but this is a place still trying to escape from its past and still not sure of its future. Here the guns can be silent and the guns can be loud. There is not yet a ceasefire silence – not yet a perfect peace.

The IRA first announced its ceasefire in August 1994. It was to be 'a complete cessation of military operations'. Within weeks, there was a response – delivered in the name of a Combined Loyalist Military Command (CLMC). Back then, this paramilitary leadership spoke for all the main loyalist organisations – the Ulster Defence Association, the Ulster Volunteer Force and the Red Hand Commando – and all three had put their names to a decision to universally cease all 'operational hostilities'. This was to be the new beginning and the start of the journey towards peace.

In the years that have followed, that peace has been far from perfect. The gun has not yet been silenced and the paramilitaries still have a place on the Northern Ireland stage. In 1996, the republican ceasefire collapsed. It was lost in the rubble of the Canary Wharf bomb and buried in the headlines that told of the IRA's return.

For months there had been a stand-off between John Major's Conservative Government and the Republican Movement. The IRA ceasefire had been delivered as a quid pro quo, in the belief that all-party peace talks would quickly follow and that Gerry Adams and Martin McGuinness would be present at the table. But subsequent events didn't run to the republican script. Major demanded that the

IRA give up its guns, the IRA responded by saying any such move would be surrender, and the ceasefire slowly withered on the vine of decommissioning. The loyalist ceasefire also crumbled, perhaps not in the same spectacular fashion as the IRA's London bomb, but there could be no doubt that the UDA, the UVF and the Red Hand Commando had resumed their 'operational hostilities'. Later, the Combined Command itself would fold, the loyalists would fight with each other, splinter factions would emerge and cover names would be used to try to hide their activities.

By July 1997, the IRA ceasefire had been restored. The political landscape had been transformed. The Major Government was gone, Tony Blair was now in Downing Street, Bertie Ahern was the new Irish Taoiseach and the peace process had impetus again. The all-party talks that had been demanded in 1994 took place before any guns were decommissioned and, at last, loyalists, republicans, unionists and nationalists moved into negotiations and towards the historic Good Friday Agreement of April 1998. Since then, hundreds of prisoners have been freed and, as a result of proposals made by a commission headed by the former Conservative Party Chairman Chris Patten, the Royal Ulster Constabulary (RUC) has been replaced by the Police Service of Northern Ireland.

Out of the political agreement of Easter 1998 a power-sharing Executive was born. This was to be the new politics as part of the new peace. For unionists and republicans, however, this has been a difficult partnership in an unhappy political home. Indeed, it has been a Humpty-Dumpty type of government, which more than once has fallen off its Stormont wall. The Ulster Unionist leader David Trimble – the Nobel Peace Prize winner with John Hume in 1998 – took his party into the Executive with Sinn Fein and with Martin McGuinness, but he has refused to stay there in the absence of continuing decommissioning. This particular battle came to be defined within the phrase 'no guns – no government'.

Northern Ireland is a place and a process that is full of such catchphrases. From the defiant writing on the wall that declared 'not a bullet – not an ounce', the IRA eventually moved to put some of its arms beyond use, but within a year of that historic move the power-sharing government was sinking in another political swamp – pulled down, unionists would say, by allegations of republican intelligence gathering at the very heart of the British Government in Northern Ireland. Just months earlier, the IRA had been linked to a robbery at the offices of the Special Branch in Belfast, and now it was being accused of stealing papers from the Northern Ireland Office – papers from the tables of the Secretary of State and the Security Minister. This was all too much for the political process to absorb and the power-sharing government came tumbling down.

This book is the story of the many battles since 1994: the battle over guns and government; the power struggles; the fights and the feuds within loyalism; the emergence of the republican dissidents, who have refused to follow the Adams and McGuinness gospel; the struggles within a divided unionism; and the continuing intelligence war involving the spooks and the spies and the IRA.

There has been a pattern to this process. Sometimes it has been two steps forward and one step backwards; at other times it has been the other way round. In my work for the BBC in Belfast I have reported the 'war', and there have been occasions when I have watched the peace live and die. Reporting that war, from before and then after the ceasefires, has meant talking to all sides: to the 'Provos', to the 'Prods' and to the 'Peelers'. I've had cold tea and heated conversations with them all and in this book I tell the story of the peace process not just through my eyes and in my words but also through their eyes and in their words.

I have watched this place change, and change it has, but the transition from war to peace is not yet complete. *The Armed Peace* charts the journey so far: the ups and downs of peace making and peace building. It has been a bumpy road and one with many bends. In October 2002, as a reaction to the latest allegations of republican intelligence gathering, Tony Blair gave the process a new route map. He wanted to move the paramilitaries beyond their ceasefires and towards what he called 'acts of completion', and he wanted the IRA and the loyalists off the stage. At the time of writing, however, Humpty-Dumpty is still broken and no one has been able to put the power-sharing government back together again.

It has been a long road towards some sort of peace – a journey that is not yet over and a journey through a place where the paramilitaries still live and people still die.

Prologue

THE 'PROVOS'

2 JULY 1992: I was on a road to somewhere and nowhere in a car with a driver I didn't know. My eyes were hidden behind sticky tape and thick dark glasses. Not a word was spoken. Hours earlier, I had been to South Armagh, where three bodies lay dumped in different parts of that bleak countryside. They had been left there by the IRA for all to see – the final humiliation for the 'collaborator'.

The journey ended in an upstairs bedroom of a house, where I was allowed to remove the glasses and the tape. The place had been stripped bare and two men in balaclavas stood before me. I was frisked, as was my friend and colleague Eamonn Mallie, and then the IRA told us why the men on the border had been executed.

The organisation's lengthy statement was written on tissue paper and it took what felt like a lifetime to copy it down. We were glad to get out of there, but, before we did, the tape and the glasses were once more applied to cover our eyes. This was pre-ceasefire, and, back then, this was the way the IRA chose to do its business. For me, this was just one of many contacts with the IRA's P. O'Neill.

THE 'PRODS'

12 OCTOBER 1994: From the window I looked out onto dark streets which had seen killing and which had produced killers. But, here on the Shankill Road – the capital of loyalist Ulster – something was changing.

Three of the men in the room sat at the top table of the Combined Loyalist Military Command (CLMC), a representative each from the Ulster Defence Association (UDA), the Ulster Volunteer Force (UVF) and the Red Hand Commando (RHC). There was speculation that a loyalist ceasefire was close, and they had asked to see me and my colleague from Ulster Television, Ivan Little.

We were joined in the room by Gusty Spence – a convicted killer, but one of the driving forces behind the new direction in which loyalism was now moving. He gave us a statement pointing to an 'unprecedented' news conference scheduled for the following morning – a news conference in which he would have the central role as the paramilitaries declared their intention to 'universally cease all operational hostilities'. A few weeks later, the new political faces in this community would journey from the Shankill to Stormont and to the table of dialogue with British Government officials. This was a whole new experience, and, to quote David Ervine, they felt like 'duds going to play Las Vegas professionals'. Some, including Ervine, have moved into the political mainstream, but others within loyalism have gone back to war. The same Shankill that produced the architects of that Combined Loyalist Military Command ceasefire also produced Johnny Adair – the most prominent and public of the paramilitaries and the man who has most destabilised and stigmatised loyalism in recent years. It took a while, but eventually his own people turned on him and he was caught on the wrong side of the loyalist lines. Adair – the man they dubbed 'Mad Dog' – was now an outcast, rejected by those he once controlled.

THE 'PEELERS'

11 NOVEMBER 2002: The worried looks and the atmosphere in the room told me all I needed to know, and those who were there told me even more – not literally but through their presence. This was a meeting that had come out of nowhere, and here I was with the Special Branch, the CID and the Acting Deputy Chief Constable in the office of a former BBC colleague who is now the director of media and public relations with the Police Service of Northern Ireland (PSNI). They knew I had been digging and they knew I had unearthed some of the secrets of the Special Branch – the secrets of Operation Torsion and how a covert human intelligence source had taken the police deep inside the IRA's hidden files.

These were matters that had not been spoken of publicly. They were the whispered secrets of another world and of a place we don't often see – somewhere inhabited by the Branch and by the spooks and the spies. Those in the room at police headquarters on that Monday afternoon in November knew that I was planning to report my findings and knew that this was imminent. They wanted me to pause – to delay my report for a week – but I refused.

But why was Operation Torsion so important to them? It was so important because it had uncovered alleged IRA intelligence gathering at the very heart of the British Government in Northern Ireland, and in the fall-out from these revelations the power-sharing Executive in Belfast fell.

CHAPTER ONE

Revenge on Castlereagh

'The spooks and the spies and MI5 and all the rest of them, their war is not over.'
Sinn Fein president Gerry Adams, April 2003

'Every time that we use a source, we take a bit of their life.'
Former senior intelligence officer, May 2003

OCTOBER 2002: The eyes and ears of the Special Branch and the British Security Service MI5 were watching and listening to the IRA. They had been inside the organisation's files, read its papers, knew where they had come from, and now they were waiting to make their catch. An informer – a covert human intelligence source – had shown them where to look.

This was Operation Torsion. The Special Branch was using all of its tools – listening and tracking devices, phone taps, surveillance and the information provided by its source – to get deep inside the IRA's hidden files. Eight years may well have passed since the original ceasefire of 1994, but the intelligence war in Northern Ireland was far from over. In this supposed peacetime, the mind games were continuing. The 'Brits', the 'Provos' and the 'Branch' were still playing with each other, still trying to get inside each other's heads and each other's systems.

All of this was far away from the familiar battlefield of old – that battlefield of 3,000 deaths and more. This fight was for supremacy in the area of knowledge, a game of who knew most about the other. For 30 years on the Northern Ireland stage this had been the stuff that usually went on behind the curtain, but in a seven-month period spanning March to October 2002 it all played out in a very public way and plunged the peace process into its deepest crisis yet.

The security assessments for that period suggested that the IRA had been behind enemy lines – inside the Belfast headquarters of the

Special Branch at Castlereagh and inside the Northern Ireland Office (NIO) at Castle Buildings on the Stormont estate. Republicans were reading what was on the desks of the British Secretary of State and the Security Minister, and when this part of the story came out in October 2002, the political process went into free-fall.

This had been building for a long time – for many months before these latest revelations of alleged IRA intelligence gathering at the very heart of the British Government in Northern Ireland. The 'peacetime' IRA, while adhering to its own strict definition of 'a complete cessation of military operations', was still an active army. It had continued to function, and now its very existence was the focus of the latest unionist demand.

The unionists wanted the IRA to disband, but the IRA said this was 'unrealisable'. The unhappy marriage, which in the period following on from the Good Friday Agreement of April 1998 had republicans and unionists as part of a power-sharing Executive in Belfast, was once more in trouble.

David Trimble and his Ulster Unionist ministerial colleagues were about to walk, but the British Government pre-empted that by once more returning Northern Ireland to direct rule from Westminster. The political Humpty-Dumpty that was power-sharing had fallen off the Stormont wall, and it was going to take something bigger than the IRA's complete cessation of military operations to put it back together again. It was at this point that Tony Blair attempted to move the peace process towards 'acts of completion'.

The roots of this latest crisis could be traced back to Saint Patrick's night – 17 March 2002 – and to a robbery in which the Special Branch in Belfast was humiliated. It was a night when some of its most closely guarded secrets were stolen right from under its nose. The raid took place at one of its offices at Castlereagh in the east of the city, in a police complex remembered for all of the controversy surrounding interrogation practices there in the 1970s, when it was the main holding centre for terrorist suspects. Back then it was a place of tight security and a place that would have sent a chill down any and every republican spine. But by 2002 the holding centre had gone, and, with the ceasefire, security had been relaxed.

On Saint Patrick's night, if the security assessments are correct, the IRA took its revenge on Castlereagh. It came back to haunt a place where some of the ghosts of 'the Troubles' still hide. On that Sunday night, its corridors were quiet and lonely. The three men who walked them knew where they were going – to room two-twenty, where a detective constable was on duty. Inside Castlereagh, room two-twenty is no ordinary office, but a place that functions for 24 hours each and every day of the year. This is the hub of the Special Branch operation, a round-the-clock contact point.

At about ten on that Sunday night, the detective constable was overpowered and his office left bare. The raiders made off with an alphabetical list of Special Branch officers and their telephone numbers, the codenames of agents and the names of their police handlers, and a log of 'addresses of interest', which lists the homes of many republicans and loyalists. As a consequence of the robbery, dozens of Special Branch officers were forced to leave their homes.

This was the most embarrassing security breach in the history of the Troubles and at first it had all the appearance of an inside job. The Secretary of State John Reid was in New York at the time and was informed by MI5. In his hotel in the company of his private secretary and his spokesman at the Northern Ireland Office, Robert Hannigan, he smoked heavily and swore a lot as they discussed the implications of the raid. It was decided that Reid would order an inquiry to establish what damage, if any, had been done to national security.

The raid on Castlereagh happened as Sir Ronnie Flanagan was about to step off the policing stage in Northern Ireland and it was the talk of the place a week or so later on 25 March, when the security and political establishment gathered to say farewell to the outgoing Chief Constable.

In the grand setting of the Throne Room at Hillsborough Castle, Reid heaped praise on Flanagan. They were all there to hear his words: the most senior army officer in Northern Ireland at that time, Lieutenant General Alistair Irwin; the British Security Minister Jane Kennedy; Flanagan's deputy, Colin Cramphorn; the Head of Special Branch in Belfast Bill Lowry; and the tall chap in the grey suit, MI5's main man in Northern Ireland, its director and coordinator of intelligence, the man who had called New York those few days earlier with the news of the break-in.

Reid had a lot to thank Flanagan for. His leadership had ensured progress towards the new beginning to policing in Northern Ireland. Flanagan, an RUC man for more than 30 years, had needed all of his powers of persuasion to coax and nurse his force through a painful period of change – change which meant an end to the RUC title, its badge, uniform and flag. On other issues important to the peace process, such as demilitarisation and decommissioning, he could have been awkward and created problems for Reid and his predecessors, but he chose not to be. In the eyes of his republican critics he was a 'securocrat', but on this night in the Throne Room in the castle at Hillsborough he was in the company of friends, and he was praised for his contribution to policing and to the wider peace process.

Before taking over the top police post in Northern Ireland, Flanagan had been Assistant Chief Constable in Belfast, and it was during this period that he became the public face of the force. This was pre-ceasefire, while his officers were still being targeted and murdered by the IRA – officers such as Johnston Beacom and Jackie Haggan. People still remember their names because Flanagan made them remember. In interviews, he made sure that his officers were not allowed to pass as mere statistics on the long list of police dead. He told us about them and their families and this was another of his important contributions.

So, at Hillsborough, he was applauded, but Reid, a Scot with a wicked sense of humour, could not resist the temptation to have a little fun with his security audience. First-time guests were told to feel free to have a look around – to roam the castle – as others had felt free to roam one of 'Ronnie's establishments' those eight days earlier. That night the joke was on the police, but soon Reid would be told that the IRA had infiltrated the Northern Ireland Office. This would be his Castlereagh, and, in terms of the joke, the shoe was now on the other foot.

Five days after that Hillsborough reception, the Castlereagh assessment changed and changed dramatically. No longer were we being told of an inside job. There was a whole new stage now and an entirely different set of actors, including the IRA's director of intelligence – a West Belfast man with a big republican reputation earned during 30 years of 'war'. His involvement goes back to the Maze prison escape in 1983, to the IRA bombing of the British Army's Northern Ireland headquarters at Thiepval Barracks in 1996 and here he was in 2002, still taunting and tormenting the republican enemy. On Saturday, 30 March, he was one of a number of republicans arrested in Belfast and Derry as part of the investigation into the Castlereagh robbery. Only one of those detained was later charged, not with the raid on the Special Branch office, but in connection with alleged IRA intelligence gathering. The organisation's director of intelligence was one of those released without charge, but the security assessment now had the IRA inside the Castlereagh frame and a Special Branch source described it as 'an act of war'.

According to this new assessment, the IRA's 'inside' help came from an American chef Larry Zaitschek – a former employee at Castlereagh – who was inside the police complex on Saint Patrick's night even though he no longer worked there. Zaitschek has categorically denied any involvement in the raid, but Castlereagh investigators sought his extradition from the United States.

In mid-April, more would emerge on the Castlereagh investigation and on why the police were now looking so closely at the IRA. The team of detectives, led by Chief Superintendent Phil Wright, was interested in a network of mobile telephones in use in the period leading up to the robbery and on the night of the raid itself. The phones had since gone quiet; according to sources, they had been destroyed and dumped below ground in a part of West Belfast. Calls to a number of coin boxes in the west of the city also formed part of the investigation and intelligence assessments led the police to believe that the stolen Special Branch documents had been moved from Belfast to Derry and then across the border into the Irish Republic. Police were also interested in the movements of a number of vehicles and people, including the IRA's director of intelligence, in the days before the Castlereagh raid.

On 19 April, Colin Cramphorn – by now Acting Chief Constable – confirmed in a BBC interview that IRA involvement was 'a major line of inquiry'. It was also on this date that news emerged that the IRA still had in its possession information on British Conservative politicians, something the politicians themselves were only told about when the Northern Ireland Office became aware that the BBC report was about to run. The night before, Reid called the MP Quentin Davies – the Conservative Party's Northern Ireland spokesman – to tell him of the find.

In all of this – the Castlereagh raid and the continuing intelligence gathering, including information being collated on British politicians – there were huge political implications. As more and more detail emerged, confidence in the power-sharing arrangements was increasingly undermined.

The IRA itself knew the damage that was being done and moved to try to address concerns. On Sunday, 21 April, I met the IRA's official spokesman. It was a meeting at his request.

We walked on opposite sides of the road. I was on the left and he was behind me on the right. Where we walked, both of us would be known – me from my television news reports, especially at this busy time, and the man on the right because of his republican credentials. He has been around the 'struggle' a long, long time. He whistled and directed me to the left. When we stopped, I bought the coffees and he found a seat at a quiet table. It was one of those fast-food places and it was about noon.

We had met many times before, the last time a fortnight or so previously, when he had dictated a statement from P. O'Neill – a statement confirming the second act of IRA decommissioning, or putting 'arms beyond use' as his organisation prefers to call it.

Ours is a whispered dialogue – a dialogue which takes place well away from listening ears, but there have been a few awkward moments along the way, like one that took place in the booth of a Belfast sandwich bar. In the middle of a briefing, we were joined by an elderly woman who slipped in beside the man from the IRA and, in typical Belfast fashion, ordered him to 'push up there, love'. I suppose it could have been an eavesdropping operation by 'MI-75', but somehow I doubt it. This was just an innocent old woman wanting to rest her weary legs and relax over a cup of warm tea; how was she to know what she had stumbled upon?

On Sunday, 21 April, there were no such interruptions and on this occasion my contact would speak as a senior IRA source. He had a number of points to make:

- The IRA ceasefire remains intact.
- The IRA is not targeting.
- The IRA is no threat to the peace process.
- The IRA did not carry out Castlereagh.
- Some section of British Intelligence did carry it out.
- The arrests and raids [in Belfast and Derry] were used to create a smokescreen.

That denial of involvement in Castlereagh has remained the IRA's public position, but privately some republicans have come close to boasting of the IRA's achievements and of the audacity which took it to the heart of the Special Branch operation in Belfast. The political process survived Castlereagh, but only just, and the revelations that would come in October would prove the final straw.

Not long after the Saint Patrick's night raid, an 'eyes and ears' source working for Special Branch in Belfast provided the lead that showed what the IRA was up to inside the Northern Ireland Office. The source's information eventually took the Special Branch to a place where it found documents it believed had been gathered by the IRA. In the intelligence war, bugging and surveillance would follow as the IRA became the target of Operation Torsion.

In this world of secrets, information is jealously guarded, and, initially, knowledge of this alleged republican intelligence-gathering operation inside the NIO was restricted to a small number of Special Branch officers in Belfast: to Bill Lowry and to those who were handling the informer. Lowry didn't tell the British Security Service

MI5 immediately, but they were brought into the loop at an early stage and their resources were used alongside those of the Special Branch during Operation Torsion. Long before an arrest operation in October, both the Branch and MI5 knew that the IRA had documents which had been taken out of the NIO. They also knew that on its intelligence files the republican organisation had the personal details of hundreds of prison officers. The IRA's files had been seen and copied. At some point and from somewhere during a long monitoring operation, the documents had been removed for a few hours and copied at police headquarters at Brooklyn in Belfast.

What was emerging was arguably bigger and more damaging than the earlier security breach at Castlereagh. When its detail became public, the political process could not absorb any more. What unionists wanted – and indeed had expected – from that process was an end to the IRA, but, now, on the heels of the Special Branch robbery, came yet more allegations of IRA activity. It was more bad news for Trimble and his party colleagues who had been prepared to operate the power-sharing government, as they were undermined by all that the IRA was alleged to have been up to.

Operation Torsion stretched out over a period of some months. The bugging warrants were signed by the British Secretary of State John Reid and at different times in the build-up to arrests in October Lowry brought more of his senior colleagues in the PSNI into the picture. Those with knowledge included Cramphorn, the assistant chief constables Chris Albiston and Alan McQuillan, senior Special Branch officers at police headquarters and the most senior detective in Belfast, Chief Superintendent Phil Wright.

During the summer, in July to be precise, Reid warned the IRA that intelligence gathering and targeting must end. The organisation's adherence to its strict definition of its ceasefire would no longer be good enough. Lowry – who as head of Special Branch in Belfast was in a position to monitor the IRA, and who was still seeing it operate while on ceasefire – believed the organisation had been given enough warnings and as Reid spoke in the House of Commons, the Branch man swore at his television. The police could have moved earlier than October to seize the documents that the IRA had gathered, but a decision was taken to let Operation Torsion breathe. Lowry was hoping that the IRA director of intelligence – the man he believed had masterminded the earlier Castlereagh robbery – would walk into his surveillance net, but he did not. The Special Branch officer would later claim that MI5 did not want arrests made, only the papers recovered. Lowry said he had come under 'constant and consistent pressure' not to take republican 'skulls' along with the documents. What he was suggesting was that

MI5 – knowing all the damage this would cause to the political process – wanted to leave the IRA the space to be able to deny any involvement in the goings-on inside the NIO. But at the end of Operation Torsion documents were seized and four arrests made.

The arrest operation finally came on Friday, 4 October, though it nearly happened earlier. In late September, the Special Branch believed the IRA was about to move its files south of the border and it came close to moving in. Their bugging operation told them that something had been moved and they had to check to see if the documents had also gone. This meant a break-in – using techniques known inside the Branch as 'alternative means of entry'. The papers had not been moved and an arrest operation was postponed. Politically, the timing could have been disastrous. All of this happened on Thursday, 19 September. It was too close to a meeting of the Ulster Unionist Council on 21 September – another difficult meeting for Trimble – and there were fears that revelations of alleged IRA intelligence gathering inside the Northern Ireland Office could finish him off.

The Branch therefore paused and the arrests were delayed for another couple of weeks. The Secretary of State John Reid, who was attending the Labour Party conference, was contacted in Blackpool on Wednesday, 2 October, and told that they were now imminent. He thought they would happen the next day, but the police waited until early on Friday morning. Based on Special Branch and MI5 assessments, Reid had already told the Prime Minister that the IRA had penetrated the Northern Ireland Office, and the British Government was now waiting for the political fall-out.

Among those arrested by the police was a former employee at the NIO and Sinn Fein's head of administration at Stormont, Denis Donaldson, who was charged and subsequently released on bail. One of the party's offices at Parliament Buildings was also searched, but nothing incriminating was found there. It was a raid that happened in a very public way and which involved a significant number of uniformed police officers who arrived at Stormont in armoured Land Rovers. It was all captured on camera and the pictures dominated the day's news coverage. This was something Reid and Northern Ireland's new Chief Constable, Hugh Orde, discussed at a London meeting that Friday afternoon. Sinn Fein was furious and Orde later apologised – not for the search itself but for the way it had been conducted.

In the raids elsewhere in Belfast, hundreds of documents were seized, many of which had been stolen from inside the NIO. A laptop computer, on which the personal details of prison officers were logged, was also discovered. For those of us looking in on that

October morning, this was remarkable stuff, but the Special Branch and MI5 were not surprised. Long before now, they had known precisely what the IRA was holding – both had copies of the organisation's documents and according to one intelligence source, this was not unusual: 'We read their books all the time,' he boasted in a conversation with me.

Indeed, in July, the Special Branch had thought about leaking the details of a significant IRA statement before P. O'Neill passed it to the media. This was the statement in which the IRA apologised for the deaths and injuries of 'non combatants', but the planned Special Branch leak was apparently blocked by the Northern Ireland Office for fear that it would damage the impact or the importance of the IRA statement. The Special Branch may well have wanted to play inside the IRA's head, but others, it seems, were looking at the bigger political picture.

The first public mention of Operation Torsion was made in a series of BBC news reports on 12 November – reports resulting from weeks of research and discussions between the author and a range of sources, security and political. The police had moved to try to delay my reports. Indeed, on the afternoon of Monday, 11 November, I found myself in a room in the company of some of the most senior officers in the Police Service of Northern Ireland and a request was made that I wait for another week.

This had all started back in late July, when over lunch in a Belfast hotel I had been told by a police source that the Special Branch had made requests for bugging warrants to be signed by Reid. I had tucked that piece of information away, but when the arrest operation happened on 4 October, I put two and two together and started asking questions. The most important conversations I had were in the period 21 to 30 October, and it was on a walk through Belfast city centre a few days after that that I briefed the BBC's most senior news editor in Northern Ireland, Andrew Colman, on the undercover operation which had led to those arrests on 4 October and the fall of the power-sharing Executive not long afterwards. Before going to air with the details of the operation, however, there were some final points to be clarified and that would take a little more time and research.

By Monday, 11 November, a decision had been taken to run with our report the following day, but then there was a surprise development. A news conference was called at police headquarters in Belfast – a news conference at which the Acting Deputy Chief Constable, Alan McQuillan, and Chief Superintendent Phil Wright would speak on the Castlereagh and Castle Buildings investigations.

At this conference they told us about the CID investigation codenamed Operation Hezz, but there was no mention of the related but secret Operation Torsion, involving Special Branch and MI5, and all the surveillance that entailed – no mention that the Branch and the spooks had been watching and listening to the IRA and no mention of the informer, the source who had shown them the IRA's hidden documents. So, what was this news conference all about?

Some have suggested it was a pre-emptive strike, something that was done to try to limit the impact of the report that was coming the following day. I don't know if that is true, but I do know that at the very highest levels of the police there was concern about the information I had gathered.

From the enquiries I was making, the PSNI's director of media and public relations, Austin Hunter, would have known that my report was imminent, but, in the background, something else had happened of which I was unaware. On Friday, 8 November, the head of Special Branch in Belfast, Bill Lowry, had reported to McQuillan that he had met me and that I had put questions to him about the operation that had ended in the arrests on 4 October. On 11 November, after the McQuillan and Wright news conference, I asked Hunter if I could use a phone to file my radio news report. There was no signal on my mobile and I needed a landline. It was as a result of this request that I ended up in a room with some of the most senior officers in the PSNI. McQuillan was there along with Wright, and they were joined by Lowry and by Chris Albiston, who was the Assistant Chief Constable in overall charge of the Special Branch and CID. Hunter and his deputy Janet Malcolmson were also present, and it was Hunter who asked me if I would delay my report for a week. I refused, but went on to say that I would be prepared to listen to any concerns they had, but not in this meeting, which had been convened without prior notice.

In conversations later that night, I was told there was a contingency plan to move the Special Branch source depending on what I was going to say in my report. It was never suggested to me that the source was a key IRA figure – quite the opposite in fact – but he was in a position to give the Special Branch access to that organisation's intelligence-gathering activities and in terms of Operation Torsion he was, to quote one source, 'the vital cog, the clue and the main man'.

These sources are people who live on the edge. They take huge risks and they know the consequences of being found out. That is why the police were so worried about my report. I was once told by a senior intelligence figure: 'Every time that we use a source, we take a bit of their life. That's the risk and they understand it.' No wonder, therefore, that there was so much worry at such a high level within the police.

Late on Monday night, Hunter asked me if I would tell him when we intended to run with our report, and, nearer the time of broadcast, could I give him some indication of what I intended to say about the Special Branch source. I offered to meet him the next day.

At 2 p.m. on Tuesday, 12 November, Hunter and Lowry came to the BBC, where they spoke to me and Andrew Colman. This was not a briefing on Operation Torsion; I had already gathered my information. Our scripts were written and nothing was removed from them. This meeting gave the police an opportunity to discuss their concerns about the safety of their source. Lowry, who as head of Special Branch in Belfast had a detailed knowledge of all the informants in the city, was best positioned to make a judgement. He told us he was 'quite relaxed'. He was not down-playing the role of the Branch informer, but he felt there was nothing in our report that would identify his source.

Lowry may have been comfortable, but others at police headquarters and elsewhere were not so relaxed. The Chief Constable Hugh Orde ordered a leaks inquiry and Lowry feels he was forced to walk the plank. On Friday, 15 November, he was accused of leaking information to the media and was advised he was the subject of an internal police investigation. He was served with what is known as a regulation 9 notice, which read:

> It is alleged that on a date and time unknown, you, without proper authority, disclosed confidential information in relation to an ongoing police operation to journalist sources within the media.
>
> This is to advise you that you are the subject of a misconduct investigation in relation to the above.

Within 48 hours, this was withdrawn as quickly as it had been introduced when Lowry decided to retire, but this was not the end of the matter. Questions continued to be asked, notably about why such a senior officer, in one of the most sensitive police posts, had retired so suddenly. Orde has rejected any suggestion that he came under pressure to bring about Lowry's departure, but the Special Branch officer clearly believed he was pushed. In a letter of complaint to the Policing Board – a committee of politicians and independent members who are the new policing watchdog in Northern Ireland – he suggested that there had been London interference, meaning MI5. Lowry complained of being 'humiliated, degraded, embarrassed and betrayed', and in his letter he said he had been 'forced out' of an organisation to which he believed he had 'a lot more to contribute'. The Police Ombudsman in Northern Ireland investigated the complaint and in July 2003 reported that Orde had not been influenced by MI5 in his decision making in the Lowry case. But what the report also told us was that there had been 'ongoing conversations regarding leaks' between the Chief Constable and the Security Service. Those coversations were about 'leaks generally' and, we were told, Lowry's name wasn't mentioned. That was until 7.15 p.m. on Thursday, 14 October – 48 hours after the BBC news reports on Operation Torsion – when Orde told MI5 that the Metropolitan Police would carry out a leaks investigation and that Lowry was being moved to other duties.

Special Branch and MI5 operate in a world in which there are competing interests – a secret, murky, mixed-up world, where it is so easy for politics and policing to collide. Lowry believes he was the victim of such a collision and that he was sacrificed. Seven months before the public revelations of alleged IRA intelligence gathering inside Castle Buildings, the Special Branch in Belfast had been embarrassed by all that had happened inside Castlereagh. But Operation Torsion had allowed Lowry an opportunity to return the serve on the IRA and he did so, he claims, against the wishes of the British Security Service. Others dispute that version of events, but what is indisputable is the fact that in this period I have just dealt with there was ample evidence of a continuing intelligence war. The Special Branch – the so-called 'Force within a Force' – and the IRA were still part of the scenery, and the future of both would be a big part of the continuing political negotiations.

The unionist demand was now for IRA disbandment and the republican demand was for policing progress to match the Patten vision of a new beginning – a new beginning in which they believed the role and influence of the Special Branch should be greatly curtailed.

In the climate of Castlereagh and Castle Buildings, the continuing existence of the IRA and the demand for the 'private army' to be stood down was always going to be the new unionist focus. After their earlier peace process demands for republican decontamination and then decommissioning, a new 'd' word became part of the unionist political vocabulary and this time it was disbandment.

Many years earlier, in August 1995, Gerry Adams had attracted a lot of criticism for an off-the-cuff remark he made at a republican rally outside Belfast City Hall. It was 12 months on from the original ceasefire and to a shout from the crowd of 'bring back the IRA' he responded by saying: 'They haven't gone away, you know.'

The problem all these years later was that there was still far too much evidence of the IRA's continued existence. It was not just what was alleged to have gone on inside the Special Branch office at Castlereagh and inside the headquarters of the NIO, there was much, much more: gun-running from Florida, the arrests of three Irish republicans in Colombia on suspicion of training FARC guerrillas and the discovery of the intelligence files which still logged the details of British Conservative politicians. It was this mix, this cocktail of alleged IRA activity, which had brought about the latest crisis of confidence in the peace process.

At least that was one way of looking at it, but in the wider frame there was much more to see. Political unionism was becoming much more fragmented and detached from the Good Friday Agreement. Trimble was reigning over a deeply divided party in which his leadership always looked vulnerable. There were also huge problems within loyalism, where the paramilitaries were still at play. Their activities included sectarian murder, confrontation with nationalists on the interfaces of Belfast and violent internal power struggles. Indeed, at one point the UDA looked as if it was about to self-destruct. This is an organisation that has been stripped of any political credibility, an organisation in which many – including some at the top – have become steeped in drugs crime. It took the British Government a long, long time to 'specify' the group, to tell it that its ceasefire was no longer recognised, but that ceasefire had long been a sham.

So, this was the mess the British Prime Minister Tony Blair walked into when he came to Belfast on 17 October 2002 to lay down some new rules and begin the rebuilding process. Forty-eight hours earlier, devolution had been suspended and Northern Ireland returned to direct rule from Westminster. The British Government had moved to prevent Trimble and his unionist ministerial colleagues from walking out of the power-sharing Executive. Here was Blair again, with all that was going on in terms of world affairs and British domestic politics, once more looking for ways of building stability into the Irish peace process. Since the British and Irish elections of 1997, Blair and the Taoiseach Bertie Ahern have become a peace-process double act. With American help, they have steered the Northern Ireland parties through the Good Friday Agreement, power-sharing and the new beginning to policing. They had also watched the IRA move to put some of its arms beyond use, but now the process that London, Dublin and Washington – under two presidents – had devoted so much time and effort to was sinking in political quicksand. If it was to be rescued, then bigger steps –

indeed the biggest steps yet – would have to be taken by Blair and the IRA.

In his Belfast speech the British Prime Minister accepted the bona fides of Adams and Martin McGuinness, and, on the loyalist side, of David Ervine, but he was in the city to tell the IRA and the loyalist paramilitaries that it was time to choose and time to get off the stage. The process had arrived at the fork in the road.

Blair was careful not to use the new unionist 'd' word, but he did speak of the need for 'acts of completion'. This was the 'crunch': the IRA could no longer be half in and half out of the process.

'Remove the threat of violence and the peace process is on an unstoppable path,' the British Prime Minister told his Belfast audience. The job now for Adams and McGuinness was to lower the unionist bar in terms of the demand for IRA disbandment, while at the same time raising the bar internally within republicanism. They had done it before. From the defiant writing on the wall, when a loud no to decommissioning was shouted out in the words 'not a bullet – not an ounce', Adams and McGuinness had moved the IRA to put 'arms beyond use'. In response to Blair, the Sinn Fein president said he could 'envisage a future without the IRA', but he set that comment in a much wider context than unilateral disbandment. Adams and McGuinness know the mind of the IRA and they know how carefully it has to be moved. They were there at the start of the 30-year 'war', and it was their joint leadership which moved the IRA out of 'armed struggle' to ceasefire and then to arms beyond use. But, they, and the leadership they are part of, are the modern-day guardians of republican ideology. In republican thinking, the ceasefires had resulted from a military stalemate, the IRA was an undefeated army and it was not now going to surrender through a process of negotiation. That is why disbandment was so quickly dismissed as an 'unrealisable demand'.

That said, McGuinness – the 'hardman' and the 'hawk' as he has often been portrayed – has publicly stated that his war is over. This, from arguably the most influential figure within the Republican Movement, has been the clearest indication of where the IRA wants to go. McGuinness has sat at the table of the IRA Army Council and has sat behind a desk at Stormont as Education Minister in the power-sharing Executive. In his personal journey it is possible to see how far the IRA has travelled – from armed struggle into the arena of political struggle. The republican objectives have not changed but the methods now being used to achieve them have.

By October 2002, Adams and McGuinness would have known that it was now time to try to move the IRA beyond its complete cessation of military operations. In IRA terms, that ceasefire had meant no attacks on the security forces, on loyalists or on so-called 'economic targets' such as city-centre bombings, but it had not meant an end to the IRA. It had continued to function, to gather intelligence, to train, and it targeted and killed a number of drug dealers under the banner of Direct Action Against Drugs. But it was the build-up of activity through Colombia to Castlereagh and then the alleged intelligence gathering inside Castle Buildings which put the IRA under a security spotlight and pushed the political process over the edge. IRA statements that the organisation posed no threat to the peace process did nothing to calm the frayed nerves of unionism, and in his response to the Blair speech this was something that Adams touched on:

> I do want to acknowledge in a very clear way that the difficulties within unionism have been severely exacerbated by the ongoing focus on alleged IRA activities. Whatever we think about the unionist willingness to embrace the process of change . . . the unrelenting concentration on activities, which it is claimed involve Irish republicans, are grist to the mill of those within political unionism or indeed within the British system in Ireland who are opposed to change. It is also destabilising those who countenance change. Whatever we, or for that matter the IRA, say about these allegations, wall-to-wall daily coverage in the media – fed by stories planted from within the British system – ensures that the denials are dismissed or doubted by even the more progressive elements. And, of course, on the republican and nationalist side, there is anger, frustration and annoyance because there is little focus on the ongoing killing campaign by unionist paramilitaries or the actions of the British forces.

Adams' reference to 'unionist' rather than 'loyalist' paramilitaries was an indication of the period of political cold war the process had now entered, but in his speech, as in the earlier Blair speech, there was an acceptance that things had to be rebuilt. If Adams and McGuinness were to move the IRA again, then Blair would also have to make a significant contribution – there would have to be British 'acts of completion' as well.

So, republicans waited for the British Prime Minister – waited to see how he intended closing the gap between the Patten recommendations for a new beginning to policing and what had been implemented, waited to see what was going to be done on the issue of demilitarisation and on other matters such as human rights and equality, waited to see how the political institutions were going to be protected and how the issue of suspects still on the run (OTRs) was going to be settled.

Instant IRA disbandment was the stuff of magic-wand politics. The republican group was unlikely to step off the stage while the British Army was still on it, while the loyalists were still killing and while the critical issue of policing had yet to be settled. Then, there was the added complication of the divisions within unionism, and who in that political family was in a position to make a deal? There were many issues to be addressed and before the IRA thought about moving forward it took a step backwards. This was republican retaliation for the British suspension of the political institutions.

It was Wednesday, 30 October, and General John de Chastelain had just stepped off the train in Dublin when his phone rang. It was 'O'Neill' on the line – not his real name – but how the head of the Independent International Commission on Decommissioning refers to his IRA contact, understood to be Brian Keenan. The two had spoken and met many times previously – a dialogue that brought together Canada's former Chief of the Defence Staff and one of the most senior figures in the IRA leadership.

Like Martin McGuinness, Keenan, the veteran Belfast republican, was considered an IRA 'hawk', but in his role as 'interlocutor' with the Decommissioning Commission he was advancing the peace process, however slowly, and this was another indication coming from the table of the IRA leadership of the direction in which the Republican Movement was moving. The discussions between de Chastelain and Keenan had led to two acts of decommissioning – to some of the IRA's arms being put beyond use – but now there was going to be a pause in those discussions. For de Chastelain, who had met the IRA in May, June and September, it was a development that came out of the blue, but it would not have shocked him. The IRA had broken off contact before, and in its new statement of 30 October it chose its words carefully. Contact was being suspended – not ended – and it was clear that in the rebuilding of the political process de Chastelain and the IRA would have to talk again, and so they did.

The Canadian General, who was born in 1937 and whose military career dates back to his late teens, is a patient man, who in his leisure time enjoys painting, fishing and walking. He has been around the Irish peace process for a long time. Indeed, his role dates back to 1995 when he, along with the United States senator George Mitchell and Finland's former prime minister Harri Holkeri, was appointed by the British and Irish governments at that time to 'provide an independent assessment of the decommissioning issue'.

General de Chastelain, as one of three international chairmen, then had a part in the multi-party talks that led to the Good Friday Agreement, and his next job was as chairman of the Independent International Commission on Decommissioning (IICD). So, given all of those years of experience in Northern Ireland, he has become accustomed to the ups and downs of the peace process and, while he may have been surprised, he would not have been shocked by the developments of 30 October and that call from 'O'Neill'.

In a statement that day, the IRA again spoke of 'unacceptable and untenable ultimatums' – another reference to the demand for its disbandment, and it was obvious that, whatever else Adams and McGuinness may be able to achieve, a formal standing down of the organisation would not be part of their agenda.

Dublin and Ahern, through all of their contacts with the republican leadership, would have had an idea of the possibilities and, at the end of November, a number of the British national newspapers ran reports predicting the IRA's next steps. Those predictions covered familiar territory – further decommissioning alongside suggestions that the IRA would promise an end to training, surveillance, punishment attacks and intelligence gathering, but, significantly, formal disbandment was ruled out.

It soon emerged that Ahern was the source behind the reports which began to lower expectations – lower the bar – in terms of the unionist demand for disbandment. Everything else that was suggested was certainly possible but by no means guaranteed, and what eventually would be doable would depend entirely on the context created by Blair and the British Government. To quote a close Adams aide, the process was now in its most crucial phase of negotiations since the Good Friday Agreement. If the negotiations were to be successful they would see the biggest decisions being taken inside Downing Street and inside the Army Council of the IRA.

In all that the IRA was alleged to have been up to through Colombia, Castlereagh and inside Castle Buildings, there was never any suggestion that the republican ceasefire was under any threat. That is the ceasefire as defined by the IRA itself, but the activities being attributed to the organisation were of such a serious nature that they were certain to have a debilitating impact on the political process and the institutions created as part of the Good Friday Agreement.

In the transition from conflict to peace in Northern Ireland, it was accepted that the IRA would still be out there, but eight years on from the original ceasefire no one expected its presence to be so obvious. Security assessments suggested the IRA's intelligence gathering was now more advanced than ever and, while there may not have been any plan to use that information for any violent purpose, it meant the IRA still had a war capability if its thinking or its intentions ever changed. What the process now needed was a less obvious IRA, a quieter IRA, a more dormant, inactive IRA and an organisation that would cease the type of activities which, in 2002, had caused so much political embarrassment and turmoil.

This was the task now facing Adams and McGuinness, but their problem was a lack of trust in the British. Previous commitments had not been honoured, deals sealed with a handshake had fallen through and now the Sinn Fein negotiating team was demanding to see the colour of Blair's money before asking the IRA to stretch itself again.

In late October 2002, Blair had been forced into making a change at the Northern Ireland Office. In London, Estelle Morris resigned as Education Secretary and, in the Government reshuffle, John Reid became Labour Party Chairman and the Welsh Secretary Paul Murphy replaced him at Castle Buildings. He and the Irish Foreign Minister Brian Cowen – reporting to Blair and Ahern – would have the job of steering the parties through this latest and toughest negotiation, which was playing out while US and UK forces fought the war in Iraq.

While the negotiations were underway, a report by Britain's most senior police officer, Sir John Stevens, confirmed collusion between elements of the security forces and loyalist paramilitaries in Northern Ireland, including in the murder of the Belfast solicitor Pat Finucane. It was a report which confirmed the worst fears that some in Northern Ireland had had for a very long time. There were also separate revelations of phone tapping in which the target was Martin McGuinness, and this prompted Gerry Adams to say that the spooks and the spies and MI5 were still at war. In recent years there had been other events which had confirmed for the republicans the continuation of the British intelligence war. The senior Sinn Fein figure Gerry Kelly had been the target of a bugging operation and so too had Adams and McGuinness during a crucial period of negotiations. While the unionist focus has been to achieve a statement from the IRA that the war is over, republicans point to another war, which they firmly believe is continuing.

By late 2002, the peace process was looking flat footed and things were moving backwards. What a contrast to the end of the previous year when a move by the IRA had put a new spring into the political step. That was the same IRA whose alleged actions in 2002 had so undermined confidence and trust, but then this has been a peace process full of confusion, full of complications and full of contradictions.

CHAPTER TWO

Saving the Peace

'We have now witnessed an event — which we regard as significant — in which the IRA has put a quantity of arms completely beyond use.'

> Independent International Commission on Decommissioning, 23 October 2001

'This unprecedented move is to save the peace process and to persuade others of our genuine intentions.'

> IRA leadership, 23 October 2001

'This was an IRA leadership initiative. It was leadership led. If it had been left to the organisation on the ground, this would not have happened.'

> Jim Gibney, Sinn Fein leadership, 11 November 2001

'It is a very, very significant move in republicanism. It represents a sea change for that organisation.'

> Sir Ronnie Flanagan, former Northern Ireland chief constable, 11 November 2001

22 OCTOBER 2001: You could feel in the room that this was an occasion of some significance – a critical moment in the peace process when the republican leadership would ask for understanding and ask for it through the persuasive voice of Gerry Adams. The IRA was about to do what many in its ranks would consider the unthinkable, and in the crumbling surroundings of the old Conway Mill it would be left to Adams – the MP in this parliamentary constituency of West Belfast – to explain why.

Conway Mill is on the Falls Road, which for years had been a battleground – a place where the guns of the IRA and the British had often been heard. The sound of that gunfire was fading now, but for the unionists the IRA's weapons were still a problem and a threat.

Inside Conway Mill, the hall was packed, and in each row there was a line of serious, solemn faces. It was wake-like, almost as if something within republicanism had died or was dying. At this difficult moment, Adams was surrounded by friends. To his left was the veteran republican Joe Cahill, a man as old as Partition itself; beside him the MPs Michelle Gildernew and Pat Doherty, symbols of Sinn Fein's growing electoral success; and to Adams' right, party chairman Mitchel McLaughlin, Stormont Assembly members Alex Maskey and Dara O'Hagan and long-time Belfast councillor Fra McCann. Adams' closest aide, Richard McAuley, was crouched in front of the table. Here in this old mill overlooking streets identified with the very start of the Troubles, the ground was being prepared for an IRA statement – a statement on the arms issue.

The audience was packed with veterans of the republican struggle, people such as Brendan McFarlane, the IRA jail leader during the 1981 hunger strike; Jim Gibney, who all those years ago had a key role in the campaign which saw Bobby Sands elected MP for Fermanagh South Tyrone; and Séanna Walsh, who was one of Sands' closest friends and one of the first IRA prisoners to benefit from the early release terms of the Good Friday Agreement. In this year, the 20th anniversary of the hunger strike, these men knew what the IRA leadership was about to do and knew it was a decision that had been taken out of their hands. Gibney later told me: 'They turned history on its head and in doing so they turned the IRA upside down as well.'

Adams spoke at length, but one sentence more than any other jumped out of this important speech – the sentence in which he told his audience:

> Martin McGuinness and I have also held discussions with the IRA and we have put to the IRA leadership the view that if it could make a ground-breaking move on the arms issue that this could save the peace process from collapse and transform the situation.

Adams and McGuinness know how the IRA leadership works and thinks, and the fact that the Sinn Fein president was prepared to go public on all of this was an indication of how confident he was about the outcome. All he was doing in Conway Mill was telling his audience, in signals they could read, that the IRA's decision had been made. He was preparing them for what would soon be publicly announced. The republican leadership – through Adams – was not asking for their permission to do something, but was asking for their understanding and acceptance of the reasons why this step was being taken.

In Conway Mill, there was applause for Adams, but no one was cheering. Republicans, and in particular the IRA, were being stretched beyond where they had thought this process would take them. For years they had sought comfort in the graffiti, in those seemingly uncompromising words: 'not a bullet – not an ounce'. As far as republicans were concerned, decommissioning was a dirty word: the IRA's guns were untouchable and to part with them would be surrender. But now they were reading a different type of writing on the wall and it was a completely unfamiliar message. Here was Adams – the father of the republican family – signalling a move that would see the IRA begin to get rid of some of its weaponry. That was now the inevitable next step, and it would not be long before it was taken. For those in the hall of that old mill there would be little time to absorb what they had just been told. Within 24 hours, the IRA, the de Chastelain commission, the British and Irish governments and Trimble would speak. It was another of those choreographed moments in the peace process.

For me, it was now just a case of waiting – waiting for P. O'Neill – and I spent much of the next day pacing, wearing out the office carpet and willing my phone to ring. His call came at around a quarter to two on the afternoon of Tuesday, 23 October. He wanted to meet within the next hour, and he asked me to contact my colleague Eamonn Mallie. As we travelled the short distance of our journey, we knew what to expect. The Adams speech in Conway Mill was still fresh in our minds. Today, there would be no sticky tape and no dark glasses. Things had changed, the IRA had changed, and the political atmosphere was changing too. This afternoon, the man from the IRA – our link with P. O'Neill – would bring with him a statement from the Army Council, which, for now at least, would end the talk of crisis and collapse within the peace process.

At about half past two, he climbed into the back of Mallie's car. We knew his routine. He would read and we would copy the words of the IRA statement onto pages of paper that would be our notes for major news broadcasts later that evening. This was a significant IRA statement, good enough for Blair and Ahern, and, after another jittery period within unionism, good enough for Trimble too. Soon, he would be restored as Northern Ireland's First Minister.

But the IRA leadership was also conscious that, in many ways, this statement was too much – too much for those in the republican camp who had not expected this day and who would have much preferred to wish it away. So, it was a statement written with those people in mind.

The IRA leadership was speaking to its own, as much as anyone else, and explaining its actions. It was a continuation of the process that Gerry Adams had begun the day before in Conway Mill. Those outside the republican family might find this difficult to understand, might wonder what all the fuss was about and why such a conditioning process was necessary, but then they would view the IRA very differently from how that organisation sees itself. In the eyes of the men and women of the IRA, you were dealing with an undefeated army and to come after its weapons was to touch a raw nerve.

So, this was a moment in which words had to be carefully chosen. There could be no hint of surrender or of capitulation to British or unionist demands, and in its statement the IRA leadership told its people and the wider political audience that it had acted to save the peace process.

IRA STATEMENT DICTATED TO ROWAN AND MALLIE, 23 OCTOBER 2001:

The IRA is committed to our republican objectives and to the establishment of a united Ireland based on justice, equality and freedom.

In August 1994, against a backdrop of lengthy and intensive discussions involving the two governments and others, the leadership of the IRA called a complete cessation of military operations in order to create the dynamic for a peace process. Decommissioning was no part of that. There was no ambiguity about this.

Unfortunately there are those within the British establishment and the leadership of unionism who are fundamentally opposed to change. At every opportunity they have used the issue of arms as an excuse to undermine and frustrate progress. It was for this reason that decommissioning was introduced to the process by the British Government. It has been used since to prevent the changes which a lasting peace requires.

In order to overcome this and to encourage the changes necessary for a lasting peace, the leadership of Oglaigh na hEireann has taken a number of substantial initiatives. These include our engagement with the Independent International Commission on Decommissioning and the inspection of a number of arms dumps by the two international inspectors, Cyril Ramaphosa and Martti Ahtisaari. No one should doubt the difficulties these initiatives cause for us, our volunteers and our support base.

The political process is now on the point of collapse. Such a collapse would certainly and eventually put the overall peace process in jeopardy. There is a responsibility upon everyone seriously committed to a just peace to do our best to avoid this. Therefore, in order to save the peace process, we have implemented the scheme agreed with the IICD in August.

Our motivation is clear. This unprecedented move is to save the peace process and to persuade others of our genuine intentions.

When the man from the IRA finished reading and we finished writing, we were told the statement was signed P. O'Neill and that it was 'stand alone'. Our contact would not be taking any supplementary questions, but he did have one more thing to say before leaving us: the O'Neill statement was embargoed until five. As he wandered off we were left with words of history burning in our pockets. This statement was like money you couldn't wait to spend. It was a story worth telling and five o'clock couldn't come quickly enough.

In its statement, the IRA did not spell out exactly what had been done; only that it had implemented the scheme agreed with the IICD in August. Back then it had told the de Chastelain commission the method it intended to use to put arms beyond use and now, after years of stalling, there had been some progress. In the blink of an eye, the IRA leadership had moved, and in doing so it had bounced its people into a reluctant acceptance of its decision. There had been no time to object. Adams spoke in Conway Mill and soon afterwards the IRA had acted. In the end, it all happened very quickly and in an interview for this book the Sinn Fein president acknowledged it was probably too quick and too soon for many republicans:

> Republicans will probably never recover in terms of their attitude to this leadership. Now, I'm not saying that they are going to run against the leadership [but] it was a move too far. I'm very conscious of that. People were not prepared for it. Even the short-term way in which we dealt with the issue of me making a speech at Conway Mill, and, before people could even absorb that, the deed was done. It was all too quick, and it was all part of us trying to do our best to deal with a very difficult issue. People actually were hurt by what happened. They will accept there is a fait accompli, it has happened, they think it's wrong, they'll tell you that now if you ask them that it was wrong and they would not have done it – surprising people, middle-class people, people who would never probably have had a gun in their possession or their

home think it was wrong, people who were at the receiving
end of loyalist violence or British Army violence think it was
wrong, people who even think it was right, emotionally have
great difficulties working with it, and even though I think it
was another one of these strategic compromises – probably as
big as any that we have ever seen – most people, by people I
mean republicans, are looking to see exactly how the quid pro
quo from unionism and the British Government comes.

Jim Gibney was one of those who struggled with the arms decision,
but he accepted it had to be done. The Belfast republican has
changed with the IRA and has been a willing participant in its
journey from war to peace. He is now part of the Sinn Fein
leadership and is his party's link to a number of influential figures in
the Protestant community. So, Gibney, more than most, knew the
importance of the arms move in building confidence within
unionism. However, he also knows the IRA, and he knows too that
if the decision had been left to the men and women of the
organisation, then things could have been a whole lot different.

In an interview with the author for a BBC documentary that was
broadcast on Remembrance Sunday, 11 November 2001 – less than
three weeks after the IRA's arms move, Gibney said:

> This was an IRA leadership initiative. It was leadership led. If
> it had been left to the organisation on the ground, this would
> not have happened . . . I just felt, emotionally, that the IRA
> blood in my veins was telling my heart that the IRA shouldn't
> have done what they did, that they didn't need to do it. Now
> my head was telling me something else. That they had to do
> it, that the peace process had to be saved . . . A raw nerve, a
> raw nerve in this Movement was touched, and it is still very
> much a raw nerve today, and the important thing from a
> republican point of view, particularly an IRA republican point
> of view, is that the massive initiative that the IRA took has to
> be, has to be, reciprocated by Downing Street and by
> Glengall Street [at the time the location of the Ulster
> Unionist headquarters in Belfast].

What Adams and McGuinness delivered on 23 October is not
something that should be taken for granted. Some have dismissed its
significance, but in republican terms this was huge and was
something that had to be chiselled out of IRA stone.

There had been a build-up to the day of arms beyond use – a period of expectation – albeit a nervous, uncertain expectation. The unionists and de Chastelain had been waiting a long time – waiting for the IRA and waiting for something to happen on the arms issue. This time it needed to be something more than the IRA talking to de Chastelain, something more than Ramaphosa and Ahtisaari looking into a number of arms dumps, and, whatever that something more was going to be, it needed to happen soon. The unionists hadn't yet settled into the new politics and were finding it difficult, if not impossible, to sustain the power-sharing arrangements with Sinn Fein while the IRA was still out there and with no progress on actual decommissioning. On 1 July, Trimble had resigned as First Minister, and on 8 October he gave details of a phased approach that would see the other Ulster Unionist ministers Sir Reg Empey, Michael McGimpsey and Sam Foster first withdraw from the Executive before formally resigning.

Their position was clear. Unless the IRA moved, unless there was decommissioning, the Executive would fail. Blair and Ahern knew the seriousness of the situation and their governments were now in regular discussions with the republican leadership – with Adams and McGuinness – and, given how the Executive was crumbling piece by piece, these were talks that had an edge to them.

In the week leading up to 23 October, I could feel what was coming, and I spoke of little else. It was a fascinating period, and in every conversation there was something that suggested that this time the IRA was going to go further than ever before. During that week I spoke to de Chastelain; to Adams; to Sir Ronnie Flanagan, who was still Chief Constable at that time; to David Ervine; to the Church of Ireland Archbishop, Lord Eames; and to a key republican contact. Conversations with him on 16, 20, 21 and 22 October were what guided me through this crucial week in the peace process. It was he who told me, a week before the arms move, that if the negotiations worked out then the IRA could do what in republican ideology was 'unheard of' – it would be 'massive'. That conversation, on 16 October, came about an hour after my meeting with de Chastelain in a hotel facing Stormont – the home of Northern Ireland's new power-sharing government – a government which by now was coming apart at the seams.

The meeting was arranged by an official of the commission – a Finn, Aaro Suonio – and took place around noon. There was a security assessment suggesting an IRA arms move was possible, but de Chastelain still had no indication when an 'event' – an act of decommissioning – might happen. Had he known, he would not have shared that information with me. He did, however, tell me that

his commission was 'fully engaged' with the IRA and he was clear
about his requirements in the event of that organisation moving:

> Unless we are there, unless we witness it, we will not verify
> that an act [of decommissioning] has taken place. I don't
> believe 'O'Neill' and his people would do it without us. They
> know if it is to be a verified act, it has to involve us.

The General had not yet seen an IRA arms dump, but when he did,
he wanted to record in an inventory what weaponry had been put
beyond use and, in line with the commission's remit, he would have
to be satisfied that the arms had been made 'permanently unusable'
or 'permanently inaccessible'. His inventory would not be made
public.

David Ervine was also in the hotel for a lunch appointment and
spotted me chatting to de Chastelain. The loyalist politician knows
me well. He knew I was digging, and later that night he called me to
pass on a piece of political gossip. He had heard a comment on
decommissioning, which was being attributed to a senior republican
– to a long-time member of the IRA Army Council: 'This is like a
computer virus. If you don't get rid of the virus, the computer will
never work.'

Those words, given who they were being attributed to, added to
the growing sense of expectation and clearly suggested that, on the
republican side, the arms penny had at last dropped – that a process
without decommissioning was not going to work.

Republicans could have killed the speculation, but they did not,
and this too was significant. Their briefing line at this time was that
no decisions had been taken. Adams and McGuinness were involved
in intensive negotiations with the governments in London and
Dublin and with the American administration in Washington.
Senior figures in Trimble's Ulster Unionist Party (UUP) were also
involved in these background contacts.

On another track, security assessments were pointing to the
probability of an IRA Army Convention – a meeting representative
of the entire organisation. Such meetings happen only rarely and are
called to rule on matters of major importance. Putting arms beyond
use would fit into this category, but, with regard to a Convention,
the senior republican source I met soon after leaving de Chastelain
had this to say: 'In order for a Convention [to happen], IRA
volunteers are called to meetings to select delegates. It hasn't
happened. Could it happen? I don't know.'

It was then that he hinted at what might be possible if Adams and
McGuinness were successful in the talks they were involved in. The

IRA, he told me, could do something 'unheard of . . . massive'. Out
of the mouth of a senior republican, it was the clearest signal yet that
a move to put arms beyond use was at last possible. Security sources,
who in the past had been sceptical, were also suggesting that the IRA
leadership was now closer than ever before to taking this step.

The direction in which the republican leadership was travelling now
seemed clear but Adams was concerned about some of the
speculation – speculation that was having an unsettling impact in the
circles he moved in. He and those closest to him knew the likely next
steps, but outside that tight-knit group there would have been little
appreciation of what was going to happen and when. Inside the
Republican Movement, the critical mass had yet to be briefed and so
Adams moved to calm things down.

On 17 October, in a tiny room at the front of Connolly House in
Andersonstown, he spoke to a number of journalists, including the
author. This was a briefing – not an interview – and his comments
were not to be attributed to him but to a senior Sinn Fein source.
The party had made the governments in London and Dublin aware
of the briefing and had also given them an outline of its content. It
was an indication of how carefully things were being managed.
There would be no surprises or unexpected developments for those
directly involved in the continuing background discussions. The
briefing format was chosen to allow Adams more time to deal with
complex issues and as it was non-attributable he could be much
more open and frank.

Connolly House is a Sinn Fein office in the heart of nationalist
West Belfast – a building that in the period leading to the republican
and loyalist ceasefires of 1994 was attacked a number of times by the
UDA. On this day in October 2001 there was no such threat. The
atmosphere – for all that was going on in the background and the big
steps that would soon have to be taken – was relaxed. There was tea
and coffee and biscuits – green and orange Club biscuits and Bounty
bars – and Adams was accompanied by Richard McAuley. For them,
the primary purpose of this briefing was to calm republicans
unsettled by reports of decisions having already been made on an
arms move and on the holding of an IRA Convention. Adams
dismissed both. He said that what he and Martin McGuinness were
trying to do was create a context into which others – meaning the
IRA – could step. It was 'work in hand' and, at this time, it was
impossible for him to give us an accurate assessment of where it was
going.

While the unionist focus was on the IRA's weapons, Adams and
McGuinness were working in a wider frame. In the discussions they

were involved in they were painting in what would be required of the unionists and the British. A crucial issue for republicans was the future stability of the power-sharing Executive and in his briefing Adams was clear that the IRA would not move if the institutions in Belfast and those which spanned the border were not guaranteed: 'There is no possibility of the IRA doing that [putting arms beyond use] unless David Trimble is prepared to commit himself to sustaining the institutions.'

In the run-up to this period, the British Government had twice temporarily suspended the Executive in August and September. These were technical moves to create space in which it was hoped that unionists and republicans could finally resolve their guns and government argument. Suspension was also about preventing a unionist walkout and the complete collapse of the power-sharing Executive. It was clear from the Adams briefing that the republican leadership knew there was all the potential for such a collapse, but if the IRA was going to move, Trimble would have to return to the Executive and unionists would have to agree to work the north–south political arrangements with Sinn Fein.

All of this would happen after the IRA's arms move, but, first, on 18 October, the Ulster Unionist Party and Democratic Unionist Party (DUP) ministers resigned from the Executive, leaving only its Sinn Fein and Social Democratic and Labour Party (SDLP) members in place. This was a situation that could not be sustained for any length of time and meant the British Secretary of State could be forced to call new elections. There was concern both in London and in Dublin that Paisley's DUP and Sinn Fein could overtake the Ulster Unionists and the SDLP, but an election was avoided.

In the background, another set of sequenced steps was being worked on. The republicans drafted a first set of position papers and in early October, Sinn Fein, the governments and the unionists started to exchange re-written statements. This was the build-up to the IRA's arms move.

A British source spoke of 'a great deal of haggling over words'. He said Adams and McGuinness wanted to be certain that the British would accord any IRA arms move 'the historic significance it deserves . . . What they wanted to make sure of in advance, if they got a move with all the difficulties it meant for their own Movement, [was] that the response would not be churlish.'

In this period, there were many publicised meetings, but others happened in private – tiresome, tedious sessions of negotiation involving the Sinn Fein leaders and the then British Secretary of State John Reid at Hillsborough that ran late into the night and resumed early in the morning. Three or four days before the IRA

statement of 23 October, Reid knew the talks had reached the end of
the road in terms of how far the British Government was prepared
to go, but he was given no guarantees by Adams and McGuinness
that the IRA would put arms beyond use. Like most of us, he had to
wait for the Adams speech in Conway Mill on 22 October for the
signal that something was about to happen.

Five days earlier, in his briefing in Connolly House, it was clear
that Adams knew exactly what would be required of the IRA if this
latest initiative were to succeed. For republicans it would mean
something bigger than the ceasefire and Adams said it would be
more difficult to achieve, but the very fact that he was prepared to
speak in these terms was another indication that an IRA move on
arms could be close. The Sinn Fein president said he had cleared his
diary to be available for the discussions that were continuing in the
background. It was later disclosed in a newspaper report that Adams
had been the source of the briefing – a briefing that, despite the
cautious tone of the Sinn Fein president, was clearly pointing in one
direction. What had long been considered unthinkable was now
looking very possible. Adams and McGuinness were moving the
IRA.

Speculation about an Army Convention continued over the next
couple of days, with one British newspaper reporting on Friday, 19
October that a Sinn Fein Irish-language conference could be used as
cover for the IRA meeting. Security sources disputed the suggested
venue, but they still believed a Convention was both likely and
imminent. Overnight Friday into Saturday, however, there was a
sudden change in that assessment. On Saturday morning, I spoke
with a senior republican source who had been following my news
reports. He asked me if I had been speaking to my 'other friends' –
meaning my security sources: 'Tell them I think they are wrong
about their Convention stuff,' he said.

He was not really suggesting that I do that; rather, in a
roundabout way, he was giving me some important guidance.
Within an hour or so, I was able to confirm it through security
sources – one of them Sir Ronnie Flanagan. I spoke to him by phone
as he travelled south for the Ireland–England rugby international in
Dublin. His assessment was clear. Everything was possible and the
IRA could move early in the week, maybe even before Wednesday,
when Reid would have to decide on the future of the political
institutions. Flanagan now believed all of this was possible without a
Convention, and he said it would be a critical weekend in terms of
the IRA coming to its decision. Within the terms of the IRA's
constitution and its standing orders, the leadership had the authority

to put arms beyond use without a Convention. It was a risky move, but it was the course that had now been chosen.

That Saturday, 20 October, I consulted with Andrew Colman at the BBC and across our output we reported the fresh security assessment that the IRA's anticipated arms move could come without a Convention. The timescale was within days and a republican source had said that any IRA decision would be a strategic one based on the future of the peace process and republican needs.

Twenty-four hours later, Gerry Adams joined in, and in an interview with RTE radio added to the belief that something was now imminent:

> If the IRA is persuaded to make some move on this issue, it will be because it wants to rescue the process. We have told them that we will continue to try with others to create a context into which the IRA and others may wish to step. The decision has to be theirs . . . The Sinn Fein leadership, working with the two governments, need to be able, with some certainty, to say that if the IRA does move – and, again, I caution, this is entirely a decision for the IRA – that the dynamic created by the historic and unprecedented nature of that will mean that a British government, whose approach has been tactical, will seize the moment.

While Adams was speaking in that radio interview, General de Chastelain was arriving back in Northern Ireland after a few days at home, where he had received an honorary degree at the Royal Roads University – a former naval location in Canada. Soon, the IRA would take him and his colleagues in the international decommissioning commission on a journey. It had been a long wait, but, at last, there was some progress.

Hours after the Adams interview, a republican source painted this picture. He said things were coming 'to something of a head', meaning the background discussions were about to close and it was now decision time for the IRA leadership. In trying to persuade the IRA, he said there would be problems for Adams and McGuinness. The British Government had 'misled' the IRA in relation to previous commitments, and the source posed this question on Trimble: 'Can they [Adams and McGuinness] persuade them that David is going to be serious or is it another bit of fuckology?'

If it all came together, the first public move would be from the IRA; there would be responses from the 'usual suspects' and nobody would be 'taking decisions in the dark'. Adams' radio interview, coupled with this latest assessment, suggested things were now at an advanced stage and that the ink was drying on a sequence of statements – statements from those 'usual suspects'.

Before that Sunday night passed, John Reid's director of communications at the NIO, Robert Hannigan, told me about a speech the Secretary of State would make in Belfast the following morning – a speech in which he would respond directly to the Adams interview on RTE. Hannigan told me I could speculate about some of its detail in interviews I would do early on Monday morning. Reid would make clear that, if the IRA acted, the response would not be 'grudging' or 'ungenerous' and that an arms move would allow the Government to push on with the implementation of other aspects of the Good Friday Agreement – issues of importance to republicans, such as demilitarisation. He would also say that he did not underestimate the difficulties that the arms issue posed for paramilitary groups.

By this stage, it was known that a number of bases and watchtowers had already been earmarked for demolition and it was anticipated that there would be an immediate security response to the now expected IRA move.

It had been a busy weekend for Adams, during which he had spoken to Blair, Ahern and to Richard Haass – the special adviser to the United States President George W. Bush. A Monday meeting was planned with Reid, and the Sinn Fein president would have talks with other key political figures including Trimble and Mark Durkan, the SDLP leader in waiting who would succeed one of the key architects of the peace process, John Hume.

In the pre-ceasefire years, Hume and his party colleagues had been prepared to talk to Adams when others had slammed their doors firmly in his face. The ceasefires and the peace process had unlocked those doors, but Adams has publicly acknowledged that without Hume there would not have been a process.

After those talks with Reid, Trimble and Durkan, Adams would stand before that republican audience in Conway Mill, in the heart of the Falls Road. By now, the IRA would have calculated the political worth of any move and its strategic advantage. Clearly it had also decided to act without a Convention. There would be no vote for the IRA membership on this most delicate of issues for republicans.

In all of the talking that had gone on, the detail of what would happen and when had been worked out, and the scene was now set for imminent developments. This was very similar to the way things happened at the end of George Mitchell's review of the implementation of the Good Friday Agreement a couple of years earlier. Then, a decision by the IRA to appoint a representative to speak to de Chastelain triggered a series of steps leading to the formation of the power-sharing Executive – an Executive in which Martin McGuinness took responsibility for education and Bairbre de Brun became health minister. Sinn Fein was now in a position of real political power. This time, in October 2001, the IRA's move would allow that Executive to be rebuilt and, for a while at least, there would be stability in the process. It would feel like the stuff of once upon a time, but Northern Ireland was not yet ready for happily ever after.

By the time Adams got to his feet in Conway Mill in front of that audience of serious, non-smiling faces, Martin McGuinness was on his way to the United States for briefings and a meeting with Richard Haass. The republican leaders had completed their business with the IRA and, now, the job was to sell the outcome at home and internationally. Someone who knows the two men well is Danny Morrison – a former IRA prisoner and once Sinn Fein's director of publicity. He is the author of that often-used phrase 'the armalite and the ballot box'. As Adams spoke, he listened from a seat near the back of the room. Morrison knew what he was hearing, as did everyone else in the hall. If the Sinn Fein president and Martin McGuinness were prepared to say publicly that they had told the IRA that an arms move could save the peace process, then they were confident of the decision. Danny Morrison knew it was only a matter of time before P. O'Neill would speak:

> It was highly unlikely that Gerry Adams would make such a public statement only for the IRA to have rejected the appeal, but I think that what Gerry Adams and Martin McGuinness and other people may have missed is the effect that that was going to have on the grassroots against a background of so many uncertainties.

In his speech, just as in the background contacts which had now ended, Adams wanted to speak not just about the IRA's weapons but about a broader range of issues, and he was addressing not just those who sat before him but a wider audience. He would touch on those 'uncertainties' raised by Danny Morrison and on the double standards, as he saw them, within the process. Because of the crisis of confidence within the political institutions, there was a particular focus on IRA decommissioning, but this was at a time when loyalist weapons were in frequent use – so frequent in fact that on 12 October, just ten days earlier, the British Government was forced to 'specify' both the Ulster Defence Association and the Loyalist Volunteer Force, meaning their ceasefires were no longer recognised.

This was one of the issues Adams addressed:

> Many republicans are angry at the unrelenting focus on silent IRA weapons. This is in marked contrast to the attitude to loyalist weapons and bombs in daily use and the remilitarisation by the British Army of republican heartlands in the north.
>
> The issue of all arms must be resolved, but not just IRA weapons – British weapons as well.

Adams said the potential of the peace process was being 'frittered away by a British Government not honouring its commitments and a unionist leadership obstructing the fundamental change that is required'.

This was thinking that would carry through into the IRA statement 24 hours later.

Adams continued:

> Unionists tell us that they are prepared to share power with nationalists and republicans. They argue that they see the issue of IRA arms as crucial to this. For this reason David Trimble says he has triggered this latest crisis.
>
> The British Government's suspension of the institutions, its remilitarisation of many republican communities, its emasculation of the policing issue and the premature movement by others [the SDLP] towards this inadequate position, along with the loyalist campaigns, have all created difficulties which are coming to a head.
>
> From this clash of positions and perceptions has emerged a threat to the peace process that risks undoing the advances of the last decade. This must not be allowed to succeed.

What Adams and McGuinness were asking the IRA to do was to move on the arms issue to try to stabilise the situation, to do something that might for the first time put some solid ground under the political institutions. And, at this difficult moment and in this difficult speech, the Sinn Fein president was asking his republican audience to understand the motivation behind this. It was not to respond to unionist demands, but to try to save the process and to protect a peace – no matter how flawed and imperfect – from unravelling. Adams knew that what he was asking for was much more than republicans thought they would have to give, and he told his audience he did not underestimate the 'difficulties this involves for the Army [the IRA]. Genuine republicans will have concerns about such a move.'

The IRA would have been concerned because it views itself, as Adams described it, as an army – an undefeated army that had viewed decommissioning in the context of surrender. That is why republicans renamed decommissioning and called it 'arms beyond use'.

Adams also knew there was the potential to lose people over this arms decision:

> The naysayers, the armchair generals and the begrudgers, and the enemies of Irish republicanism and of the peace process, will present a positive IRA move in disparaging terms. That is only to be expected.
>
> Others will say that the IRA has acted under pressure. But everyone else knows that the IRA is not an organisation that bows to pressure or which moves on British or unionist terms. IRA volunteers have a view of themselves and a vision of the Ireland they want to be part of. This is what will shape their attitude to this issue . . . I would appeal to republicans to stay united. I would particularly appeal to IRA volunteers and their families, and to the IRA support base, to stay together in comradeship. This is the time for commitment to the republican cause. It is a time for clear heads and brave hearts . . . None of this will be easy. Those of us who want the most change, who seek the transformation of society, are called upon to stretch ourselves again and again.

The language that Adams used told us everything. He would not be putting republicans through such trauma in the hope that the IRA might do something. This was a speech signalling a decision that had already been taken, a decision made at the level of the IRA leadership and now being communicated downwards. By now, Adams knew the timing of the sequenced steps, and his speech was preparing the ground for the IRA statement that would soon follow. It was a speech in which the Sinn Fein president spoke directly to the membership of the IRA and in which he asked them to accept what the Army Council had decided. The last time Adams and McGuinness had so publicly called on the IRA leadership to do something was in 1997, when they urged a restoration of the ceasefire. Inside 24 hours that had happened, and the IRA would not dilly-dally this time either.

An evening darkness had fallen as republicans left Conway Mill with the words of that Adams speech swimming through their heads. They had all been around the 'struggle' for a long, long time – long enough to know the inevitability of the next move. It was now just a case of waiting for the IRA statement.

Republicans had successfully delayed the day of decommissioning. They had found a way into all-party talks without it happening, had negotiated the Good Friday Agreement without it happening and had stretched things out beyond the target date set in that agreement of May 2000 for the arms issue to be settled, but now there was no room for further delay. Something had to happen, and that something would have to involve de Chastelain and his fellow commissioners – the American Andrew Sens and the Finnish brigadier Tauno Nieminen.

This was now one of those pacing moments as everyone was made to wait outside the IRA's delivery room. It was a moment of great expectation, but one of those nervous moments in the process when people were unable to relax. It had been such a long wait and, while there was now that inevitability about what the IRA was going to do, people just wanted to hear that it had happened.

Overnight Monday into Tuesday, I was unable to sleep. I was waiting for the IRA to deliver and waiting to be able to tell that news. It was just before two o'clock on Tuesday afternoon, 23 October, when the pacing stopped. I would soon be on my way with Eamonn Mallie to that meeting in West Belfast at which the IRA statement would be delivered. As we made our way there, we had no idea that a five o'clock embargo would be placed on the information given to us, and before leaving the BBC building I advised my editors, Andrew Colman and Michael Cairns, to be ready for a possible breaking story.

Mallie and I had been together in August 1994, when the IRA ceasefire statement was read to us, but this was bigger – a step beyond ceasefire to arms beyond use and a move that was taking the IRA ever closer to ending its 'long war'. That end has not yet been declared, but the sound of the armalite is fading and within republicanism politics now has primacy.

No army, to use Adams' term, with an intention of continuing war allows its arms dumps to be inspected or puts weapons beyond use, but that is not to say that the IRA's capability for violence has been removed. It has not – something Northern Ireland's then Chief Constable, Sir Ronnie Flanagan, said at the time, but he also knew the significance of the IRA's decision:

The big problem for us is their engineering capability, that they can manufacture mortars, that they can crush fertiliser, that they can manufacture shoulder-mounted rockets. So, I don't know how you decommission engineering knowledge, and that's why clearly decommissioning has always been a political issue, it has always been a question of building confidence . . . So, in terms of the threat, it's not the case that the actual act of decommissioning has debilitated them from any future terrorist activity they might choose to re-engage in, but it is a very, very significant move in republicanism. It represents a sea change for that organisation.

The meeting in West Belfast with the spokesman for the IRA leadership did not take long. It was over as soon as he had dictated the 17 sentences of the statement signed in the name P. O'Neill, and I was back in my office just after three. Then came that long wait until five – the embargo set by the IRA leadership. As I wrote my scripts for the various news outlets, one of my colleagues, Michael Cairns, stood guard at my doorless office. I was not to be disturbed by the many other BBC newshounds who were trying to sniff out exactly what had been said in the IRA's embargoed statement. Across the city in the Belfast offices of the Independent International Commission on Decommissioning, the phones kept ringing, but the Finnish official Aaro Suonio decided he too would not be disturbed. He chose to make himself 'permanently unavailable', or as unavailable as he needed to be until the IRA had spoken. By four, Suonio had been joined in the office by the three commissioners who had witnessed the IRA put some of its arms beyond use. General de Chastelain, the former Clinton aide, Andrew Sens, and the military man from Finland, brigadier Tauno Nieminen, got down to the business of writing their report, which would be faxed to the British and Irish governments around seven – an hour or so before the commissioners would meet with Trimble.

When the clock struck five and the story of the IRA statement could be told, the importance and significance of the development could be judged by the responses it brought. The British Prime Minister, the United States President, the Irish Taoiseach and the Ulster Unionist leader all reacted positively. That is how important it was – important enough for Tony Blair and George W. Bush to find time, in the middle of all that was going on in terms of the military response to the terrorist attacks in the United States on 11 September, to recognise publicly the significance of what had happened in the Irish peace process. The British Prime Minister responded:

I pay tribute to the republican leadership, to Gerry Adams, to Martin McGuinness in particular, for the boldness and the courage of this move. It has been done not out of weakness, but from the strength that comes from recognition that there is a new dispensation.

In a formal statement, the British Government described the IRA's move as 'unprecedented and genuinely historic'. It had greatly enhanced the prospects for peace in Northern Ireland and for the full implementation of the Good Friday Agreement. The statement continued:

> In particular, the British Government believes that it is essential that there is the full, stable and uninterrupted operation of the political institutions – the Assembly, the Executive, the North–South Ministerial Council and the British–Irish Council – which are the democratic core of the agreement.

The IRA's move had represented 'by far the most significant progress in the resolution of the arms issue'. The statement added:

> Together with the Irish Government and the parties, we will implement fully the Good Friday Agreement, including through the proposals which the Prime Minister and the Taoiseach made after the Weston Park discussions. This includes:
> –further progress in implementing the agreement's provisions on human rights and equality;
> –the implementation of the Patten report [on police reform], including through a review of the new arrangements and the introduction of legislation to amend the Police Act 2000 to reflect more fully the Patten recommendations and ensure the achievement of the new beginning in policing as set out in the agreement;
> –the implementation of the Criminal Justice Review;
> –a progressive rolling programme reducing levels of troops and installations, as the security situation improves . . .
> We are grateful to the IICD for their patient work to discharge their important responsibilities under the terms of the agreement and to secure the putting of all paramilitary arms beyond use.

The Taoiseach Bertie Ahern said:

> I would like to express my appreciation to all those who have played a part in moving the process to this point. I believe that we can now move forward on the basis of this development. I believe that all the other parties will recognise that this move offers the breakthrough that we have all sought for a long, long time.

The main players in the peace process were responding to two things: to the IRA statement and to the report from the Independent International Commission on Decommissioning – a report that was short on detail but packed with significance:

> On 6 August 2001, the Commission reported that agreement had been reached with the IRA on a method to put IRA arms completely and verifiably beyond use. This would be done in such a way as to involve no risk to the public and avoid the possibility of misappropriation by others.
>
> We have now witnessed an event – which we regard as significant – in which the IRA has put a quantity of arms completely beyond use. The material in question includes arms, ammunition and explosives.
>
> We are satisfied that the arms in question have been dealt with in accordance with the scheme and regulations. We are also satisfied that it would not further the process of putting all arms beyond use were we to provide further details of this event.
>
> We will continue our contact with the IRA representative in pursuit of our mandate.

General de Chastelain and his commission colleagues have kept to themselves the detail of what happened and this has meant that information on the method used to put arms beyond use and the amount of weaponry involved has not been disclosed. These have become two more secrets in a hidden process. What is known is that the 'event' witnessed by de Chastelain, Sens and Nieminen happened in the period between the Adams speech in Conway Mill on Monday, 22 October and the IRA statement that was passed to Mallie and the author at just after two the following day. The commissioners had been to one location in the Irish Republic – possibly to one of the bunkers previously examined by the arms inspectors Cyril Ramaphosa and Martti Ahtisaari. Their role as part of a confidence-building process before decommissioning began was now over. Ahtisaari's aide, Matti Kalliokoski, called Suonio in Belfast on the evening of 23 October to advise him they would be issuing a statement the following day ending their role and Ramaphosa would later speak directly to de Chastelain. The IRA had now moved beyond arms inspections to the beginning of a process of putting arms beyond use and, although the Canadian General saw that as significant progress, he still had some concerns, which he outlined to me in a conversation for this book:

> The commission was pleased it had taken place and it recognised the significance of the act given the IRA's history and all that it had said about arms previously. But we were concerned at the lack of transparency and that that might deflect from its public impact. So, in a sense, while the commission was pleased, its elation was muted.

In terms of putting the pieces of the political jigsaw back together, the most important of the responses on 23 October would be from Trimble. Unless the Ulster Unionists were prepared to buy into what was developing, it would not work. All of this, however, had been settled beforehand.

Remember what the republican source had said about 'no one taking decisions in the dark'. Trimble's party was onboard and quickly acknowledged the 'significance and importance' of the de Chastelain report: 'Today's announcement means that the IICD is fulfilling its mandate. All aspects of the Belfast Agreement are now being implemented.'

A meeting of the party executive had been arranged at which Trimble would recommend that the Northern Ireland Executive be re-established. This meant he would put himself forward for election as First Minister, Empey, McGimpsey and Foster would return to their posts and the North–South Ministerial Council would function as intended under the terms of the Good Friday Agreement:

> We remain committed to, and will play our full part in, securing the full implementation of the agreement and the full functioning of all the institutions, including North–South Ministerial Council and British–Irish Council. An agreed schedule of meetings can now proceed smoothly and normally.

In his briefing in Connolly House six days previously, Adams had outlined what would be required of Trimble. The Sinn Fein president working with Martin McGuinness and the IRA leadership had delivered the republican side, now Trimble was making the expected unionist response.

In all of what was developing, McGuinness had made a key contribution and, according to security sources, had played the lead role in the internal IRA debate. The man who now has such a public role in the new politics of Northern Ireland still holds considerable influence over the republican 'army' and on the issue of arms he had made possible what had long been considered the impossible:

> I think it was fairly late in the day, if the truth be told, whenever people would have had any indication that there was a possibility that this could be resolved, and I think what you also have to factor into that is the fact that this was such a huge thing, that this was an issue that maybe even they felt wasn't going to be resolved, and so, even up to the last minute, there would have been many, many doubts – I think in both governments and in many other areas – as to whether or not we were capable of getting a result from our deliberations, but fortunately we got a good result . . . I saw it as a decision of great strength on behalf of the IRA, because the IRA, at one fell swoop, have effectively liberated everybody within this process. I thought it was a very courageous thing for them to do, I thought it was a very patriotic thing for them to do and I think it was a much needed thing for them to do.

So, why do republicans place so much significance on the events of 23 October and why for them was this such a massive initiative on the part of the IRA leadership? Perhaps it is because republicans are best placed to read between the lines of that P. O'Neill statement and because they interpret much more than was actually said in its 17 sentences.

> People realise in their hearts, even though I cannot ever see the IRA saying that the war is over – and Sinn Fein does not have the power either to wage war or declare it on or off – I think that most people, most republicans, deep down inside know that they cannot return to armed struggle.

This is Danny Morrison speaking – once Sinn Fein's director of publicity and once a senior figure in the IRA leadership:

> In the 200-year history of physical-force republicanism, never before were weapons actually destroyed, and again to resort to an old phrase of putting the pike in the thatch because there will be another day [of possible conflict], republicans appear to be saying, quite decisively, that there

will not be another day, that it is these days that we are going
to work for and we are going to have to live with political
realities.

In October 2001, one of the realities that republicans had to deal with
was that the political institutions were not going to function as
intended unless there was a move from the IRA on arms. There was
also the reality of a new world context after the events in New York and
Washington on 11 September – a context in which the major powers
had declared war on terrorism. This was not a time for republicans –
and in particular the IRA – to be caught on the wrong side of the lines.
It is also true that weeks earlier, in August, the IRA had agreed a
scheme with the de Chastelain commission for putting arms beyond
use. The one outstanding issue was when that would occur. Was the
IRA's original plan to move in October, or were things speeded up by
changing world attitudes – particularly in the United States – after the
attacks on the World Trade Center and the Pentagon?

There was, of course, another matter – the arrests in Colombia of
three republicans who had been in territory controlled by FARC
guerrillas. Washington was appalled and back in Ireland Sinn Fein
was clearly embarrassed – one of those detained was the party's
representative based in Cuba. It would be foolish to believe that the
events in the United States and in Colombia did not have some
bearing on the IRA's decision, but these were only pieces in the
jigsaw and not the whole picture.

Adams and McGuinness knew that an IRA arms move would
probably save the peace process and that the decision would be
applauded in London, Dublin and Washington. If Trimble failed to
carry his party, the likelihood was an election which Sinn Fein would
contest with the applause of three governments ringing in the air.
The IRA's move was timed for best strategic advantage, and what
pressure there had been was gone – at least for now.

In summary, the IRA move put Trimble in a position to rebuild
the political institutions. He returned to his position as First
Minister, but only with backing from the Alliance Party and
Women's Coalition members in the Northern Ireland Assembly,
who, as part of complicated technical arrangements, were able to
temporarily re-designate themselves as unionists. The loud, anti-
Good Friday Agreement voice of Ian Paisley was raised in anger. His
Democratic Unionist Party said Trimble's election lacked credibility,
but on 14 November unionist, nationalist and republican ministers
met again as an Executive and the political Humpty-Dumpty was
back up on the Stormont wall.

Four months before the IRA's arms move, Sinn Fein had had its

best ever elections in Northern Ireland. Adams, McGuinness, Pat
Doherty and Michelle Gildernew all won seats in the British general
election, and in both this and the local council elections Sinn Fein
won more votes than the SDLP to emerge as the largest nationalist
party in the north of Ireland. From this position of strength,
republicans could have been tempted to do nothing about
decommissioning, but Adams accepts that would have been a
dangerous road to travel:

> After the last elections, Sinn Fein could have hunkered down.
> Sinn Fein could have let the institutions collapse. David
> Trimble could have been allowed to fall on his own sword.
> The only certainty we can say about all of that is that within
> a year of that happening we would almost certainly have been
> back in conflict.

So, in October 2001, the IRA moved on arms and saved the process,
but five years earlier in 1996 continuing demands for
decommissioning had brought that organisation's first ceasefire
tumbling down. It was buried in the rubble of a bomb explosion in
London, buried with the bodies of two men – the latest victims of
the IRA's 'war' with Britain. In one of a number of interviews for this
book, I asked Adams to think back on this period:

> It was more a sense of resignation and also to some degree a
> sense of loss. Sinn Fein had been in the driving seat up to that
> point and we were doing OK, but I knew we were now no
> longer in the driving seat. So, you had a sense of, almost as
> the news came, of being put into a spectating role once again
> and that is not a criticism of the IRA. I regret the fact that the
> cessation broke down, but it was always in the quid pro quo
> that the IRA would have a cessation and there would be
> substantive negotiations.
>
> It is to the great tribute of the IRA that they maintained a
> very genuine cessation for so long . . . The decommissioning
> issue may have been the straw that broke it, but had it not been
> that it would have been something else, because it wasn't about
> decommissioning. It was about a British Government being
> unprepared to engage with the type of will and capacity that's
> required anywhere in the world to build peace.

Gerry Adams was speaking about the Conservative Government led
by John Major – a government swept away in the British general
election of May 1997. Tony Blair and Labour took power with a

massive majority. There would be a new approach, a new ceasefire, all-inclusive negotiations before decommissioning and the type of political engagement necessary to build peace. It all took time, much more time than was originally intended, but eventually Adams and McGuinness were able to deliver the IRA and arms beyond use. The IRA move on 23 October 2001 was not a one-off, but something that would be repeated, but despite these acts – hugely significant as they were within republicanism – they were not enough to persuade unionists that the IRA had changed, and down the road Trimble would ask for more. We now know that the ceasefire of 1994 was only a starting point. For many years since, we have observed the fight over guns and government and the long struggle for some sort of peace in a place still haunted by its history and still not certain of its future.

CHAPTER THREE

The Fatal Ingredient

'You can't be a human being with any sensitivity and minister to people who are burying their dead in plastic bags, seeing what's in the plastic bags, and answering, or trying to get alongside little children of seven or eight, who say, "Where's my daddy gone?" You can't do that without realising the importance of getting the gun and the bomb out of this.'

Church of Ireland Archbishop Robin Eames, September 1997

'It is my opinion that the decommissioning question was fatal to the peace process.'

Jim Gibney, Sinn Fein leadership, November 1996

For seven years from the first ceasefire of August 1994 through to that day in October 2001, republicans had managed to push away the day of decommissioning. They did so by accusing the unionists and the British of seeking the surrender and the humiliation of the IRA, and, rather than bend, that organisation returned to a battlefield on which it knew there could be no winners.

From February 1996 to July 1997, the IRA was back at 'war' – first in Britain and then in Northern Ireland, and in each of those theatres of operation people were killed. After the August 1994 declaration of a complete cessation of military operations, there were no substantive negotiations, and, like an elastic band that is stretched too far, the patience of the IRA leadership finally snapped and the ceasefire crumbled.

Unquestionably there were those who saw the weapons issue as a tool to break the IRA, but there were others – not interested in victory and defeat – who approached the arms question from an entirely different perspective. For these people, getting rid of the gun was about trying to build confidence in a place where trust is sometimes hard to find. One such person was the Church of Ireland leader, Archbishop Robin Eames, who had coaxed the loyalists towards their ceasefire of 1994 and who later involved himself in a private dialogue with Sinn Fein – with Jim Gibney and his party colleague Tom Hartley. The discussions later developed into private talks between Eames and Gerry Adams. It is a dialogue that neither side has publicly confirmed, but it is an important piece in a wider process of two communities beginning to meet each other and trying to understand each other after long years of hurt. There may have been those who sought the surrender of the IRA, but there were many others who still feared that organisation and who, long after the ceasefire, still felt threatened by its guns.

Archbishop Eames has not been able to hide from the horrors of life and death in Northern Ireland. On too many occasions, he has had to bury the dead of its conflict. He has had to step forward when others have been able to stand back, step forward into homes where widows and children have asked why. For him there has been no hiding place and in the loneliness and sadness of those situations he has had to search for words that might console. When we spoke in his office in Armagh on 3 September 1997, he found powerful words to explain the importance of decommissioning. They were the words I quoted at the top of this chapter and are worth repeating:

> I can understand, in a human sense, why decommissioning took on the importance it did . . . You can't be a human being with any sensitivity and minister to people who are burying their dead in plastic bags, seeing what's in the plastic bags, and answering, or trying to get alongside, little children of seven or eight, who say, 'Where's my daddy gone?' You can't do that without realising the importance of getting the gun and the bomb out of this.

The Archbishop was speaking two months or so after the IRA had restored its ceasefire. For much of 1996 and throughout the first half of the following year, the IRA had been active. London was its first target and when it resumed its activities in Northern Ireland, it bombed the headquarters of the British Army at Thiepval Barracks in Lisburn. The loyalists responded, but the UVF, the Red Hand Commando and the UDA chose not to own up to their actions. Instead, they played a game – sometimes a deadly game – which came to be described as 'no claim – no blame'. It was obvious what was happening, however, and those who wanted to could see exactly what was going on. Others, though, looked the other way.

Throughout this process there has always been a sharper political focus on the IRA and its weapons, even at times when loyalist guns were in frequent use. The republican Jim Gibney – the man who reluctantly accepted the IRA's arms move in October 2001 – holds the view that the ceasefire collapsed in 1996 because of the demands of the Major Government for decommissioning:

> It is my opinion that the decommissioning question was fatal to the peace process. When the British Government introduced it into it, I think it inevitably led to the collapse of the peace process, because republicans look at the question of decommissioning in this light. It is a surrender they're looking for. They are trying to humiliate the republicans. And what the British Government must realise is that the IRA was not defeated in August 1994. The British Government know that, their generals know that. Everyone accepted that there was a stalemate and what the British Government must realise is this, that they cannot get pre-conference table or at the conference table what they didn't get on the battlefield, and that is an IRA surrender.

Those words were spoken in November 1996 by a man considered to be one of the 'doves' of the Republican Movement, and in Gibney's statement it is possible to see the distance that the IRA had to travel to get to October 2001 and the position of putting arms beyond use. They had fought a 'war' and they were not going to allow the ceasefire to be stigmatised by any suggestion of surrender. So, despite the military stalemate that had previously existed, the IRA took the decision in February 1996 to end its ceasefire, even though some senior republicans, including Gibney's close friend Danny Morrison, had long accepted that this was a war which neither side could win:

> I was in prison in 1991 when I wrote a private letter to Gerry Adams at that time, and I believed that given the admission by [the former Conservative Northern Ireland Secretary of State] Peter Brooke and also by a number of senior army figures that there was a military stalemate, I felt that there was also a stalemate from the republican point of view, that, despite all of those weapons that were there, that the IRA could fight on for ever but without necessarily changing the situation any further, and that was the time to strike for negotiations.

Brooke made his comments in November 1989, in an interview with

Deric Henderson of the Press Association in Belfast. He said it was 'difficult to envisage a military defeat' of the IRA and believed that if a ceasefire was declared the Government 'would need to be imaginative'. In an interview with the author in January 2000, Danny Morrison gave this interpretation of Brooke's comments and the republican response:

> When Peter Brooke made that statement, and later when it became clear that the British Government was thinking along the lines that there was a stalemate, it couldn't defeat the IRA . . . there was interest in the way the Brits were thinking. I think there was a slow realisation amongst republicans . . . that it was a military stalemate, even though the IRA had all of these weapons it was difficult to see what it could achieve, and once the British Government went into a negotiation mode, there was a responsibility on the republicans to explore it . . . I think that over a period of time, as the war was fought . . . it was seen that basically both sides had fought each other to a military stalemate, and once you acknowledge that, then that places an onus on you to find an alternative to it and I think . . . this was the seeds of the peace process.

Brooke had gone when the IRA ceasefire finally came in 1994 and republicans saw the response of the Conservative Government at that time, of the then Prime Minister John Major and Secretary of State Sir Patrick Mayhew, as anything but 'imaginative'. The substantive negotiations that republicans were looking for in return for their ceasefire simply did not happen. Instead, beginning in December 1994, they got an 'exploratory dialogue' with Government officials – a dialogue in which the issue of decommissioning would not go away.

The loyalists were also involved in these talks. Billy Hutchinson of the Progressive Unionist Party (PUP) said their mandate within the discussions was 'the silence of the guns', but Martin McGuinness pointed to a mandate of a different kind: 'We are here and we are entering these discussions on the basis of our electoral mandate. We hope to move speedily through these discussions towards inclusive peace talks with all parties to the conflict involved.'

There would be no such speedy movement; rather it would take the best part of three years, a change of British Government and another IRA ceasefire before Sinn Fein would gain entry to multi-party talks. Within the developing political process, exploratory dialogue became a type of purgatory out of which republicans and loyalists would not pass until there was progress on the arms issue.

At least that was the plan back then, but the script has been modified on numerous occasions. A demand for guns before talks was changed to guns during talks, then no guns – no government and then there could be government for a while before decommissioning. It has been a make-it-up-as-you-go-along-type process, and on the journey out of the long war and towards something new perhaps that was always going to be the way of it. In this process, nothing has been set in stone and all sides have been prepared to shift positions.

In the exploratory dialogue there were two sets of Government officials – one dealing with McGuinness and his Sinn Fein colleague Gerry Kelly, and the other with the two small loyalist parties, the PUP and the Ulster Democratic Party (UDP), led by Gary McMichael. The dialogue with the loyalists began on 15 December and just eight days later they had been presented with a paper on decommissioning. I read it during my research for this book. A loyalist source had kept all of the documents that had passed between his party and the Government team. The papers had been filed in chronological order and many of the documents were headed either 'In Confidence' or 'Confidential'. My source took me through the file and then allowed me to leave with it. The weapons paper was titled 'Modalities of Decommissioning Arms: Paper by the Government Side'. This was one of the file documents marked 'In Confidence' and it ran to five paragraphs. I want to set out its detail in order to show what Government officials were attempting to achieve at this time. Remember this was 1994 and the two ceasefires were only a few weeks old.

> 1. All sides wish to see the normalisation of political and community life in Northern Ireland. The issue of illegal weapons, along with other issues, must be addressed as part of that process. The Government believes that, as a matter both of principle and of political reality, substantial progress on decommissioning of arms held by loyalist groups would be necessary before the Progressive Unionist Party and the Ulster Democratic Party could and would be included in a realistic and meaningful political dialogue.
>
> 2. Against that background, the Government believes that it would be useful to develop an understanding of the modalities of decommissioning illegally held arms. All sides note the relevance of progress in respect of decommissioning IRA arms.
>
> 3. This paper sets out some headings to promote discussion of this issue.

4. Areas which would need to be considered include:
  (i) Possible methods of decommissioning, including:
    -Depositing arms for recovery and subsequent
    destruction.
    -Direct transfer of arms to the authorities for
    destruction.
    -Rendering arms inoperable prior to handover.
  (ii) Verification/validation, including:
    -Possible role of intermediaries.
    -Independent supervision of destruction of arms.
  (iii) Practical considerations, including:
    -Safety factors.
    -Preventing agreed arrangements for decommissioning
    being exploited by others.
  (iv) Legal considerations.
  (v) Timetabling.
5. The Government side looks forward to discussing these
issues further, whether in full meetings of the exploratory
dialogue or in a sub-group.

NORTHERN IRELAND OFFICE
23 DECEMBER 1994

It is understandable that the then Conservative Government would
have wanted to make early progress on the arms issue, but the reality
of 1994, and for a considerable period afterwards, was that progress
would not be made. Organisations coming out of a 25-year conflict
and only recently persuaded to move to ceasefire positions were not
about to dispose of their weapons. The IRA didn't trust the British and
the loyalists didn't trust the IRA. In that stand-off, guns would not be
given up. Indeed, at the time of writing none of the main loyalist
organisations has decommissioned any of its weapons. But, back in
1994, their political representatives took the Government paper and
agreed to consider its content. Martin McGuinness did not.
Republicans viewed decommissioning as a British precondition to
talks and saw the proposals in the document as a means of processing
that precondition. McGuinness refused to accept the paper.

Despite what the paper said about the need for 'substantial
progress on decommissioning of arms' before loyalists would be
included in 'a realistic and meaningful political dialogue', the
obstacle of guns before talks was eventually overcome. The loyalist
parties and Sinn Fein were part of the Good Friday Agreement
negotiations,   negotiations   which   proceeded   without
decommissioning and which failed to resolve this most difficult of
issues. In the future this would give rise to the 'no guns – no

government' stalemate, but for now it is important to concentrate on
the exploratory dialogue.

For the political representatives of loyalism, this was the beginning
of a journey – a journey which brought many of them out from
behind closed doors and into the public eye. These were the people
who would give a voice to loyalism and who, a little further down the
road, would join their republican 'enemy' at the negotiating table.
Loyalism was now ready to speak for itself and had people who
would do so – people such as David Ervine. There had been some
preparation for this day. In one of a number of interviews for this
book, Ervine spoke to me of loyalism 'getting ready for a wedding it
was never sure was coming'. The wedding was the ceasefires of 1994
and the talking that would inevitably follow.

They had been getting ready since 1991, when the Combined
Loyalist Military Command first emerged and offered a truce to
cover the first phase of a protracted political dialogue that came to
be known as the Brooke–Mayhew talks. At that time there were no
places at the table for loyalists or republicans and no prospect,
therefore, that these talks could deliver a peace of any kind. But, the
period spanning the late 1980s into the early 1990s was significant in
terms of developments within loyalism. The different paramilitary
elements were pulled closer together under an umbrella of sorts –
the Combined Loyalist Military Command. Coinciding with this,
the loyalist leadership also began to look for people who could
represent them politically.

William Smith, who chaired the 1994 news conference at which
Gusty Spence read the loyalist ceasefire statement, spoke to me
about how loyalism was developing in that period: 'They [the
CLMC] recognised that some day there would have to be an end to
the war, that people would have to try to make an agreement, and
they wanted people there from their own community to develop a
political strategy for that day.'

David Adams, of the Ulster Democratic Party, was one of those
people. When he spoke to me for this book, he said the groundwork
for the 1994 ceasefire could be found in the 1991 truce: 'It reminded
people that this was a political conflict. It pointed volunteers' minds
towards the need for a political settlement.'

In other words, the truce in 1991 began to help establish the
primacy of politics over violence and people such as David Adams
began to position themselves to play a part in any future talks:

> Loyalism had been used and abused, or [loyalists] saw
> themselves as having been used and abused, so often by

mainstream unionism that they decided – and quite rightly and very positively in my view – that from now on if political decisions have to be made regarding loyalism, regarding initiatives taken by the Government, that analysis and those decisions will be taken exclusively by people within loyalism.

Adams, Ervine, Smith, Gary McMichael and Billy Hutchinson all became part of that exploratory dialogue with Government officials in December 1994 and this was when Ervine told me that they felt like 'duds going to play against Las Vegas professionals'.
He went on to say:

> Certainly I have been disabused of the notion that government and civil service has a big blackboard that everything is plotted and schemed out on. They can so easily be derailed. They work with the issues day and night and if you do too there's no reason why you can't be their equal.

David Adams also told me he took time to find his feet in those exploratory talks. Initially he felt intimidated but, as the dialogue progressed, he found himself gradually being able to relax:

> What really did help the confidence, and I'm speaking personally but I know I'm speaking also for other members of the party, is often being proved right within negotiations or discussions with those who, in earlier days, we would have thought to be our intellectual betters. Now, there's nothing like that sort of experience to boost your confidence.

So, as part of a learning curve, loyalism saw some worth in this dialogue, but republicans believed the Government was merely going through the motions – that the exploratory dialogue was there as part of a stalling process. Martin McGuinness and Gerry Kelly would have known that talks in this format were not going to produce a result and would have viewed them as an unwanted and unnecessary preliminary to the all-party, all-inclusive negotiations that Sinn Fein sought. The two republicans would also have been suspicious because of a previous bad experience in negotiations with the British. The exploratory dialogue was out in the open, but prior to the August 1994 IRA ceasefire announcement McGuinness and Kelly had been involved in secret 'back channel' contacts with the Government – contacts which only became a matter of public knowledge in November 1993. When this information came out, the then Northern Ireland Secretary of State Sir Patrick Mayhew claimed the Government's involvement was in response to a message that had been received from Martin McGuinness in February that year – a message from the IRA leadership asking for British advice on how to end the conflict.

In his autobiography, John Major said the message was brought to him while he was working on papers in the Cabinet Room. It had come through an 'intelligence link which we and they maintained for private communication'.

Major wrote:

> The Northern Ireland Secretary Patrick Mayhew and I were assured by Northern Ireland Office experts that the secret channel was reliable and the message was authentic; but it could still be a trap.
>
> The political risk should we proceed was high. Even entering into a preliminary dialogue with Sinn Fein was a dangerous political minefield. For uncertain gain we risked the alienation of the unionist majority of the population in Northern Ireland and outright opposition from many Unionist and Conservative Members of Parliament; it was not fanciful to reflect that if it went wrong, this could have ended both Paddy's and my careers.

Martin McGuinness has always maintained that he never sent the message, and nor did he. It was, in fact, written by a former priest, Denis Bradley, who is now vice-chairman of Northern Ireland's Policing Board, which is overseeing the 'new beginning' to policing negotiated as part of the Good Friday Agreement.

Back in 1993, Bradley was one of three men from Derry who formed a link in a chain between the then British Government and the republican leadership. He has spoken to a number of journalists, including myself, about his role in the 'back channel' and his part in that message which Major and Mayhew attributed to McGuinness.

I met him at his home in Derry on 27 March 2000. Throughout the interview, Bradley puffed on his pipe. Our conversation was punctuated by the sound of matches being struck on a box and then being flicked into a nearby bin. He told me he wrote that February 1993 message based on 'his interpretation of what the Provos wanted to happen'. What he believed they wanted was a negotiated end to the conflict:

> BRADLEY: You are no good as a mediator if all you do is mediate. At one stage or other you have to make a big decision and you have to say, well, these two people

> want to move but they are incapable of moving. Now
> how do you get rid of that roadblock? . . . The three of
> us got together, and I sat in my office and I wrote the
> thing, but we made it up. We didn't say where it came
> from. We just said this is where the Provos are at. We
> didn't say it came from McGuinness . . . We were no
> good to anybody unless we actually interpreted what
> was going on.
> ROWAN: Why does Mayhew then attribute it to McGuinness?
> BRADLEY: Because he attributed everything to McGuinness.
>   If it came from us, it came from McGuinness.
> ROWAN: But that specific message did not come from
>   McGuinness?
> BRADLEY: No. Martin McGuinness never wrote that.
> ROWAN: Or said it?
> BRADLEY: Or said it.
> ROWAN: Nor did anyone in the Republican Movement?
> BRADLEY: Correct, but they were all saying it indirectly.

That was Bradley's interpretation: that republicans wanted to end
the conflict and were looking for negotiations. He confirmed the
republican version of events, that as part of the 'back channel'
contacts a two-week ceasefire was sought by the Government in
return for negotiations between the two sides, but he said the British
'got scared and they didn't go for it'.

In all of this there were huge risks for Major. This was pre-1994
and pre-ceasefire, and the contact was maintained in a period
remembered for a number of IRA 'blunders' – attacks that went
horribly wrong. There was the explosion in Warrington in which
two young boys were killed and then the slaughter on Belfast's
Shankill Road. In a botched attack aimed at loyalist paramilitaries,
the IRA took the lives of nine civilians, including children. They
died in a bomb explosion on a busy Saturday afternoon, just weeks
before the revelations of the secret link between the Government
and the republican leadership. Northern Ireland's former chief
constable, Sir Ronnie Flanagan, was the senior police officer in
Belfast at that time and was on the Shankill Road that afternoon as
bodies were pulled from the rubble; but, in one of a number of
interviews for this book – this one recorded in August 1997 – he
accepted that the outcome of the attack was not what the IRA had
intended:

> You had the Shankill bombing in October '93, but from their
> perspective, and this is not to give any credence to the sort of

people who carried out such an atrocity, but their intention, under tremendous pressure [as a result of increased loyalist violence], was to carry out an attack against the UFF [another name used by the UDA]. They never intended what actually was the outcome of the Shankill bombing and largely the campaign had shifted to direct attacks against us – the police and the Army. But internally there was this growing belief that if they couldn't be beaten by military means alone, neither could they win by military means alone. So, perhaps they could actually make more progress towards their overall objective, which hasn't changed and isn't likely to change, along a political path.

Back in late 1993, the IRA may well have been considering that possibility, but no decision had been taken at that time and the violence continued. That was a problem in itself, but Major also had to think of the unionist community, and there was an additional concern. Numbers-wise, he was weak in parliament and this meant there was little room for boldness. Further down the road, a massive majority would allow Tony Blair's Government to be much more adventurous.

So, the 'back channel' did not produce the type of negotiations that republicans were looking for, but Bradley believes the fact that the IRA was prepared to offer a ceasefire at that time was hugely significant:

> The most important historical thing in that was that for years the word ceasefire was a dirty word. They were not even going to use the word . . . I knew that once that psychological barrier had been crossed, that this was the beginning of the end. I didn't foresee all the difficulties, I didn't see all of that, but . . . we'd crossed the Rubicon, because they would not tolerate even the mention of the word up to that moment.

In our interview, Bradley said it was 'a long time later' before he told McGuinness that it was he who had written the February 1993 message. So, what was McGuinness's reaction? Bradley told me: 'I can't remember.'

I'm sure he can, but, moving on, the 'back channel' contact ended in claim and counter claim and in a very awkward news conference for Mayhew. The way it all ended was not a good backdrop for what would follow after the ceasefires of 1994. Gerry Adams saw the exploratory dialogue as part of a tedious, tactical approach by the Major Government, which he said lacked will, conviction or momentum.

That was the republican experience of those post-ceasefire talks with British Government officials, but the loyalists used the exploratory dialogue to their own advantage – used it to learn and, according to Gary McMichael, used it to widen the talks frame out beyond the guns issue:

> The Government was working along a very specific agenda. There's no doubt about that, but we changed that . . . We insisted that the debate be widened, that we look at and examine and deal with all of the issues which were involved in the conflict – community issues, social matters, relationships, about structures of government as well as the political prisoners and the decommissioning . . . We were wary, at each stage, that the Government were quite happy to see us be presented as a political prisoner–decommissioning party . . . We also wanted to make it plain that our role within the process wasn't just because we were the ones who were sitting at the front of a table when the loyalist ceasefire was announced, that loyalism wasn't just about paramilitarism, that there was an ethos there, there was a community that was very distinct and separate from all different other strands of our wider community in Northern Ireland, and that it had a role to play in the process and that role wasn't just about the decommissioning of weapons any more than it was just about the release of political prisoners . . . but that we had to be treated and accepted on equal terms with other parties.

Up to the point of the exploratory dialogue of 1994, there was little indication coming from the loyalist community that it would want to engage across such a wide range of issues and David Ervine believes the agenda the loyalist parties brought to these discussions clearly surprised those sitting at the Government side of the talks table. This was 1994 – there had been 25 years of killing – and this was a new experience not just for the loyalists but for all involved. No one really knew where this process was going or how long it would take to find its way into a more structured and stable political arena.

David Ervine believes the exploratory dialogue had a purpose and that the talks played a useful part in those very early days of the peace process:

> What I felt was in some respects like going through the motions almost to the point where you didn't get your pay rise until your apprenticeship was served, some sense like that, and I'd have to say that I believe that the Provos'

attitude of going for three meetings of exploratory dialogue
and running away from the table was wrong. We went for
many, many more than that . . . I think it was a learning curve.
It was also very important to understand that the
Government didn't really know fully where it was going. I
think that's the lesson out of that, they didn't know where it
was going, not only with us, the whole process . . . I think
they were also surprised and shocked when we demanded to
talk about economic issues and education and issues in
relation to the department of the environment, things like
that. I think they were shocked that that would be something
that we would want to talk about.

What the loyalists also did, through a number of papers tabled in the
exploratory talks, was try to take some control of the discussion on
arms. They wanted the Government to slow down and they were
spelling out in their responses to the NIO document of 23
December 1994 the real world position as it was viewed from the
Shankill. In one of its papers, the Progressive Unionist Party wrote:

We have moved a long way . . . and we believe that we have a
long way yet to go before we can even begin to talk about real
peace. We must progress slowly. We must not rush too far
ahead of those who have laid down the guns and entrusted us
with a task of creating and developing conditions whereby
the guns can be finally removed from the conflict.

Another PUP paper, headed 'The Issue of Arms', made a number of
observations and listed a number of conditions that would have to be
met before loyalists would consider moving.

–The INLA (Irish National Liberation Army) have not
declared a ceasefire and still maintain an armed stance.
–The issue of PIRA weapons would have to be resolved first.
–Loyalists would have to be absolutely convinced that the
constitutional position of Northern Ireland as an integral
part of the United Kingdom was absolutely safe and inviolate.
–The crucial issue in the whole debate about arms must be
the building of trust throughout the whole community,
particularly between protagonists to the armed conflict.

The document continued: 'Until such times as these issues are
resolved, both Her Majesty's Government and the other political
parties must be satisfied with the fact that war materials are not

being used and that a genuine cessation of the armed conflict exists.'

For now, the UVF, through its political representatives in the Progressive Unionist Party, was making it clear to the Government that its ceasefire was all that was on offer. There would be no move on arms.

In its discussions with Government officials, the Ulster Democratic Party – representing the other main loyalist paramilitary group, the UDA – was making similar arguments. The party also argued that the issue of arms should not be linked to prisoner releases and said there were no 'historical precedents in the conflict for the handing over of arms or war materials'. In one of its documents, the party wrote:

> In conclusion, the UDP believe that arms and war materials are symptoms of the conflict. We believe the Combined Loyalist Military Command is committed to peaceful dialogue, in the hope that such dialogue will in turn serve to allay the fear and apprehensions engendered by both the physical and political conflict, and, by doing so, finally remove causes for the retention and possible use of weapons and war materials.

These position papers, produced as part of the exploratory dialogue, clearly show there was no prospect of loyalist decommissioning at this time. They remained deeply suspicious not only of the IRA but also of the Government. That is why in their papers they were seeking guarantees about Northern Ireland's future constitutional position. Could they – would they – be sold out as part of a deal to silence the IRA and finally end its long war?

The loyalists were nervous then and have remained nervous on their journey along this unknown road. In the exploratory dialogue, they set out a position which demanded that the IRA move first on decommissioning, but, back then, in the political cold war that followed the ceasefires, that was not going to happen.

By March 1995, the Conservative Government had defined its position within three demands. Speaking in Washington, Mayhew set a test for the IRA and spelled out the steps that organisation would have to take if Sinn Fein was to be allowed a place within all-party talks. The three demands were: a willingness in principle to disarm progressively; an understanding of the modalities of decommissioning; and as a demonstration of good faith, the actual decommissioning of some arms as a tangible confidence-building measure and to signal the start of a process.

Those were the demands of March 1995, but they were not met. The IRA did not agree a method for decommissioning until August 2001 and did not move to put some of its arms beyond use until October of that year. By then Major and Mayhew were long gone in terms of having any involvement or influence in the Irish peace process. But, in 1995, they were still in a position to shape that process and back then Mayhew's Washington test was the route the IRA would have to travel on decommissioning if Sinn Fein was to gain entry to all-party negotiations.

At the same time there was no guarantee – even in the event of decommissioning – that there would be a place for the loyalists at the main talks table. This was linked to the issue of electoral mandate or, in the case of the two loyalist parties, the absence of such a mandate. In its opening statement in the exploratory dialogue, the Government said:

> Neither the PUP nor the UDP currently command a sufficient electoral mandate across Northern Ireland, comparable to that of the other political parties already involved in the talks process, to secure formal participation in such a talks process. However, the Government would want to keep the PUP and UDP . . . in touch at the appropriate level with its general thinking and in broad terms with the development of political dialogue, and to take account of their views.

In one of his interviews for this book, David Ervine described that position as 'massively and wholly unacceptable'.

> This game was getting played. These scenarios, we think, were being played out by government, but I think they got quickly disabused of that for two reasons. One, it was not tolerable, but, two, I think they found that there was more movement and talent within the loyalists than they imagined existed.

With their move into mainstream politics after the ceasefires of 1994, the loyalist parties did build on their electoral mandate, but it was a case of baby steps rather than giant strides. Ervine was elected to the Northern Ireland Assembly and to Belfast City Council, as was his party colleague Billy Hutchinson, and, as I mentioned earlier, the PUP and UDP were part of the negotiations which led to the Good Friday Agreement in 1998. Three years earlier, however, with the peace process sinking in a decommissioning swamp, it was difficult to envisage such an agreement – especially an agreement emerging from all-party talks which had proceeded and concluded before the disposal of any weapons.

This was eventually made possible by the Blair Government, which managed to lift the process out of the swamp, but as 1995 developed, there was a growing concern that the IRA ceasefire would sink in the sands of the argument over arms. Some months after Mayhew's Washington proposals, there was still nothing to suggest an IRA move, and, writing in the *Irish Times* in June 1995, the Sinn Fein president Gerry Adams set the demands for decommissioning in this context:

> The demand for the surrender of IRA weapons as a precondition to negotiations was never mentioned by the London Government before August 31st [1994]. In fact the British were engaged in intensive contact and dialogue [through the back channel] with Sinn Fein prior to the IRA cessation and never at any time was the issue of decommissioning raised. In my view, had a surrender of IRA weapons been imposed as a precondition to peace negotiations prior to the cessation, it is possible that there would have been no IRA cessation . . . It has been argued that the British Government is simply asking for a symbolic gesture. But it is a gesture that would symbolise an IRA surrender.

Here again you get an idea of the psychological journey that republicans had to travel to get to October 2001. Whatever way the arms issue was going to be dealt with, it was not going to be settled on Mayhew's terms. This was going to take time and the talking would have to come before the guns; not the other way round. What is also clear in everything we have watched develop since 1994 is that there would not have been a ceasefire by the IRA had it been known in advance that decommissioning was going to be raised as such an immovable obstacle in the way of multi-party negotiations.

The IRA ceasefire of 1994 grew out of a process – much of which was private – and which involved Adams, John Hume, influential Irish Americans and Albert Reynolds' Government in Dublin. And it was the fall of Reynolds as Taoiseach in late 1994 that, in Adams' view, allowed the British to so firmly establish the weapons issue as a precondition to all-party talks. The Sinn Fein president clearly holds the view that Reynolds would have resisted the British push to make negotiations conditional on prior decommissioning, but that his successor John Bruton had not been sufficiently robust and this had allowed the Major Government room to establish its talks precondition. This is what Adams had to say on the fall of Reynolds, in an interview recorded for this book in October 1997:

> Well, at the very least it meant that the decommissioning issue came onto the agenda, and, in my view, once the British Government saw that the new Bruton Government was soft on the issue, that allowed them that entire year almost. Even though Mr Bruton, I think, came round to the right position, it was after the summer [of 1995], and I think what Albert Reynolds understood totally was that you had to keep running at the Brits, you had to keep jigging at them, you had to keep moving them forward. So, it gave them breathing space and allowed the subversion of the process to continue, because even though the British had been subverting the process before that, there was some confidence around the broad nationalist and republican family, because John Hume and I were still there, because President Clinton was taking an interest, because Albert Reynolds all the time, or very regularly, was asserting [the need for all-party talks]. So, I think, that's the very least of the cost to the process.

The process was like a broken record – stuck on decommissioning – and after months of deadlock the IRA ceasefire would finally collapse. The exploratory dialogue between Sinn Fein and Government officials progressed to meetings between Mayhew, the then Political Development Minister Michael Ancram and Adams and McGuinness, but while the faces had changed the agenda had not. The British position was fixed on decommissioning before talks, something Mayhew repeated before his first meeting with Adams in Washington in May 1995: 'I shall make clear again that substantive political talks with Sinn Fein will only be possible when there is a satisfactory outcome to exploratory dialogue, including the progress on decommissioning which we have already publicly stated to be necessary.'

What was considered necessary in 1995 was quickly swept away when Labour came to power, and, given all we now know about how long it took to make even some progress on the arms issue, we have to conclude that the position outlined by Mayhew was both unrealistic and unrealisable. The IRA was not going to move on decommissioning until there was substantial political progress.

By August 1995, the loyalists had moved – not on decommissioning

– but to expand on their cessation of 'operational hostilities'. There would be further explanation of what that ceasefire meant and a public declaration from the Combined Loyalist Military Command that there would be 'no first strike' from them. The statement from the loyalist leadership was passed to me and to Ivan Little of Ulster Television at a meeting on the Shankill Road on the afternoon of Friday, 25 August. This happened in a small back room at offices where we were met by two men, one a member of the UDA's inner council – its then West Belfast brigadier – and the other the most senior figure on the UVF's brigade staff. This was at a time when loyalism spoke with one voice, but years later that Combined Command would disintegrate and the office chosen for this August 1995 meeting would be blown apart in a UVF bomb attack that came during a feud with the UDA. The latter group – or at least a significant part of it – would become an enemy of the peace process and an enemy to its own community before descending into a spiral of bitter in-fighting.

Back in August 1995, however, there was common purpose, a joint approach and major policy decisions were agreed among the leaderships of the UVF, the UDA and Red Hand Commando before being announced in the name of the Combined Loyalist Military Command. In this, its latest statement, it was still questioning the IRA's commitment to peace, but it was prepared to add to the ceasefire it had announced the previous October. The statement said that, provided the rights of the people of Northern Ireland were upheld, the CLMC would not initiate a return to war – there would be 'no first strike'.

> The retention of weaponry by the CLMC is a purely defensive measure. We are committed to removing the cause for the retention of arms in our society, thereby removing for ever the gun from Ulster politics. However, much will be dependent on the mutual establishment of goodwill, trust and confidence between all concerned. It is inconceivable for the CLMC to decommission weapons with a fully operational, heavily armed republican war machine intact and refusing to relinquish their arsenals.

There was little or no trust back then, and in those circumstances there was no prospect of moving the decommissioning issue forward.

That the loyalists were prepared to move this far and to this new position of no first strike had much to do with the prompting of Archbishop Eames. In a meeting with Gary McMichael and his party colleague John White, Lord Eames had spoken about continuing fears in the community and of the need for the paramilitaries to move beyond their ceasefires and to do something more to demonstrate a commitment to peace. There were limits to what was possible and McMichael knew that decommissioning was out of the question. He began to think, however, about the type of statement the CLMC might be prepared to issue and what parallel developments would be necessary to achieve it.

He would turn to another churchman, this time to the Presbyterian minister Roy Magee, who along with Archbishop Eames had been involved in the background work that led to the loyalist cessation.

The release of prisoners was a huge post-ceasefire issue and Magee had already suggested that a commission be established to look at this. McMichael asked him to lobby the Northern Ireland Office to restore 50 per cent remission for paramilitary prisoners. In other words, to restore the position whereby sentences would be cut by half. A position of 'no first strike' would more easily be achieved if there was something with which to persuade the loyalist leadership. McMichael briefed David Ervine on developments and the 25 August statement emerged out of these contacts. On the same day, Mayhew announced that remission would be returned to 50 per cent. It had been one-third.

So, Archbishop Eames was talking to the loyalists back then, and later he would engage Sinn Fein in a private dialogue. These are the talks with Jim Gibney and Tom Hartley mentioned earlier. The churchman who had buried the dead of this conflict and who knew the importance of decommissioning in a confidence-building sense would speak directly to the republican who believed the Major Government was using the arms argument to try to break the IRA. In terms of where they stood they were miles apart, but this dialogue was important. For years, there had been a stand-off – a situation in which people spoke at each other rather than to each other – and this dialogue, and other similar discussions, was the beginning of some bridge building.

Gibney has never confirmed to me that the dialogue with Eames took place, but in broader terms he spoke of the importance of Sinn Fein engaging the unionist community. He told me that 'privacy allowed for a wide-ranging and very honest discussion' with a range of contacts in the unionist community. It was a dialogue that Sinn Fein, even before the IRA ceasefire of August 1994, took a very deliberate decision to involve itself in: 'At the start of the engagement, political unionism refused to speak with us,' Gibney told me, 'but we refused to be paralysed by this reluctance. We were determined because of the importance of this area of work to speak to those unionists who would speak with us. We found representatives from the mainstream Protestant churches very helpful in this regard.'

Gibney continued:

> The exchanges were and are worthwhile and valuable. Today republicans have a better understanding of the unionist and Protestant people, and we hope they have a better understanding of republicans and nationalists. Republicans believe we cannot have a lasting peace on this island without the active participation of the northern Protestant and unionist population in the shaping of that peace.

Before the ceasefires of 1994, Eames had taken the risk of speaking to the loyalists, to appeal to them, in God's name, to end their violence. Exactly when he began speaking to republicans has not been established, but before decommissioning and before it was politically acceptable and comfortable to do so he was stressing to them – to Gibney and Hartley – the need for something more than a ceasefire. This is what he told me in an interview recorded for this book back in September 1997:

> We can all handle the war situation because we know the problems, we know who to condemn and this is for me a problem, but handling this peace is full of traps for loyalism and Protestantism given its siege mentality, and, I think I haven't really spent enough time thinking this one out, but in my own thinking, I believe that that's the real reason why loyalism and Protestantism finds this peace so hard to deal with. We haven't yet got the language. We haven't yet got the vision . . . It's no use talking among friends. It's when you go to talk to your enemy and I go and talk to my enemy and try and come alongside him, it's asking an enormous, a momentous step to do that, but we're on the verge of it and I can't see why republicanism cannot make the step of recognising that what they have done so far [the ceasefire] has been right, but that their biggest step has still to be made.

It would take time, but eventually republicans would take those bigger steps – arms inspections, arms beyond use, an apology to the families of 'non-combatants' killed and injured by the IRA and an acknowledgement of the 'grief and pain' caused to the relatives of 'combatants' who had lost their lives. All of these things were about building on the ceasefire and building some more trust.

It was the changing political landscape of the late 1990s which made these things possible, but in the stand-off which characterised the process during the Major years, there was not a chance of the IRA moving – something that organisation made abundantly clear in a statement issued on 29 September 1995:

> John Major's Government know enough of Anglo-Irish history to understand that there is no possibility of disarmament except as part of a negotiated settlement. Given that history, and the reality that they and their loyalist death squad allies hold the largest stock of licensed and unlicensed weapons, the demand for an IRA handover of weapons is ludicrous. There is no possibility of the IRA meeting these demands.

What was equally clear at this time was that Major was serious about his position, and in this stalemate you had the slow slide towards the ending of the IRA's cessation of violence. Not even a visit by the US President Bill Clinton to Ireland in late November 1995 could save the ceasefire, although it probably did delay its collapse by several months. What Clinton's visit also did was concentrate the minds of the Major and Bruton governments, and late into the night on the eve of the President's arrival they came up with a new initiative. This time, there would be a twin-track process aimed at making parallel progress on decommissioning and on all-party negotiations. On the political track, there would be preparatory talks with a remit 'to reach widespread agreement on the basis, participation, structure, format and agenda to bring all parties together for substantive negotiations aimed at a political settlement based on consent'. The target date for the beginning of those all-party talks was the end of February 1996.

As a second element of this latest initiative, an International Body was created to provide an independent assessment of the decommissioning issue. It would be chaired by the former United States senator George Mitchell and would also include the Canadian General John de Chastelain. This would be the beginning of his long involvement in the decommissioning process. The International Body was asked to:

> –report on the arrangements necessary for the removal from the political equation of arms silenced by virtue of the

welcome decisions taken last summer and autumn [the IRA
and loyalist ceasefires];
–identify and advise on a suitable and acceptable method for
full and verifiable decommissioning;
–report whether there is a clear commitment on the part of
those in possession of such arms to work constructively to
achieve that.

By 22 January 1996, the International Body had reported its
findings, Gerry Adams had accused John Major of discarding the
suggested approach and within three weeks the IRA had ended its
ceasefire and part of London was targeted in a bomb attack.

All of this was far removed from the euphoria that had surrounded
the Clinton visit to Ireland, when Belfast, Derry and Dublin had
celebrated so publicly in the presence of the President and the First
Lady. The New York-based publisher Nial O'Dowd, who had been
part of the network of confidants and go-betweens involved in the
process leading to the ceasefire, was watching two scenes: the one we
could all see on the streets – the joy, the singing, the cheering and a
sense, as Christmas approached, of some new hope. Behind the
scenes, however, there was something entirely different going on:
'As time went by and nothing was happening you were getting the
distress signals,' O'Dowd told me.

> By the time of the President's visit, in the lead-up and during
> it, the message we were getting from Sinn Fein was this is
> great, but we are in trouble. And that was more an appeal to
> us, amidst the euphoria, to keep an eye on reality. I didn't get
> a sense that it [the ceasefire] was gone, but people were under
> pressure.

People were under pressure because the IRA ceasefire had been
delivered in the belief that negotiations would quickly follow, but,
here, late into 1995, there had been no discussions of any real
significance and nothing to suggest that that situation might change.
Now, however, there was a presidential visit and, alongside it, this
eleventh-hour initiative from the British and Irish governments.

There was no guarantee that it would work, but Adams believed
there was at least a chance that the ceasefire could still be saved. This
is what he had to say in an interview for this book:

> It could have been saved on the back of the Clinton visit. I
> remember saying jokingly to some of the Americans, it's a
> pity you couldn't stay for a month. My view of the public

euphoria over Clinton is because people realised . . . it wasn't
that they were so glad to see the US President, it was because
they saw it [the peace process] going down the tubes, they
saw the Taoiseach and the Prime Minister scuttling together
over at Downing Street at the midnight hour, they saw
something coming out of it, they didn't know quite what, but
it looked as if there was a chance . . . so, I think, the euphoria
you saw in Derry, the euphoria you saw here in Belfast and
then in Dublin was entirely, entirely because people
recognised that the US President's visit, which was an event
on its own, but the US President's visit was what had created
the possibility of saving a process, which for the previous year
had not made any significant progress whatsoever. That's why
you had that type of response as opposed to say the response
there was to Ronnie Reagan. Also, and it's important just to
note, there would not have been a presidential visit to the
north without the IRA cessation. It wouldn't have happened.

As mentioned earlier, the International Body established as part of
the Major–Bruton initiative reported on 22 January 1996 and it was
out of this report that the Mitchell Principles emerged. These would
be the standards expected of all participants in the talks, and those
involved in the negotiations would have to endorse them – a
stipulation that further down the road would cause a schism within
the Republican Movement. The authors of the report of the
International Body wrote:

To reach an agreed political settlement and to take the gun
out of Irish politics, there must be commitment and
adherence to fundamental principles of democracy and non-
violence. Participants in all-party negotiations should affirm
their commitment to such principles.

Accordingly, we recommend that the parties to such
negotiations affirm their total and absolute commitment:

A. To democratic and exclusively peaceful means of
resolving political issues;

B. To the total disarmament of all paramilitary
organisations;

C. To agree that such disarmament must be verifiable to
the satisfaction of an independent commission;

D. To renounce for themselves, and to oppose any effort
by others, to use force, or threaten to use force, to influence
the course of the outcome of all-party negotiations;

E. To agree to abide by the terms of any agreement

reached in all-party negotiations and to resort to democratic
and exclusively peaceful methods in trying to alter any aspect
of that outcome with which they may disagree;

    F. To urge that 'punishment' killings and beatings stop
and to take effective steps to prevent such actions.

Just to focus on that final point for a moment, paramilitary
punishment attacks continued long after the ceasefires in both the
republican and loyalist communities, and, using the cover name
Direct Action Against Drugs, the IRA also killed a number of drug
dealers. These were acts of violence that the republican group would
not have considered to have been in breach of its 'complete cessation
of military operations', which in IRA terms had a very strict definition;
and while governments have repeatedly told us that all violence is
unacceptable, these attacks continued without any political
punishment or sanction being introduced. The message that this sent
out was that the ceasefires were being judged by how republicans and
loyalists defined them; not on standards set by others.

These were matters that would be confronted down the road
when Tony Blair demanded 'acts of completion' from the
paramilitaries, but in 1996 the primary purpose of this report from
the International Body was about finding a way out of the
decommissioning maze. As expected, the authors also produced a
compromise position:

> One side has insisted that some decommissioning of arms
> must take place before all-party negotiations can begin. The
> other side has insisted that no decommissioning can take
> place until the end of the process, after an agreed settlement
> has been reached. This has resulted in the current impasse.
>
> The parties should consider an approach under which
> some decommissioning would take place during the process
> of all-party negotiations, rather than before or after as the
> parties now urge. Such an approach represents a
> compromise. If the peace process is to move forward, the
> current impasse must be overcome. While both sides have
> been adamant in their positions, both have repeatedly
> expressed the desire to move forward. This approach
> provides them that opportunity.

The report went on to make a number of other recommendations:

> –the decommissioning process should suggest neither victory
> nor defeat;

–the decommissioning process should take place to the satisfaction of an independent commission [this would be the arms body that General de Chastelain would later take charge of];

–the decommissioning process should result in the complete destruction of armaments in a manner that contributes to public safety;

–the decommissioning process should be fully verifiable;

–the decommissioning process should not expose individuals to prosecution.

Senator Mitchell and his team also reported that several written and oral submissions made to them had raised the idea of once more having an elected body in Northern Ireland and in paragraph 56 of their report, they wrote:

Elections held in accordance with democratic principles express and reflect the popular will . . . If it were broadly acceptable, with an appropriate mandate and within the three-strand structure, an elective process could contribute to the building of confidence.

The three-strand structure was the settling of relationships within Northern Ireland, between north and south and between Britain and Ireland.

Gerry Adams believes it was the response of the British Prime Minister to this report that brought the ceasefire crashing down. John Major was not prepared to move immediately, but instead he offered a choice. The talks could begin after a start to decommissioning or alternatively there would be an election in which the parties would seek a mandate for negotiations. Republicans saw it as yet more delay and as a sop to the unionists. In an interview for this book Gerry Adams reflected:

The US administration came up with a way of resolving the decommissioning issue insofar as the presidential visit by Clinton to Ireland brought about the twin-track process. There you had a proposal where you dealt with the politics and you tried to look at this whole question of decommissioning. When Senator Mitchell then came back with the proposition that he came back with, John Major put it in the bin. So . . . it had been a waste of time from November through to January, and I think it was John Hume

> who said that when he listened, I think he was in the House
> of Commons that day, that when he listened to John Major,
> he knew it was over.

After 17 long months of argument over guns and talks, this was a defining moment. The ceasefire was withering on the decommissioning vine and soon it would be over. In an interview for this book, Northern Ireland's former chief constable Sir Ronnie Flanagan said that by the end of 1995 and the beginning of 1996, the police were beginning to see 'a real prospect of a resumption of violence'. But he admitted to being surprised that the IRA moved before the end of February, which had been the target date for all-party talks. By now, however, it was obvious that that target was not going to be met.

On decommissioning, Major – the Prime Minister who survived a republican mortar bomb attack on Downing Street in 1991 – proved as stubborn as the IRA. He had set his entry standards for Sinn Fein's participation in negotiations and on this issue he remained consistent.

Once it crumbled, the ceasefire was not restored until Major had gone. The 'complete cessation of military operations' had taken years to achieve, but it disappeared in a flash. In February 1996, the IRA bombed Canary Wharf, flattened part of the British capital and left two men dead. The IRA was back, and in all of this there was another inevitability. It would not be long before the hawks on the loyalist side would swoop.

CHAPTER FOUR

One for Sorrow

'From a position of confidence, strength and sophistication, we have withstood the recent provocation of IRA bombs on the mainland which have killed our innocent British fellow citizens. These atrocities cannot be permitted to continue without a telling response from this source.'

Combined Loyalist Military Command, 12 March 1996

7 OCTOBER 1996: The setting was so depressing – a prison car park, a grey sky full of rain and, for those of superstitious mind, a single magpie present in the picture. This is a place of many ghosts. It is the jail which held the prisoners of the Troubles and it is remembered for protest, for hunger strike, for murder and escape. Its history still haunts the present day, the ghosts have not been exorcised and it is a place that will never be forgotten.

The Maze Prison, or Long Kesh as many prefer to call it, is closed now; its men of war set free into the new Northern Ireland. But for years this was another battlefield and on its wings the Maze held those associated with some of the worst of what went on during the Troubles. These were prisoners whose affiliation was to the IRA, the UDA, the UVF and the Red Hand Commando – men who, even behind bars, remained hugely influential.

It was in the Maze that the IRA prisoner Bobby Sands died in 1981 after refusing food for 66 days. His hunger strike led to him being elected an MP and made him a martyr in the eyes of the republican community. Sixteen years later, his sister Bernadette would emerge as one of the fiercest critics of the Adams and McGuinness peace strategy. It was here too, inside this same jail, that the loyalist Billy Wright was murdered – shot dead by another inmate, a member of the Irish National Liberation Army. Wright was the leader of the Loyalist Volunteer Force (LVF), a splinter faction that emerged in opposition to the ceasefire and to the peace process.

Just weeks after this shooting, and in the midst of another crisis in the process, it was to this prison that the then Secretary of State Mo Mowlam came to speak to loyalist leaders including Johnny Adair and Michael Stone. This was January 1998 and the meeting was a measure of the importance of the men held inside the Maze. Adair was there for directing the violence of the UDA and Stone was a convicted murderer. Three of his victims died in a gun and grenade attack on an IRA funeral in Belfast in March 1988, when Stone was captured on camera during a killing rage inside Milltown Cemetery. The loyalists who met Mowlam were among hundreds of prisoners later released as part of the Good Friday Agreement. This was the Blair Government responding to the new peace – albeit a peace that was imperfect.

There was no peace on Monday, 7 October 1996, when I stood in the car park of the Maze Prison. That single magpie had shown itself and this would be one more day of sorrow in a place that had endured so many. Eight months earlier, the IRA had ended its ceasefire, but up to this point it had restricted its activities to attacks in Britain. Parts of London and Manchester had already been devastated by explosions and now the IRA would turn up again in Northern Ireland.

Even before this point there had been signs of splintering within loyalism. After an unsanctioned sectarian murder, Wright and his associates were expelled by the UVF and it was from these seeds that the new Loyalist Volunteer Force would grow. The victim of that killing in July 1996 was Michael McGoldrick. He was chosen at random and killed because he was a Catholic. In a place of such bitterness and raw sectarian hatred, Michael's father has emerged as one of the most forgiving voices of the Troubles.

Three months after that murder, I was in the car park of the Maze to report on a meeting that would take place inside the jail, well away from the watching eyes and listening ears of the media. At around two o'clock, the first of a number of cars pulled into the visiting area. David Ervine was there along with William Smith and Jim McDonald, all of whom had been given seats at the top table on the day the loyalist ceasefire was announced in October 1994. That ceasefire was now almost two years old, but it was coming under increasing strain. Weeks after the ending of the IRA's complete cessation of military operations, the loyalists had threatened a 'telling response', and the events of this day in October 1996 would bring closer that inevitability.

Inside the Maze, UDA prisoners had already withdrawn their support for the peace process. They accused republicans of hypocrisy 'in that they preach to the world about peace, whilst they practise war'. History will, however, show us that the biggest hypocrites in this process rested within the ranks of this loyalist organisation.

Ervine, Smith and McDonald, all of whom are members of the Progressive Unionist Party, came to the jail to speak with another set of loyalist prisoners – those affiliated to the UVF and the Red Hand Commando. Before going inside, they stopped for a while and answered some questions from journalists, but all of this was a distraction and out of view of our cameras members of the loyalist paramilitary leadership filed through a turnstile and into the jail. Inside, a political and paramilitary delegation numbering 12 would meet with 30 prisoners. This was remarkable: that such a meeting, involving such characters, would be accommodated inside Northern Ireland's top security jail. Indeed, a prison source I spoke to that day quipped that some of those coming in should not be allowed back out again.

The talks got underway shortly after two and we were told the meeting would last about two hours. At least that was the plan as the visiting loyalist delegation disappeared out of sight and into the jail. Things, however, would change as that grey, depressing afternoon unfolded.

It was just after four o'clock when the afternoon calm was shattered by the sound of an explosion and minutes later there was a second blast. Not far away, two bombs had exploded without warning inside the Army's headquarters at Thiepval Barracks in Lisburn. The IRA was back in Northern Ireland and this was the first attack here since the ending of the complete cessation of military operations. There were casualties – some of them seriously hurt – and four days later Warrant Officer James Bradwell would die.

It would be five hours, not two, before the loyalists would return from their meeting inside the Maze. Their ceasefire had been able to absorb the IRA bombings in London and Manchester, but this was different. This was much closer to home and the attack on the army barracks had clearly been carried out with a body count in mind. In the car park of the jail, after that long meeting inside, David Ervine summed up the loyalist mood: 'We came here to try to salvage something for the betterment of all of the people of Northern Ireland, and as we were doing that others were planning skulduggery and evil with horrible intent in their minds.'

On the talks that went on inside the jail, he added: 'I would say that today is one element of a consultative process, and I would be telling you lies if I was to suggest that the two bombs in Lisburn would not make a difference.'

In a conversation for this book, Ervine told me there had been no 'jumping up and down' inside the talks. The IRA was not on ceasefire and in that situation there was always the possibility of an attack inside Northern Ireland. It was only a matter of time and therefore the mood was one of 'angry resignation'. That said, he was 'fearful of the implications' of this attack and he, like everyone else watching what was developing, knew the inevitability of what would flow from this. The two bombs at Thiepval Barracks did make a difference – a difference which in the weeks ahead would see a gradual return to violence by those groups under the umbrella of the Combined Loyalist Military Command.

There had been a gaping hole in the intelligence picture. The Special Branch and the security services, who so often know so much about the IRA, appeared, on this occasion, to know nothing. Just as with the London Docklands bomb in February 1996, there was no prior knowledge of the IRA's intentions. Not one, but two bombs were taken inside the Army's Northern Ireland headquarters and this was an incredible breach of security. Sir Ronnie Flanagan commented in an interview for this book:

> Of course it has to be considered embarrassing. We had always felt that if violence was to be resumed by the IRA that it would resume in Great Britain first. We'd always felt that they felt a need to condition people and that that would bring about attacks on the mainland first and foremost for a number of reasons, because: (a) they would think it would have greater impact on the British Government, but (b) there would be less resistance to it amongst those who might be inclined to support them here in the province. And, therefore, as part of the conditioning process, to bring those people back to an acceptance of violence, there would have been care taken that attacks would start on the mainland, and when they started here, they would be seen very clearly as attacks against military targets. Thiepval was carried out very much with that in mind. But, in terms of a bomb being taken right into the heart of the headquarters of the British Army in Northern Ireland, I suppose one would have to say, yes, it is embarrassing, but embarrassment is the least of your worries when somebody has actually lost their life in the attack.

The bombs in London in February 1996 and at Thiepval Barracks eight months later which marked the return of the IRA first in

Britain and then in Northern Ireland were of a type which had come to be described as 'spectaculars'. Here the IRA was using big bombs, choosing prestigious targets and doing so in the knowledge that these attacks would have maximum impact. That said, this latest phase of the IRA's military campaign, which would stretch through to July 1997, prompted suggestions that this was a 'phoney war'. There were many attacks which were far less 'spectacular' and which had much less impact than those I have just mentioned, but between then and the next ceasefire others would die and the notion of a 'phoney war' is not something that Flanagan would endorse:

> I think when they resumed violence, and it started of course in February '96 with Canary Wharf, but when they resumed violence in the province, we had talk here, amongst people who should have known better, of a phoney war, and while there were a whole range of attacks carried out against us that were unsuccessful, it wasn't because they were meant to be unsuccessful. There were a whole variety of reasons – the flow of information to us was very good, our ability to thwart their intentions was very high, but included in those reasons for the lack of success, undoubtedly was a rustiness, if you like, caused by the relative inactivity of all of the prior period. So, to that extent, the period of inactivity probably meant that, when they resumed, their ability to be successful had been reduced.

In the days immediately after Thiepval, the loyalist leadership was meeting regularly. Indeed, the Combined Military Command met on 8, 11 and 18 October. The 'telling response' threatened as far back as March had not yet come and there would not be an immediate reaction to the bombing of the Army's headquarters. In my research for this book I spoke to one of the most senior figures on that loyalist command, a man whose contribution to the process that delivered the ceasefire was described by David Ervine as 'mammoth'. He told me 'it couldn't have been done without him'. To this day, the man remains the most senior figure in the UVF leadership. He has been to jail, has been the target of a number of murder attempts by republicans and, given the position he holds, he would have given direction to the violent loyalist campaign before its ceasefire was declared. Our meeting was arranged through a third party, who was also present, and during our conversation I got some insight into the thinking of the loyalists in that period immediately after Thiepval: 'It didn't look like it [the ceasefire] could be saved, but people were of the view that it shouldn't just be crashed there and then. A reaction after Thiepval would have been seen as reacting to the IRA agenda.'

So, the loyalist leadership was prepared to hold back a little longer, but it had now decided that there would be a so-called 'measured response' to any further IRA actions. Another source – this one in the UDA leadership – spoke to me of the hawks sitting on the wire waiting to swoop.

At this time loyalism was a much more cohesive force and its ceasefire was much more disciplined. There was no knee-jerk reaction to the attacks in London, Manchester and Lisburn and, whilst this 'measured response' was certainly coming, things could have been a whole lot worse. Maybe the fact that the most volatile and unthinking figures, such as Adair, were still in jail helped the Combined Command to hold things back.

This is certainly one possibility and there were other restraining influences at this time. In the Forum elections at the end of May, the two loyalist political parties – the PUP and the UDP – had achieved an electoral mandate in which their combined share of the vote amounted to a little over 5.5 per cent. Without decommissioning, both had also become part of all-party talks, which had begun on 10 June. Sinn Fein, however, was still on the outside because of the absence of an IRA ceasefire. So, politically, the loyalists now had something worth holding onto and they were being urged from the highest political level not to respond to republican violence. But the strain was showing – showing on the faces and in the words of David Ervine and Gary McMichael. Twenty-four hours after the Thiepval bombing, Ervine publicly appealed to the loyalist leadership not to do what its 'enemy' wanted: 'The first thought in my mind is where are we going to get another miracle from, because we have been living a miracle for the last couple of years and certainly since February.' His advice to the Combined Loyalist Military Command was to let the IRA commit 'hari-kari'.

McMichael also admitted that the situation was out of his hands: 'It can only be decided by the CLMC, who have ownership of the ceasefire.'

In this peace process, David Ervine has established himself as one of the principal thinkers on the loyalist side and in a 'broad, sweeping analysis' of the period that included the breakdown of the IRA ceasefire and the eventual loyalist response he described it as 'pain that we all had to go through'. This was the journey from the euphoria of 1994 into the world of reality. The ceasefires were only a beginning, not an end; peace making would take time and there would be periods such as the one we were now in. In one of a number of interviews for this book, I spoke to him about the events of 1996 and the impact the breakdown of the IRA ceasefire had on loyalism:

> *ERVINE*: It was an incremental, debilitating circumstance each and every time something happened, but at Thiepval I thought, yeah, we're going to lose it here.
>
> *ROWAN*: What held it together then?
>
> *ERVINE*: I think the recognition, or the belief, that they were expected to lose it. I remember making the comment, don't do what your enemy wants you to do, and fundamentally that's what they believed their enemy wanted them to do. So, they didn't do it.
>
> *ROWAN*: You also said, 'let the IRA commit hari-kari'. Is that what you think they did?
>
> *ERVINE*: Well, I think they were making, if not mistakes, they were perhaps pandering, I think, to their membership – quite brutal when you consider there were people killed. It couldn't have been pleasing for Adams when he ends up in the position he is in, because, at that point, it could have all fallen apart for Adams, both nationally and internationally.

Thiepval was the latest crisis the loyalist leadership had to manage, but before now there had been cracks in their ceasefire. The two main organisations under the umbrella of the Combined Loyalist Military Command – the UDA and the UVF – had been behind bomb alerts in Dublin in May and July.

These were warning shots, but much more serious was the murder of the Catholic taxi driver Michael McGoldrick – the unsanctioned shooting which led to Billy Wright and others being ejected from the UVF. This killing came at a time when the atmosphere in Northern Ireland was polluted by a parades dispute in Portadown – a stand-off at Drumcree, where, for a few days, the police and the army had prevented Orangemen from marching through a predominantly nationalist area. As a result of this stand-off, Northern Ireland was thrown into chaos and eventually the Orangemen were allowed to walk. The police and the army buckled under huge pressure. It was in this highly charged, highly tense and hostile climate that Michael McGoldrick lost his life – murdered, we would later learn, as a birthday present for Billy Wright.

Wright, like Adair, seemed to thrive on notoriety. They both wanted to rule the loyalist roost and between them, at different times, they totally undermined the efforts to remodel loyalism and to move it in a new direction. The UVF dealt quickly with Wright and his closest associates by almost immediately expelling them from the organisation, but under the new banner of the Loyalist Volunteer Force, these men continued to threaten the peace.

None of what has just been outlined in relation to breaches of the loyalist ceasefire was part of the planned 'measured response'. This was something that was only agreed in those meetings of the Combined Loyalist Military Command that followed the Thiepval bombing, and it was eventually triggered by an IRA attack on police officers inside a children's hospital in Belfast on 20 December 1996.

The officers were there to protect the Democratic Unionist Party politician Nigel Dodds, the city's former Lord Mayor and now an MP, who was visiting his young son. The child, Andrew, died from his illness two years later in December 1998. In a hospital corridor, the IRA opened fire, injuring one of the police officers, and television news reports the following day showed pictures of an incubator that had been pierced by a bullet. It was empty at the time, but something used to nurture young life had been shattered in this attack.

There was confusion about the IRA's intentions. In a statement afterwards, the organisation said its target was the police, but others believed it was Nigel Dodds. One source told me the shooting was viewed within loyalism as 'a deliberate and calculated effort by the IRA to target a unionist politician'. That is not, however, the police view of this shooting.

In an interview for this book, Sir Ronnie Flanagan had this to say:

> With Nigel's son being ill, we had set a pattern of officers being there regularly to make sure that he was safe while visiting the child, and we have no doubt whatever that the attack was an intended attack against our officers, and, indeed, it was only the alertness of our officers that prevented the attack being more successful than it was. We had one officer slightly injured, but it was the action of our officers seeing people at a distance wearing very obvious wigs and confronting them at an early stage which caused them to open fire from a distance and then immediately flee. We never had any doubt that the attack was planned as an attack against the police officers.

It was obvious that the situation was now worse than at any time since the breakdown of the IRA ceasefire, and loyalist sources were painting a very black picture. The 'measured response' could no longer be held back and within 48 hours of the hospital shooting we saw the first evidence of it. In North Belfast, a senior republican, Eddie Copeland, was injured in an under-car booby-trap explosion and within a week a similar device was discovered under a car in Derry. Both these incidents were linked to the UDA, but no one owned up to the attacks, at least not publicly.

By March 1997, the UVF and the Red Hand Commando had joined in. Bombs were placed near Sinn Fein offices in Monaghan in the Irish Republic and in Belfast, and also that month the UDA was linked to the murder of a Catholic man, John Slane. Based on security assessments and conversations with loyalist sources, I was able to report what was going on and who was behind these attacks, but the Combined Loyalist Military Command said nothing. Their ceasefire was never declared over and the political representatives of loyalism were allowed to remain inside the talks process – the same process from which Sinn Fein was barred because of IRA violence. The loyalist ceasefire may not have fallen in the same 'spectacular' way that the IRA cessation did, but its ceasefire was being broken and a political double standard was in evidence.

Probably the most candid assessment of this period that I have heard came from David Ervine in an interview for this book which I recorded back in August 1997. By then the IRA ceasefire had been restored, the Major Government had gone and Tony Blair was preparing the ground for new all-party negotiations that would include the loyalists and republicans. It was safe now for Ervine to give this assessment, but had it been given publicly during Major's stewardship of the process then the loyalists may well have been expelled from the previous talks. I put it to Ervine that loyalism had been living a lie:

> In absolute dotting i's and crossing t's form, then you're right, but one had to understand that it was not as that simple, straightforward, living a lie suggests. It was a much more complex and much more difficult circumstance than people imagined. There was a simple choice . . . either there was a full-blown resumption of loyalist violence or there was a measured response. That was not dictated by the PUP or the UDP. That was dictated by the Combined Loyalist Military Command and we have to accept and acknowledge the difficulties that they worked under . . . and there will be some people who will not want to believe what I am about to say, but in my heart of hearts I know that it is totally true. Had the loyalists succumbed to the easiest option of a resumption, which would have satisfied the emotions, would have satisfied

the machismo and would have satisfied the history that is a
litany of one piece of violence carried out [then] immediately
reacted to, had the loyalists succumbed to that we would have
been into a cycle of violence and goodness knows where it
would have taken us. I think that assuring that that cycle of
violence didn't happen gave us all another chance.

That second chance was a long time coming, and in the end the
process had to wait for Blair. There had been some speculation after
the Forum elections of May 1996 that the IRA could restore its
ceasefire to clear the way for Sinn Fein's entry into all-party talks the
following month, but the speculation proved unfounded. The
Forum elections had demonstrated that the breakdown of the
ceasefire had not damaged republicanism in terms of electoral
support. Sinn Fein's share of the vote was 15.4 per cent – its best ever
performance in any election in Northern Ireland, but that mandate
alone was not going to be good enough to take Adams and
McGuinness to the negotiating table, not yet anyway. In the House
of Commons on 21 May, Major had outlined what would be
required before his door would be opened to Sinn Fein:

> We believe that it is extremely important that the talks on
> Northern Ireland are successful, but the only way in which
> Sinn Fein will find themselves a part of those talks is if there
> is a clear-cut, unequivocal ceasefire by the IRA. In the
> absence of that, Sinn Fein will not be part of the talks. I hope
> that is entirely clear to Sinn Fein, to the IRA and to every
> member of this House.

Major was prepared to park the decommissioning question for a
period of a few months, but the issue of arms would have to be
addressed at the beginning of negotiations. In all of this, republicans
sensed another decommissioning trap and there would be no new
ceasefire.

It became increasingly clear that the IRA was not going to be
moved in the lead-up to those talks on 10 June. Twice in the week
before I met the official spokesman for the leadership of that
organisation – first in a house and then in a café. These were
briefings, and this was the IRA inserting and asserting itself within
the process as Major and Bruton moved the Northern Ireland
parties towards negotiations. On 3 June, my wife drove me to a
rendezvous point in Belfast, where I was collected and taken to a
house where the IRA's spokesman was waiting. We talked in the
front room. It was a Monday night and I noted the briefing on a

church bulletin I had picked up the previous day. On the same piece of paper which listed the mass times and the winners of the weekly parish draw, I now copied down the words of the IRA's spokesman. These were to be attributed to a senior IRA source and he had two main points to make: that the IRA remained 'ready and willing to enhance the potential for real and meaningful peace talks', but the possibility of his organisation doing anything before 10 June as regards a new ceasefire was 'extremely remote'. The IRA believed the talks were being shaped as a decommissioning conference and the source accused the British of 'playing' with the process.

Late that night, I went to the office to prepare reports for the early-morning radio and television output. On 4 June, Sir Patrick Mayhew and the then Irish Foreign Minister Dick Spring were meeting in London to try to agree an agenda for the talks due to begin in six days' time, but their meeting was overshadowed by the IRA's intervention and by the use of words which virtually dismissed any possibility of an imminent ceasefire. It was a message the IRA would repeat 24 hours later.

On the afternoon of 5 June, I went to the café where my IRA leadership source was waiting. We had tea in a quiet corner and this time the message he delivered on the ceasefire and on decommissioning was much more blunt. He had no notes, but had memorised the points his organisation wanted to make and when I had copied them down he asked me to read them back to him.

The first thing he did was put the ceasefire of August 1994 into this context:

> We became persuaded by a number of parties in Ireland and abroad that a real potential existed for substantive negotiations without preconditions.
>
> The British Government committed themselves to facilitate direct entry into those negotiations. We undertook our initiative to enhance all of this potential.

The failure to get to those talks because of the deadlock on decommissioning is what republicans blame for the collapse of the ceasefire, and the IRA was not prepared to renew its cessation for the type of negotiations now being planned. While the British Government was prepared to delay decommissioning for a short time, the IRA believed this obstacle would soon be erected again, and in this situation the likelihood of any new ceasefire was 'remote in the extreme'. That was the public position, but off-the-record my source went much further, suggesting there was not 'a snowball's chance in hell' of the cessation being restored at this time: 'What is required is immediate entry without any preconditions whatsoever into substantive negotiations involving all parties and with all matters on the table,' he told me.

His comments on decommissioning were kept to last, but in three short sentences the IRA's position was made absolutely clear. There was no room for misunderstanding: 'Let us nail completely the position on decommissioning. The IRA will not be decommissioning its weapons through either the front or the back door. We will never leave nationalist areas defenceless this side of a final settlement.'

If they did not already know, then Major and Bruton could have no doubts now. Their planned all-party talks, now just five days away, would not include republicans and therefore this phase of negotiations could not deliver peace. The IRA had made clear that it would not be meeting the British Government's terms for Sinn Fein's entry to talks and in this stalemate there would be a continuation of violence.

The main British and Irish newspapers all reported on the briefing the IRA had given to the BBC – their headlines telling a story of a continuing and dangerous stand-off. The *Daily Mail* went with 'Peace dream shot down by the IRA', *The Guardian* with 'IRA deals new blow to peace' and the *Daily Telegraph* had 'Bomb fears after IRA rejects talks'.

In his opening remarks in a paper setting out the agenda for those 10 June talks, Sir Patrick Mayhew said Sinn Fein had excluded themselves: 'We regret that greatly. But good faith negotiations cannot take place in a democracy if one group is inextricably linked with those who threaten to carry out atrocious acts of violence while negotiations are proceeding.'

Within five days of the start of the talks, the IRA detonated a bomb in Manchester. The huge device, packed with one and a half tons of explosives, sent a shower of glass and debris sweeping through the streets of the city centre and 200 people were injured. There would be another year of IRA violence and a year of talking without Sinn Fein.

Gerry Adams and John Hume – the creators of the 1994 ceasefire – continued to work to find a way out of this, but in an interview for this book the Sinn Fein president told me he had little confidence of things changing while the Major Government was still in power: 'Probably the sense was that it couldn't be rebuilt,' he told me. 'At different times there would have been some little reason to hope that there could be some change in the British Government's position, but I would say the underlying opinion was that this Government wasn't interested . . . but, anyway, whether there was a chance or not, the onus was on us to keep pushing it.'

The IRA believed the British were still looking for a victory and in a statement after the Manchester bomb it claimed the Government had used the period since August 1994 'trying to secure the surrender of IRA weapons and the defeat of the republican struggle'.

The statement continued:

> If there is to be a lasting peace, if the conflict is to be resolved in Britain and Ireland, then the British Government must put the democratic rights of all of the people of Ireland before its own party political self-interest.

John Hume had met the IRA soon after its ceasefire had fallen in early 1996 and in an interview for this book he told me he believed there was still 'a window of opportunity', that the IRA leadership remained 'very committed and interested in the whole new approach'. Hume believed that, in the right political circumstances, the IRA could be persuaded to restore its ceasefire, but by the end of 1996 there were moves underway inside the organisation itself to tie the hands of the leadership in terms of its approach to any new cessation. Within weeks of the Thiepval bombing, there was an IRA Army Convention. This meeting in November 1996 brought into being 'resolutions' which meant that any new ceasefire called by the seven-member Army Council would be reviewed within four months by the larger twelve-member Army Executive. There would also be another Convention within a year of any renewed ceasefire for the organisation's membership to review the situation and to have its say. These were secret developments within the IRA – not things that surfaced publicly at the time – but based on what we now know we can tell that at this point there were tensions within the organisation and a questioning by some of the leadership's strategy. This was a critical internal debate and some senior figures would later part company with the IRA. It is in these developments that you have the birth of what is now labelled dissident republicanism – used to describe those who have dissented from the Adams and McGuinness gospel. The schism would come in late 1997, just months after the restoration of the IRA's 'complete cessation of military operations' and after Sinn Fein had endorsed the Mitchell Principles of democracy and non-violence. Some within the IRA saw this as a repudiation of armed struggle and a betrayal of the organisation.

The first ceasefire had not followed the republican script, and in that period of 17 months or so much had gone wrong. Decommissioning had been an insurmountable obstacle, Albert

Reynolds had fallen, there were no all-party negotiations and when it resumed its campaign, there was a security assessment that the IRA was 'rusty'. Now, inside the organisation there was a questioning of strategy and an effort by some to hold back Adams and McGuinness. Those behind this move would always have been anti-ceasefire and would have viewed the peace process as a sell-out in terms of the traditional republican position. Inside the IRA, these men and women were a minority – but a minority that included a number of highly significant figures.

Despite the bad experience of the 1994 ceasefire, Adams would argue that throughout 1996, including the period of the Thiepval attack, he was working with others, including and most specifically John Hume, to create the political circumstances into which a second cessation could be fitted. This was work that was happening in the background, out of vision, while the foreground was filled by the barracks bombing – how close it had come to being a bloody massacre and how near it had come to pushing the loyalists right over the edge. There were many questions for Adams when I spoke to him the day after the attack on the Army's Northern Ireland headquarters, but he said he wanted to be measured, he wanted to be circumspect, and he was not going to speculate 'about the authors of yesterday's explosions'. Everyone else had, and everyone knew it was the IRA, whether Gerry Adams was prepared to speculate or not.

When I interviewed the Sinn Fein president on 8 October 1996, I put it to him that people would be amazed that someone like him, with his ear so close to the ground in the republican community, would not have some idea about who was behind this bombing:

> Well, what I have to do in terms of my public utterances in all of this is to say what I have to say in a very measured way, and the focus of what I want to say today is not about speculating about the authors of yesterday's explosions, but in the first hand to extend my sympathy to those who were injured and in the second hand to stress my willingness to reach out to those who are our opponents, to those who have sought to exclude us, to those who have sought to marginalise us, and to say to them, whether it be in the British Government or the unionist establishment or the loyalist groups, to say to them all, let's build now a proper peace process based upon inclusive dialogue.

I then asked the Sinn Fein leader if he would call on those responsible for the Thiepval attack to desist.

Well, what I want to see are the conditions in which everyone engaged in armed actions stop those armed actions. I think the best way to do that is to continue doing what I have been doing and I haven't stopped doing it, even yesterday I was about the business of trying to re-create the conditions wherein there can be proper talks in a peaceful, or at least a non-conflict, climate, and my commitment today, after last night's explosions, is double what it was yesterday.

When we spoke, Adams must surely have known, as everyone else did, that it was the IRA that was behind the Thiepval bombing and he must also have known the potential in all of this to bring the loyalists back in. That they had stayed out this long had been quite extraordinary. What Adams also knew was what it was going to take to recreate the ceasefire: a date for Sinn Fein's entry into all-party talks, a time-frame for the negotiations, the removal of the decommissioning precondition and confidence-building measures by the British on issues such as prisoner releases and demilitarisation. This would be the context into which a new ceasefire would be set and in November 1996 I explored this in a little more detail with Jim Gibney, one of Adams' colleagues in the Sinn Fein leadership. Back then, Gibney believed a realistic period for talks was something in the region of six months and it is worth noting that the Good Friday Agreement was later negotiated in the period between September 1997 and April 1998 – close enough to the time-frame that Gibney had suggested. In this interview Gibney also spoke on the question of decommissioning. Back in November 1996, he was in charge of Sinn Fein's press office in Belfast. So, at this point he would have been articulating not just his own views but also a party position and wider republican thinking on this matter. A general election was now only months away and it is also possible that Sinn Fein was using interviews like this one to speak out to the next British Government. They had long ago given up on Major and they were now hoping and waiting for Blair.

On the arms issue, Gibney said the Major Government had created a roadblock which republicans could not get over:

> GIBNEY: It totally undermines the notion that you can have a
> credible peace process if the British Government is
> going to insist on prior decommissioning or
> decommissioning in the process of talks.
>
> We have stated our position clearly on it. We accept
> that the issue needs dealt with, but it has to be dealt
> with to the satisfaction of everyone. What we are now

seeing . . . [is] that it has been imposed on the peace
process. In my view, it was fundamental to the collapse
of the peace process on the ninth of February this year.
ROWAN: Decommissioning is a non-starter basically?
GIBNEY: Well, in terms of the way the British Government
are dealing with the question, then, yes, it is a non-
starter. In terms of republicans realising that it is a
crucial element which needs resolved as part of a wider
package of issues that need resolved, then republicans
are committed to resolving it at that stage, but the way
in which it is being used [makes it] a roadblock which
republicans cannot get over.

So, what republicans had to do was demolish the roadblock, slowly
remove the pieces of the barrier – prior decommissioning, parallel
decommissioning, guns before government – and as they dismantled
the obstacles, they slowly introduced into their internal debate
proposals that would eventually begin to address this issue. This
would not be on the terms that had been dictated by the unionists or
the then Conservative Government, but in a way that would be
tolerated inside the IRA. This would be the journey to arms beyond
use, but long before that point could be reached there was the
business of getting the ceasefire restored and doing so in
circumstances in which all-party negotiations were guaranteed:

GIBNEY: What Sinn Fein is saying is needed is a comprehensive,
credible peace process wherein then the IRA cessation is
fitted. But if you talk to republicans today, there are very,
very few of them who would say there is a mood for a
unilateral cessation by the IRA because of what has gone
on during the IRA cessation itself. But that is not to say
that republicans are not committed to trying to find a way
back to a credible peace process. They are, and, as I said
earlier, the republican door is open to the British
Government and to the unionists, but peace is, ending
conflict is, a two-way street.

Unilateralism, in my view, can be taken as a sign of
weakness and I think that's what republicans would be
concerned about: that a second cessation without the
British Government putting in place a credible peace
process would be taken by them as a sign of weakness.
ROWAN: There would need to be some guarantees this time
that circumstances would change, that it would be a
different playing pitch, if you like.

GIBNEY: The one thing that was very striking in the lead-up to August 1994: there was a great sense of hope and expectation. People were arguing on the basis of let's try this as an opportunity to move away from armed conflict into dialogue, and I think that we did test, if you like, the British Government's commitment to that and their commitment to it was found wanting. So that's very much in the minds of republicans these days and it's not something that you are going to overcome simply by issuing a statement. Action is required to convince republicans that the British Government is serious about trying to move away from armed conflict into a negotiating process that will lead to a negotiated settlement.

That context for ceasefire and talks would become available soon after Tony Blair's arrival in Downing Street, but throughout the remainder of Major's term in government the IRA remained active, and in the run-up to the general election there was a tactical switch in its campaign, which saw its activities being concentrated in Britain. This meant that Major, Blair and the then Liberal Democrat leader Paddy Ashdown were constantly being dragged into the Irish question.

Before then, a young soldier was killed in Northern Ireland in a sniper attack at Bessbrook in County Armagh. The shooting was on 12 February 1997 and the victim was Lance Bombardier Stephen Restorick. He was the first soldier to die in Northern Ireland since the Thiepval bombing and the last to lose his life before the restoration of the IRA ceasefire in July 1997. Just ten days after this shooting, Gerry Adams said he was of the firm view 'that an opportunity to rebuild the peace process and secure a permanent peace' still existed, and he repeated that Sinn Fein wanted to see an end to all 'armed actions' and that his party was committed to 'inclusive democratic negotiations'. All of this would be too late for Stephen Restorick and for the others who would lose their lives before the IRA returned to ceasefire. In the wait for Blair, the killing continued, and Sinn Fein kept emphasising the need for negotiations without preconditions. Adams said these would 'best be conducted in a wholly peaceful environment'.

But even if there was such an environment at this time no one knows when Sinn Fein will be admitted into substantive talks. The British Government has retained a veto over our entry into substantive negotiations and neither myself, John Hume

or the Irish Government have so far been able to elicit a
direct answer from London. When a meaningful and
inclusive process of negotiations is genuinely being offered
we could, with credibility, seek to persuade the IRA to restore
the cessation of August 1994.

Adams again spelt out the republican context for any new ceasefire.

–The removal of preconditions to and in negotiations. [This
is a reference to decommissioning.]
–The issue of a time-frame for the negotiations.
–Confidence-building measures on the part of the British
Government.
–A date for Sinn Fein's entry into dialogue.

We all knew by now that none of this was going to make an
impression on John Major, and Adams would have known that this
was business to be done after the elections – that realistically this
could only happen once the Tories had left office. Speaking to the
author in October 1997, Adams said:

What was for sure – and again this was proved when Blair
came in – was when the British, or if the British, had moved
on the issues which we had identified as being necessary for
the IRA leadership to bring about a cessation, then the result
would have been a cessation.

Blair had moved because Labour's landslide election victory meant
he had the parliamentary numbers to act decisively. Major never had
that luxury. The Westminster arithmetic and his dependence on the
unionists had always ruled against the prospect of any bold initiative
in Northern Ireland. So, it was a long wait from August 1994
through to '97. Major and Adams never met. They spoke at each
other rather than to each other and in this phase of the peace process
they never moved beyond an enemy relationship. In contrast, Blair
and Adams have met many times and out of this a peace of sorts has
grown. Blair got a second ceasefire, the IRA then moved to put some
of its arms beyond use and then the British Prime Minister asked for
'acts of completion'. All of this is the steady progress of
developments beyond the 1997 British general election, but before
then the IRA again advertised its presence in Britain and then it
killed in Northern Ireland.

Polling day in the 1997 general election was 1 May and from late
March you could see a very deliberate raising of the IRA's profile in

Britain. The attacks came in the form of low-risk activities – in that there was little chance of those involved being caught – but, given the period and the closeness of the election, these were high-impact actions. Clearly the IRA's intention was to disrupt the day-to-day routine of normal life and this meant targeting the rail and road networks, a number of airports and then one of the jewels in the British sporting crown. On Saturday, 5 April 1997, the Grand National at Aintree had to be abandoned after coded bomb warnings were made. No device was found, but the Saturday race was delayed until Monday. The IRA was a big part of every news report and Major, Blair and Ashdown were forced to respond to events on the ground. In the same period, the IRA switched off in Northern Ireland. On 10 April a policewoman was shot and wounded in Derry, but then the organisation went quiet.

The loyalists, however, were reacting to the IRA and to what was happening in Britain. In late March and then again in late April large bombs were positioned close to Sinn Fein offices in North and West Belfast. Through their actions the loyalists were saying two things to the IRA: that 'bombs in England count as well' and that the 'brinkmanship' had 'come as far as it dare'. The UDA also murdered a man during this period and there were other shooting incidents in which Catholic families were targeted. This was the so-called 'measured response' and this was the most active the loyalists had been since their ceasefire of October 1994 – a ceasefire they had still not declared over.

In the general election, Adams regained the West Belfast seat he had lost to the SDLP's Joe Hendron in 1992, and Martin McGuinness topped the poll in mid-Ulster. In Northern Ireland, Sinn Fein's share of the vote was 16 per cent – its best ever showing, which grew to almost 17 per cent in local council elections a few weeks later. So, the pattern through three elections – all of them in a period of non-ceasefire – showed increased support for Sinn Fein, but more importantly for republicans Major and the Tories were now gone and very quickly the conditions for a new ceasefire were created.

In interviews for this book, Adams spoke of Major being 'dumped' in 'such style' – a reference to Blair's huge majority. The Sinn Fein president believed the increased vote for his party 'vindicated' its peace strategy, and contacts between London, Dublin and Sinn Fein would soon put in place the necessary pieces for Adams and McGuinness to call on the IRA to restore its 'complete cessation of military operations'. On the increased vote for his party, in October 1997 Adams said 'people had been radicalised and understood that Sinn Fein's peace strategy was not a vote for violence, contrary to what others have said, but was an endorsement of a strategy'.

ROWAN: A peace encouragement?

ADAMS: Yes, absolutely, but a peace with justice encouragement. It would be wrong to suggest that this was anything other than a vote for a peace settlement which was democratic, which would have justice as its basis and which would have the republican analysis being put by our party. So, it was a strong vote for the republican position to be put in real peace talks.

ROWAN: Given what you've just said about a vote for peace, how taken aback were you with John Hume's intervention before the '97 election when he talked about a vote for Sinn Fein being a vote for violence?

ADAMS: I made the point that it appeared to me that the SDLP were going to fight a very robust election campaign and I made the point, actually, in a number of pieces, that what John Hume and I had been able to do was not to join each other's parties or to set aside our own particular analysis, but find areas of common agreement and to set aside party political advantage to do this. So, I actually said to people because we're contesting an election, and this election will be a temporary intervention, if you like, into the necessary task of finding peace, and because we do so from our different positions, it doesn't mean that we have given up on the necessary task of working together.

So, I think all of those who took up that position, and I think it was a mistake for them . . . it is untrue, or it's inaccurate or whatever word you want to use, and John Hume, John Bruton, all the rest of them were proved to be wrong.

ROWAN: But were you angered by that sort of comment?

ADAMS: Well, anger doesn't come into it. The task of politics is, in terms of this stage of the whole political process, that parties which are rivals electorally compete; we're competing for each other's votes. So you do it with an eye to the longer term and it would be wrong to get angry or to get sidetracked or to get caught up in an electoral squabble.

I'll give you a little example which hasn't been used very often. When I lost the West Belfast seat in 1992, I was talking to John Hume during that period, privately, and he told me afterwards that one of the things that reassured him totally that I was serious was that I didn't leak that I was talking to him, because clearly had I done that we would have been able to thwart the loyalist tactical voting in the Shankill, because obviously nationalists would have welcomed that type of initiative which had me playing a central part in it. So, the point I'm trying to make is that in '92 the seriousness of the task that I was involved in with John Hume was more important than the election and, similarly, '97, the task of trying to bring about a democratic peace settlement and recognising John Hume's pivotal role in all of that, while we fight robustly in the elections, we have to do that in a way which sees beyond the elections.

Beyond the election of 1997 is when it all started happening again. On 16 May, on his first visit to Northern Ireland as Prime Minister, Tony Blair said he was prepared to allow officials to meet with Sinn Fein 'provided events on the ground, here and elsewhere, do not make that impossible'. The Prime Minister said the 'settlement train' was leaving and he wanted the talks process to include Sinn Fein: 'The opportunity is still there to be taken if there is an unequivocal IRA ceasefire. Words and deeds must match and there must be no doubt of commitment to peaceful methods.'

These were the first public signals that things were about to change. While Blair had stressed the need for an unequivocal ceasefire, there had been no mention of decommissioning as a precondition to negotiations, and the guns and talks stand-off was about to end. But this was not just about reaching out to republicans, and the Blair speech – at Balmoral in Belfast – included the things that the unionists needed to hear, particularly about consent – meaning that any constitutional change would require the backing of a Northern Ireland majority. None of this came as a surprise to David Trimble. He had spoken to Blair before the election and had urged him 'to pick up the Northern Ireland issue rapidly' and 'to run with it', and the Ulster Unionist leader had also outlined what was possible in terms of a potential agreement. In March 1999, Trimble discussed how his sense of Blair was that he was strong on the issue of consent but not so solid on decommissioning, in terms of it being a precondition to talks.

> TRIMBLE: So, there we had a new Prime Minister in, a huge majority, adopting on the crucial consent issue similar views to our own, who is anxious to push things forward . . . but I knew he wasn't solid on decommissioning. So,

> it was not altogether a surprise when a few weeks after
> Balmoral he signalled that they were going to move.
> *ROWAN*: That Sinn Fein could get into the talks without that
>   precondition?
> *TRIMBLE*: Yes.

It was not a question of Blair being weak or solid on decommissioning as a precondition to talks, but more a case of a new British government, in a position of considerable strength, knowing what it was going to take to move things forward and prioritising in terms of what needed to happen first. Blair and his Secretary of State for Northern Ireland, Mo Mowlam, had been watching things long enough to know that the IRA was not going to decommission on unionist terms. So, for the moment they would settle for a new ceasefire and push the arms question further down the road. Once the Government had made its mind up, there was then a choice for Trimble – particularly when the IRA ceasefire was restored.

> I can remember some really tight manoeuvring in a confined
> space in interviews in July when we were saying that there
> were possibilities for progress which we were exploring and
> all the rest of it . . . and that we were going to consult the
> party.

This is the Ulster Unionist leader speaking in an interview for this book:

> Now, Blair could have pushed me into a corner and he didn't,
> in fact he went out of his way and was briefing, Downing
> Street was briefing, the press in ways that were basically
> helpful to us. Again that was important to us in the run-up to
> September [the date for new all-party talks] because we did
> our consultation exercise over the summer, and particularly
> in September. We'd had time, through the summer, for
> people to think about it, without being heavily pressurised,
> and for people then to work their way through. We could not
> have stayed in the talks on the entry of Sinn Fein if it hadn't
> been the clear view of the greater number of the party and the
> party wouldn't have come to that view had the matter been
> pushed.

For republicans, the real signal that Blair meant business came in a private document passed to Sinn Fein on 13 June. If the IRA restored its ceasefire, the party could be in talks by the end of July.

Blair later told the Commons that he expected substantive talks to be underway by September and that the target date for reaching a settlement was May the following year. The plan, at this stage, was for the negotiations and decommissioning to happen in parallel – the latter to be handled by an International Commission. So, Sinn Fein now had its entry date to the talks, a time-frame for those negotiations and the arms precondition had been removed. But, as is so often the case in Northern Ireland, the momentum of this period was punctuated by 'events on the ground' – by more killing and by the continuing controversy over the Drumcree march in Portadown.

On 16 June, just three days after that Government position paper had been given to Sinn Fein, two RUC officers on the beat in Lurgan – not far from Portadown – were shot dead by the IRA. This was the backdrop to the July marching season, when, once again, the air was filled with all the tension associated with Drumcree.

Based on a number of conversations I had with senior security sources in the run-up to the parade on Sunday, 6 July, the very clear impression I had, and felt I had been given, was that the police would prevent the Orange march from reaching the nationalist Garvaghy Road. At this stage, decisions to allow or ban marches still rested with the RUC, but this responsibility was later passed to a Parades Commission. Late into the night on 5 July, the impression I had hardened when the army began working in the fields below the Drumcree Church. It appeared that those fields were going to be dressed in coils of razor and barbed wire and that the parade would be stopped, but I was wrong. In the early hours of 6 July, police and soldiers moved on to the Garvaghy Road to clear a route for the marchers – a decision which sparked a period of street violence in nationalist areas, but a decision still defended by Sir Ronnie Flanagan – the then Chief Constable:

> ROWAN: I assume you thought long and hard about it, and there had been an impression beforehand that the march might not go down. What changed all of that?
> FLANAGAN: The decision was arrived at late on the Saturday night [and I had] to balance two evils. And I'm not saying that a march is an evil, I'm not saying a protest against a march is an evil, but clearly there were evil outcomes going to arise following the decision either way. I had to balance that and I have no doubt that at that time and in those circumstances had that parade not gone down many innocent lives would have been lost.

ROWAN: Through loyalist violence?

FLANAGAN: I have no doubt that there would have been
many innocent Catholic lives lost and, assessing all of
the intelligence that I had at my disposal, I came to the
view, late on that Saturday night, that that was the
decision that was appropriate. Now, bear in mind that
up to that time and, indeed right to after midnight on
the Friday night, the Secretary of State was working to
try and bring about an accommodation; the church
leaders had worked, politicians of all views had
attempted to work to bring about an accommodation
and I was left, if you like, with 24 hours in which to
arrive at a decision, a desperately difficult decision, and
the whole thrust was to engage in absolutely the
minimum of force required and the further thrust was
to be out of there and to subject the people of Garvaghy
Road to the minimum disruption possible, and if you go
back and review the policing operation you'll see the
police and army withdrawing as soon as the parade is
through. The one thing that is a source of bitter regret
for me is the disruption that was caused to people who
wanted to attend mass at St John the Baptist Church. It
was something we failed to take into account,
something I deeply regret and something that if you
were winding the clock back I would certainly take into
account. We were just beginning to make arrangements
to convey people when it was decided they would hold
an open-air mass instead, but that was an unpredicted
effect, if you like, that we should have predicted.

What happened on the Garvaghy Road could in no way be described
as 'minimum disruption', and in the eyes of nationalists in
Portadown and elsewhere Flanagan and Mowlam were now
damaged goods.

In the situation that developed from the decision to force the
Orange march through there was all the potential for a security
nightmare. The main day of the marching season, 12 July, was just
around the corner, and in some areas nationalists intended to play
the numbers game. There would be a 'mobilisation' and some
parades would be confronted. This was to be the revenge for
Portadown.

On 10 July, Flanagan and other senior police officers met Orange
Order leaders at their Belfast offices. In terms of the security
assessment, the then Chief Constable told it as it was. Flanagan

painted a black picture and in some areas the Orange Order was faced with a simple choice – to walk away or to have their route blocked by the security forces before they arrived at potential flashpoints. In an interview for this book, I spoke to Flanagan about this period and that meeting with Orange leaders:

> FLANAGAN: I left them in no doubt what the consequences would be.
> ROWAN: Very serious consequences?
> FLANAGAN: I have no doubt that there would have been dire consequences.

On the evening of 10 July, I sat outside the Ballynafeigh Orange Hall on Belfast's Ormeau Road with my colleague Mervyn Jess and we watched the comings and goings. Local Orangemen were being informed of the decision of their district officers to withdraw from the main Belfast demonstration on 12 July. It would mean no march into the predominantly nationalist lower Ormeau Road – one of the areas where there had been plans to confront a parade. A statement released by the Ballynafeigh District read: 'This action has been taken to avoid the enemies of our Protestant heritage being given the opportunity to create a situation resulting in major civil disorder with a possible loss of life.'

In Newry, Armagh and Londonderry, the Orange Order also altered its plans. The Drumcree parade may have got through, but at a price now being extracted elsewhere.

At a news conference in Conway Mill on the Falls Road the following day, Gerry Adams welcomed the decision taken by the Orange Order. I remember him also making a comment about working in the background on the bigger picture – meaning the peace process – but, in the heat of all that was going on in relation to the marching season, the significance of this remark was missed. We heard it, but did not take it in. On the decisions taken by the Orange Order, Adams said:

> They have created a welcome breathing space and I understand that the many mobilisations which were planned in response to these parades have now been cancelled. As details emerge of how the Orange Order's decision came about I think it will show that there were two factors at work: the mass mobilisation of nationalists and the debate within Orangeism as it came to terms with this. In commending the Orange Order I would like also to praise the stand taken by the people of the Garvaghy Road. Although brutalised by the

RUC and British Army, they stood firm for their own rights and secured the rights of beleaguered nationalist communities in areas like the lower Ormeau Road. I want to commend those who supported these beleaguered communities . . . The British Government, following the events on the Garvaghy Road, has a genuine credibility problem with nationalists and republicans. They have to address this. Tony Blair needs to demonstrate good faith in dealing with republicans and nationalists by accepting that nationalists and republicans have equal political and civil rights.

This was the last time the Orangemen were allowed onto the Garvaghy Road. In every year since 1997 their path has been blocked by the security forces. But, let us leave Drumcree for now, and return to that passing comment Adams made about working on the bigger picture. What none of us knew at the time was that we were just nine days away from a new ceasefire – a ceasefire brought about by those background contacts involving Sinn Fein, the British Government and a new Irish Government headed by Bertie Ahern. Sir Ronnie Flanagan believes there were other contributing factors – that the reaction to the murders of his officers in Lurgan in June and then the decision taken by the Orange Order in the lead-up to 12 July forced the IRA to move sooner than anticipated. Instead of waiting till September to restore the ceasefire, the IRA found itself having to move in July:

> I think at that time, if you go back to the murders of my two colleagues in June in Lurgan and the utter and absolutely widespread revulsion that that brought about, my colleague Commissioner Pat Byrne in Dublin saw to it that flags were flown at half mast in his stations in the Republic. There was worldwide complete condemnation. I think the Republican Movement at that time was beginning to move towards a restoration of their cessation of violence. I think, to be quite frank, they thought that the marching season would ease the pressure that was brought to bear on them following the murder of my two colleagues . . . and they thought that probably that would give them through to about September, and they would have seen that as a period during which they could, if you like, portray hurt and simply use the marching season and undoubtedly the disorder that would flow. I think the decisions the Orange Order arrived at in relation to 12 July denied them, in a sense, that opportunity . . . and I have

no doubt that precipitated an earlier decision than might
otherwise have come about.

The ceasefire decision did come quickly – quicker than many
expected – and out of the dark of all that happened in Lurgan in June
and then around Drumcree in July there was now new light, new
hope and a second chance. By Tony Blair's September target date,
republicans, loyalists, unionists and nationalists would be at the
negotiating table and the former United States senator George
Mitchell would skilfully steer the talks participants towards a historic
agreement reached without prior decommissioning or
decommissioning in parallel with the negotiations. There would be
a new target date of May 2000 for the decommissioning process to
be completed, but still there was no commitment from the IRA to
put its arms beyond use.

CHAPTER FIVE

Good Friday, Black Saturday

'We have ordered the unequivocal restoration of the ceasefire of August 1994. All IRA units have been instructed accordingly.'

IRA leadership, 19 July 1997

'We all have reasons to be suspicious of each other, but we have to rise to the occasion that is before us and lead the people of this island into a new and peaceful future.'

Sinn Fein president Gerry Adams, 20 July 1997

FRIDAY, 18 JULY 1997: The hotel at Redcastle just across the border from Derry in County Donegal was a happy place. It had that wedding-day feel to it – loud chat and laughter as family and friends celebrated something special in the summer sunshine. It would be a big day too for the peace process, its biggest day since 1994. I was just passing through the hotel with my wife Val and the kids. We had called in for a coffee and an ice cream before heading back to Brigid McGuinness's house at Moville – our base for a short summer break. Just after five, however, my mobile phone rang. It was Noel McCartney, one of my colleagues back at the BBC in Belfast, and he was calling with big news. Sinn Fein had just issued a statement telling us that Gerry Adams and Martin McGuinness had briefed the IRA and had urged its leadership to restore the ceasefire of August 1994. Earlier in the day, there had also been a Hume–Adams statement. This had also happened before the 1994 cessation, but in 1994 the ceasefire had been signalled well in advance, while what was unfolding on this day – 18 July 1997 – was a surprise to say the least. Perhaps had we listened more carefully to Adams at that news conference on the Orange marches a week or so earlier, and specifically to his remark about working on the bigger picture, then we would not have been caught so unawares by these developments.

I had to abandon Val, Elle and PJ in Moville and I headed for the BBC's Foyle studios in Derry with my oldest son Ruairi. McCartney had arranged for a jacket, shirt and tie to be ready for me. Things were moving quickly – more quickly than anyone would have thought possible those few weeks earlier when the news was about murder in Lurgan and all of the controversy attached to Drumcree.

At Foyle, I called a key security contact, someone who I knew would have knowledge of the most up-to-date intelligence assessments. He gave me a clear and convincing read out. It was inconceivable that Adams would issue such a statement if he was not certain of a positive outcome. A ceasefire announcement was imminent. It could come by midnight and would certainly come within hours. This was information I used in my early reports and in interviews with presenters back in Belfast, and it was information I became more certain of when I spoke to a republican source sometime between nine and ten. He suggested I should head for Belfast early the next morning and I did.

In his statement of 18 July, Gerry Adams clearly indicated that he believed the conditions for a new ceasefire had been met: 'I have made it clear over the 18 months since the collapse of the peace process that I would only approach the IRA to restore their cessation if I was confident that their response would be positive.'

If Adams was confident then there was good reason for everyone else to be so too. He was confident because he believed the 'two pillars on which the peace process was initially constructed' had been rebuilt. The Sinn Fein president now believed there was a commitment to inclusive negotiations without preconditions and that these talks would take place within a stated time-frame.

There would be a comprehensive agenda for the negotiations, there would be no attempt to predetermine the outcome and no outcome would be precluded. The decommissioning issue would not be allowed to block negotiations and he said the talks 'would be enhanced by specified confidence-building measures with a particular focus on the equality agenda and demilitarisation, including the issue of prisoners.' All of these things were part of the first pillar and they all became part of the negotiations leading to the Good Friday Agreement. His statement continued:

> Secondly, following intensive contacts, it is clear that there is a shared commitment to significant and substantial change, to issues of equality and to demilitarisation on the part of Sinn Fein, the SDLP, the Irish Government and Irish-American opinion. In addition, I am confident that the mistakes that were made by the former taoiseach John Bruton

will not be repeated and that Sinn Fein will be accorded full
equality of treatment.

This statement from Adams, endorsed by Martin McGuinness, was
preparing the ground for the IRA's announcement. This was
something the two would repeat in October 2001 just ahead of the
IRA's decision to put some of its arms beyond use, and what these
public pronouncements did, if you like, was whet the appetite before
the IRA delivered the main course.

Given their positions, Adams and McGuinness would have
known, of course, what was on the IRA's menu and, to this day, they
remain the two most influential leaders within the broad Republican
Movement. Here is how a former chief constable, Sir Hugh
Annesley, described their roles in an interview with me in June 1996:

> *ANNESLEY*: There is no doubt in my mind that, at the top,
> the Republican Movement – the Provisional IRA and
> Sinn Fein – are inextricably linked. So, I do not see this
> artificial distinction that's been drawn. I believe Messrs
> Adams and McGuinness are very, very influential
> people and I think they have a major say in the conduct
> overall of the republican thrust.
> *ROWAN*: So, you don't buy this line from Gerry Adams that
> Sinn Fein is not the IRA and the IRA is not Sinn Fein.
> Is that what you are saying?
> *ANNESLEY*: I'm saying that categorically. They are
> inextricably linked, particularly at the top. There are
> people in Sinn Fein who devote themselves purely to
> politics, but the control of the Movement at the top is
> clearly linked. There are members of provisional Sinn
> Fein who are on the Army Council and there are
> members of the Army Council who are on the political
> talks level of Sinn Fein.

So, it was with a sense of expectation that I left Moville at around
eight o'clock on Saturday morning, 19 July 1997, and about an
hour or so into my journey back to Belfast my phone rang. It was
the republican I had spoken to the night before. The IRA's
ceasefire statement had just been issued to RTE in Dublin, and
within a few minutes of that phone conversation a BBC newsflash
carried the details of a restoration of the cessation of August 1994.
It would begin at midday on Sunday. The full text of the IRA
statement read:

On 31 August 1994, the leadership of Oglaigh na hEireann announced a complete cessation of military operations as our contribution to the search for a lasting peace.

After 17 months of cessation, in which the British Government and the unionists blocked any possibility of real or inclusive negotiations, we reluctantly abandoned the cessation.

The Irish Republican Army is committed to ending British rule in Ireland. It is the root cause of division and conflict in our country. We want a permanent peace and therefore we are prepared to enhance the search for a democratic peace settlement through real and inclusive negotiations.

So, having assessed the current political situation, the leadership of Oglaigh na hEireann are announcing a complete cessation of military operations from twelve o'clock midday on Sunday, 20 July 1997.

We have ordered the unequivocal restoration of the ceasefire of August 1994. All IRA units have been instructed accordingly.

P. O'NEILL

After all of the dilly-dallying of the Major years, things were now moving at a swift pace. This new ceasefire would open up a path for republicans into the type of multi-party negotiations that Adams and McGuinness had long argued were necessary if an end to conflict was to be achieved, but it also opened up divisions within republicanism. This is the schism that gave birth to the so-called 'Real' IRA (RIRA).

Sinn Fein joined the talks in September and by 10 April the following year agreement had been reached. It was a Good Friday for the peace process, but just four months later a car bomb produced the blackest Saturday of the Troubles. The explosion in the County Tyrone market town of Omagh, on 15 August 1998, claimed 29 lives. It was a bloody reminder of just how difficult it would be to find peace in a place more used to war.

It was Sinn Fein's entry into multi-party talks, and more specifically the party signing up to the Mitchell Principles of democracy and non-violence which prompted some within republicanism to move against the policy of the central leadership. Remember, one of the Mitchell Principles was to renounce the use of force, and some within republican ranks interpreted this as a condemnation of the IRA's 'armed struggle'. It was a step too far, and it would lead to an IRA Army Convention in County Donegal in October 1997 – a meeting to which the emergence of the dissident 'Real' IRA can be traced.

What happened could not be characterised as a major split, but 'senior' and 'serious' people left the organisation. As details of the secret meeting began to emerge, a senior Northern Ireland Office security official gave me this assessment of developments: 'The situation is that Adams and McGuinness still have the Movement. It's not a split. There are no bodies on the border.'

The security view was that the IRA leadership had emerged from the Convention with a grip on its organisation and with its ceasefire intact. That said, the IRA was now looking over its shoulder at some of its own and at some of those who had been central to its 'war' effort, and in what was unfolding there was a new threat to the peace.

At the time all of this was emerging publicly, some newspaper reports suggested that a former IRA chief of staff had resigned along with the entire 'engineering department' – those responsible for developing IRA weaponry – and that the organisation had lost many in its South Armagh brigade. Had all of this been accurate, it would have represented a huge split in the IRA and a rejection of the Adams and McGuinness strategy by some of the most significant elements of the organisation, but, while confirming resignations, security sources said these reports were 'exaggerated'. The situation was, however, serious – serious enough for the IRA itself to move to put these developments into context.

So, on Sunday, 9 November 1997, I met with a senior IRA figure in a house in Belfast. We had spoken before, but this was the first time I had met him in his new role as spokesman for the IRA leadership, and this would be one of many contacts we would have in a period spanning a little over two years.

Our first meeting was on that Sunday afternoon in November 1997 and I was taken to it by another republican. The IRA spokesman confirmed that:

- The organisation's Army Executive had called a Convention in October.
- It was called to debate the situation around the ceasefire and the current strategy.
- The vast majority of those present endorsed the strategy and the Army Council position on the cessation.
- A small number of those present took an opposing view.
- Among the issues discussed was the Mitchell Principles.
- The IRA leadership had previously made it clear that the Mitchell Principles were a matter for Sinn Fein.
- Since the Convention, a small number of individuals had chosen to resign from the IRA.
- The numbers in the media were inflated.

The source was adamant that no former chief of staff had resigned and he dismissed as 'nonsense' the media reports that the entire engineering department had resigned and that there had been big losses in South Armagh: 'The position of the Convention was that all brigade areas supported the leadership decision [on ceasefire and strategy].'

Another republican, whom I spoke to five days later, said the leadership was 'managing' the problem. He said he would not describe what was happening as 'haemorrhaging' but 'erosion', and on the issue of those who had left the IRA, he said they were 'serious people' who had been around a long time and who had held 'senior posts' in the past – the recent past. My source said they had opposed the leadership's strategy and their main argument was over the Mitchell Principles. He said it was a 'shallow analysis' and that no alternative strategy was offered. The source said the IRA Army Council had allowed the Convention, even though it was a minority on the Army Executive who had pushed for it, and he described the situation as 'largely a southern problem'. 'The Army [IRA] in the north is solid, northern command is solid, Army Council is solid,' he told me.

Before this Convention, the IRA had given its view on the Mitchell Principles. This was back in September 1997 in an interview in the weekly republican newspaper *An Phoblacht/Republican News*, which came just before the start of all-party talks and which also dealt with decommissioning and the thinking behind the renewal of the ceasefire in July. On that matter, a spokesman for the IRA leadership said:

> The key elements which influenced our decision were that the new British Labour Government moved with some speed after taking office to deal with the need for all-inclusive negotiations and the new Fianna Fail-led Government in the south moved to help put a peace process back on the rails from an Irish point of view. The previous British Government under John Major had imposed a number of blocking mechanisms or obstacles to prevent inclusive and meaningful peace talks taking place. The British Government had known for some time that before the IRA would again consider a cessation of military activity they would have to address four key issues:
>
> 1. The removal of the precondition of decommissioning.
> 2. Setting a time-frame for any talks.
> 3. Immediate entry into talks for Sinn Fein on the basis of its democratic mandate.

4. Confidence-building measures by the British Government.

The new British Government moved publicly and speedily to address these issues. They removed the precondition of decommissioning, they set a time-frame for substantive talks of between now and May next year, they made it clear that such talks would be substantive and inclusive when they were convened on 15 September and that bilateral meetings would start almost immediately after any announcement of an IRA cessation. They also gave public commitments to move on a series of confidence-building measures including POWs, the Irish language and issues of equality of treatment.

In the *An Phoblacht* interview, the IRA spokesman again made clear the organisation's position on decommissioning. Sinn Fein would soon be in all-party talks, but in this commentary from the IRA we appeared no nearer a resolution of the arms question:

I don't think anyone has ever realistically expected us to agree to decommissioning this side of a political settlement. There is no historical precedent in Ireland for such a demand. Those who raised the issue in the first instance and who continue to hype it are interested only in creating an excuse for their own refusal to engage in meaningful negotiations. The seriousness with which they take the issue can be fairly well measured by their lack of focus on any need to decommission the guns of the RUC, the British Army or the 100,000 and more other 'legally' held guns in the Six Counties.

Decommissioning on our part would be tantamount to surrender. It was irresponsible of the last British Government to try to use the opportunity provided by our initiative in August 1994 to secure an IRA surrender. It would therefore be doubly irresponsible if the present British Government went on that same fruitless pursuit again. Decommissioning should not be allowed to become a distraction from the need for meaningful negotiations. Those with a genuine interest in developing a peace process which has the potential for producing a just and lasting peace will have no interest in decommissioning beyond the point where all guns are silent.

Given its timing, the British and Irish governments would not have found any of this particularly helpful. The negotiations – scheduled for 15 September – were now just a few days away and Trimble's Ulster Unionists and the two loyalist parties were still considering

whether to join Adams and McGuinness at the talks table. Because
of Sinn Fein's presence, a significant chunk of political unionism had
opted to boycott the talks. Ian Paisley's Democratic Unionist Party
and Robert McCartney's United Kingdom Unionist Party would not
be participating. So, the governments would have been anxious to
get to the talks as quickly and quietly as possible, but this unexpected
IRA intervention had caused a problem. It was not just because of
the hard line taken on decommissioning, but also because of what
was said on the Mitchell Principles and the distinction the IRA
spokesman made between the decisions of Sinn Fein and the
position of the IRA itself:

> Sinn Fein is a political party with a very substantial
> democratic mandate. What they do is a matter for them. But
> I think all republicans should understand and support them as
> they do what they believe is right and necessary to bring
> about a lasting peace. Sinn Fein's stated commitment is to
> secure a peace settlement which both removes the causes of
> conflict and takes all the guns – British, republican, unionist,
> nationalist and loyalist – out of Irish politics. The Sinn Fein
> position actually goes beyond the Mitchell Principles. Their
> affirmation of these principles is therefore quite compatible
> with their position. As to the IRA's attitude to the Mitchell
> Principles per se, well, the IRA would have problems with
> sections of the Mitchell Principles. But then the IRA is not a
> participant in these talks.

It had the feel of double-talk. Sinn Fein was saying one thing and the
other arm of the Republican Movement something else. Certainly as
far as unionists were concerned, it was possible to read into this that
the IRA was leaving open the option of returning to violence. It was
one of many times in the process when there was a lot of political
huffing and puffing. Unionists called for Sinn Fein to be expelled
from the talks and loyalists claimed that the IRA was trying to wreck
the negotiations by ensuring that loyalism and unionism did not
participate. Undoubtedly Trimble had genuine concerns about all of
this, but the public anger expressed by loyalists may well have been
used to shield their private relief. Why? Because there was nothing
to suggest that the paramilitaries in that community were ready to
embrace those principles of democracy and non-violence.

At the time, Davy Adams was a senior figure in McMichael's
Ulster Democratic Party – the political representatives of the UDA.
This is what he told me, when I asked him to think back on that
period: 'It would have created a bigger problem for the loyalists if

the IRA had come out and immediately and boldly signed up to the Mitchell Principles, for the spotlight and weight of expectation would have immediately shifted onto loyalism.'

The start to the talks was never going to be easy and this was the difficult beginning that many would have anticipated, but the storm blew over and Trimble, Ervine and McMichael joined republican leaders at the talks table. Given the absence of Paisley and McCartney, it was vital for Trimble that this happened and that he was not left totally isolated within the negotiations. Indeed, in the end, the UUP, the PUP and the UDP delegations entered the talks arena together. Trimble himself said: 'Technically, we needed Ervine and McMichael under the ground rules of the talks.'

He needed them as part of the numbers game – to guarantee that a majority of unionist/loyalist political opinion was represented inside the talks, and the combined electoral mandate of the three parties ensured this:

> TRIMBLE: Now, that was an embarrassment, so it was, because when they suggested to us that we all walk in together, we could scarcely say no, go away, we don't want you, when in fact we needed them.
> ROWAN: Was it difficult for you to walk in with them?
> TRIMBLE: It was not the easiest thing in the world . . . [but] not as difficult as what was waiting for us on the other side.

Adams and McGuinness were waiting on the other side, and for Trimble and the political representatives of loyalism these were big steps – their biggest steps in the process so far. So, was Trimble concerned that significant unionist figures had chosen to stay outside? 'The Paisley–McCartney thing, while it may have weighed on the minds of some other people, didn't bother me one iota,' he told me.

'In fact I expected as a consequence that for us, myself personally and for the UUP, life would be easier without them and our bargaining position would be strengthened without them.'

What Trimble meant was that the other talks participants would have to take on board the tensions within unionism and, given those tensions, the fragility of his position within the talks:

> The disappearance of Paisley and McCartney simplified things, enabled us to concentrate purely on dealing with nationalism, and in dealing with nationalism then, as you say, the weakness and strength argument came in because we

would say, now, look, you can't do this without unionism,
they're away [Paisley and McCartney], you can't do this
without us.

So, Trimble believes the absence of the other unionist parties
actually strengthened his negotiating hand and that nationalist
demands had to be diluted in order for agreement to be reached.

I will deal with the negotiations and the outcome of the talks later,
but for now I want to concentrate on what was going on within
republicanism in late 1997. What the IRA had to say in its September
interview in *An Phoblacht* is likely to have been the position outlined at
the Army Convention a few weeks later. It is also possible that the
public commentary on the Mitchell Principles was not intended to
upset the talks applecart, but had more to do with calming things
internally. This was the IRA trying to settle those within its ranks
who were starting to sense a 'sell-out'. The security assessment is that
Adams and McGuinness and the central leadership used the occasion
to out-manoeuvre their critics – that even though there were
resignations after the Donegal meeting, the Convention had been a
success in terms of the overall objective of avoiding significant splits.
When I interviewed Sir Ronnie Flanagan for this book in March
1999, I asked him for his assessment of the meeting:

FLANAGAN: I think that you have to consider that particular
            Convention as having been sought by dissidents, if you
            like, or potential dissidents, having been sought by
            people who were opposed to the signing up to the
            Mitchell Principles. But those people were completely
            outflanked by the central leadership as a result of which,
            it's well documented now, some of them, including the
            then quartermaster general, stood to the side. What
            they did in those early stages was raise, if you like, a
            rallying flag just to determine how much support would
            rally to that dissident cause. But, even though that
            Convention resulted in [the] movement of a number of
            dissidents away from the mainstream organisation, . . .
            [it] has to be considered, I guess, a success in terms of
            avoiding significant splits.
ROWAN: In a sense, did Adams and McGuinness call the bluff
            of the dissidents? Would that be a reasonable summary
            of what happened then?
FLANAGAN: I have no doubt that that could summarise what
            happened in that particular Convention.
ROWAN: You mentioned the quartermaster general, but other

serious and senior people, as republicans would
describe them, left at that time, was that a signal to
Adams and McGuinness that it wasn't going to be an
easy journey in terms of taking their people along in
this process?

FLANAGAN: There undoubtedly were a few significant
people, including those with engineering expertise, who
stood to the side, but [and it was Flanagan who coined
the phrase before that] what was always important was
the critical mass and certainly not then and not since
did the critical mass move away from the policy being
delineated by the leadership. So, certainly it was a
warning signal but there was never anything that
changed it from being a trickle of movement away
towards it being a stream of movement away.

ROWAN: Did the departure of these people make it easier for
the central leadership to manage the process?

FLANAGAN: I think you could say that. I think that would be
fair to say.

In this same period, there were developments within loyalism which
also threatened the movement towards some sort of peace in
Northern Ireland. The murder of Billy Wright inside the Maze
Prison in December 1997, and what followed, put everything at risk
– every little bit of progress that had been achieved during the
negotiations that had begun in earnest just a few months earlier.
Wright was shot inside a prison van on his way to a Saturday
morning visit – shot by an INLA prisoner with a gun that had been
smuggled into the top-security jail. The Portadown loyalist was hit
several times in the chest. In the emergency control room, a report
of the shooting was received at 09.59 and by 10.53 that same
morning, 27 December 1997, Wright was pronounced dead. The
news spread quickly beyond the walls of the prison. I was called first
by Richard McAuley of Sinn Fein, who had heard rumours of the
shooting, and as soon as we finished our conversation I got to work
trying to get confirmation of what he had told me. I spoke first to
my colleague, Mervyn Jess, at the office and asked him to contact the
police, while I started chasing a number of loyalist sources – one of
them a close associate of the man lying dead inside the Maze. He
confirmed that Wright had been shot and a short time later a police
source, who called me at home, told me the shooting was fatal. My
phone just kept ringing and ringing. Ian Paisley Jnr called and so too
did Davy Adams of the loyalist Ulster Democratic Party.

By now, details of the shooting had reached the political

grapevine. At around twelve o'clock, I had joined Jess in the office. One of our editors, Andrew Colman, was also there and the news was about one thing only – the jail shooting and murder of Wright.

On a number of occasions, the IRA had attempted to kill the loyalist known as 'King Rat', but it was the smaller splinter faction, the Irish National Liberation Army, which eventually took his life. In the inevitable loyalist reaction, others would die as not only Wright's LVF but also the UDA went on a killing spree. It all came at a time when loyalism was having one of its political wobbles. The Progressive Unionist Party, aligned to the UVF, was considering pulling out of the talks. Indeed, there was a proposal that it should do so from its chairman William Smith. He complained of 'one-sided concessions' to republicans and his party was also unhappy about how it was being treated inside the talks process. It believed that on some issues it was being kept in the dark – that other parties had papers that were not made available to the PUP. David Ervine told me this gave 'an angry impetus' to developments within loyalism at this time. So, the party was considering its place in the talks and, at the same time, some of the loyalist prisoners – those affiliated to the UDA – were once again reviewing their support for the peace process. It was with all of this going on in the background that the Wright shooting happened inside the Maze.

The response of the LVF to the murder of its leader was predictable, but the UDA, which had given its support to a threat issued against Wright after the Michael McGoldrick murder in 1996, now used the prison killing as an excuse to bring out its guns. Here we saw the first evidence of a relationship between the anti-peace process Loyalist Volunteer Force and elements in the UDA – a relationship which involved the UDA, supposedly on ceasefire, hiding behind the title of the other group to carry out one of the sectarian murders that followed the Wright shooting. It would not take long for the truth to emerge, and the UDA's involvement in this and other killings forced the British Government to suspend the Ulster Democratic Party from the talks process – a move which came on 26 January 1998. This was a period of real crisis and, here, I want to set out the sequence of events which followed the Wright killing:

27 December 1997: LVF gun attack at hotel in County Tyrone. One dead, several wounded. The man killed was a former republican prisoner.

29 December 1997: Secretary of State Mo Mowlam, Chief Constable Ronnie Flanagan, Security Minister Adam Ingram, Chief Executive of the Northern Ireland Prison Service Alan Shannon,

Director of Security Policy NIO John Steele and Maze Governor Martin Mogg meet to discuss weekend events.

31 December 1997: Loyalist gun attack on a North Belfast pub. One man killed and several injured. Attack admitted in the name of the LVF, but the shooting was carried out by the UDA based on the Shankill Road.

4 January 1998: Details emerge of UDA prisoner vote at Maze. Majority vote to withdraw support for peace process.

5 January 1998: I interview Sam McCrory, one of the UDA's jail leaders who was serving a 16-year sentence for conspiracy to murder. He said the prisoners wanted peace ' . . . but we want to send a clear message to the Government that we don't want to play second fiddle to Sinn Fein–IRA or any republicans. We want to be treated equally. If they are going to give concessions to republicans, they have to give them to loyalists also.

> *ROWAN*: If the leadership on the outside was to take the decision to end the ceasefire, is that something the prisoners would support?
>
> *McCRORY*: We would support it 100 per cent.
>
> *ROWAN*: So, are you saying there is that possibility – that the ceasefire could end?
>
> *McCRORY*: All things are possible.

6 January 1998: Ulster Unionist leader David Trimble and UDP leader Gary McMichael meet Maze prisoners.

7 January 1998: UDP delegation, including the UDA's South Belfast brigadier, Jackie McDonald, meets Mowlam in London. Mowlam decides to meet UDA prison leaders.

8 January 1998: Media is given access to Maze prisoners, including UDA and IRA leaders.

8 January 1998: The executive of the Progressive Unionist Party meets and postpones vote on its future in the talks.

9 January 1998: Mowlam meets UDA jail leaders, including McCrory, Michael Stone and Johnny Adair. The prisoners agree not to block the Ulster Democratic Party's participation in talks when they resume on 12 January. Two weeks later, the UDP is suspended from the negotiations after the UDA admits to breaches of its ceasefire.

11 January 1998: LVF gun attack at nightclub in Belfast. Terry Enright shot dead. His widow is related to Gerry Adams. The owner of the nightclub is related to the PUP politician David Ervine.

11 January 1998: At a news conference at a hotel in East Belfast, the Progressive Unionist Party said it would be returning to the multi-party talks at Stormont the following day. Since William Smith had proposed the party withdraw from the negotiations, the PUP had held meetings with Mowlam, Security Minister Adam Ingram, the then Irish Foreign Minister David Andrews and the Ulster Unionist Party.

It is difficult to say exactly what was going on within loyalism at this time. They would say their basic grievance was over concessions to republicans, but, in truth, these did not amount to a great deal. There was a slight reduction in troop levels, army patrolling was stopped in some areas, a number of prisoners were transferred from Britain to Ireland and in the Republic some had been released. This hardly justified the type of crisis that was allowed to develop through Christmas and into the New Year, but a crisis was created and it continued to a point where the IRA became involved and Sinn Fein was put out of the talks.

The Maze vote by the UDA had all the appearance of an attempt to push the issue of prisoner releases further up the talks agenda and also had the appearance of attention seeking. The involvement of the prisoners in such a public way and at a time when they were threatening to withdraw their support for the peace process damaged McMichael and his Ulster Democratic Party. What we saw was who was in charge and where the real authority rested within this particular section of the loyalist family – not with the UDA leadership on the outside, certainly not with its political representatives, but with those inside the Maze, including Adair, who we were once again seeing in a destructive role. Never in the course of the peace process have the IRA or the other main loyalist organisation, the UVF, allowed their prisoners such a central and public role and such control.

It was not the first time McMichael and his colleagues were undermined. It happened again, later in January, when the UDA was forced to admit to its involvement in a number of sectarian killings. The weekend after the talks resumed, the LVF killed again and there was an almost immediate response from the INLA. On Monday, 19 January, that organisation killed Jim Guiney, a member of the UDA in South Belfast. Within 24 hours, two Catholics, Larry Brennan and Ben Hughes, had been shot dead.

The UDA did not own up to the killings, but, quoting security and loyalist sources, I linked that organisation to the murders in my news reports on Tuesday and Wednesday, 20 and 21 January – reports which McMichael dismissed as media speculation based on anonymous security sources. Within a few days, however, the UDA had admitted its involvement, describing it as 'a measured military response' to a phase of 'republican aggression initiated by the INLA'. It was the UDA's way of trying to dress up and justify sectarian murder. The loyalist group only spoke after being publicly accused of the killings by the Chief Constable Sir Ronnie Flanagan.

The naming of the UDA came in a series of interviews he gave on 22 January 1998. Flanagan blamed the loyalist organisation for the killings of Eddie Treanor (31 December), Larry Brennan (19 January) and Ben Hughes (21 January). His assessment, which had been given privately to the Secretary of State Mo Mowlam before being made public, meant the loyalist group had been smoked out and forced into a position where it had to own up to its actions. On 23 January, the UDA admitted its ceasefire had been broken and three days later the group's political representatives were out of the talks – talks they were allowed to rejoin before the completion of the negotiations on Good Friday. The relationship between the UDA and the UDP finally broke down in 2001 when the paramilitaries withdrew their support for the Good Friday Agreement – the very agreement their political representatives had helped negotiate. It was no longer possible for the two to live under the same roof with any credibility and as a result of this clash of positions McMichael's Ulster Democratic Party was dissolved.

Over a number of years since the original loyalist ceasefire of 1994, we have watched the UDA become more and more involved in drugs and other criminality, and in between murdering Catholics and Protestants, this organisation has fought with itself and with other loyalists. Its ceasefire, questioned in 1998 and shown to have been broken, has been questioned many times since, and in October 2001 the organisation was eventually 'specified' by the British Government – an action which meant its cessation of violence was no longer recognised. I will deal with all of that in more detail later, but for now I want to concentrate on those early weeks of 1998.

Dr Mowlam said the Government viewed the UDA statement of 23 January with 'grave concern'. It could mean only one thing – for now at least, the UDP's participation in the negotiations was at an end. The Secretary of State said:

> I acknowledge commitments that Mr McMichael and his colleagues have made to peaceful means and his statement today that his party has used its influence in a positive manner. Nevertheless, the two governments have always made clear that the position of political parties must be considered in the light of activities of paramilitary organisations with which they have clear links.

The decision to suspend the UDP was taken when the talks moved to London and it came as no surprise to the loyalist party. Davy Adams told me there was never any doubt what the outcome would be:

> I said to our people going over on the plane, don't be getting too comfortable in the hotel. Anybody who thought we were going to be staying in the process wasn't looking at the big picture. As soon as the UFF admitted it, which I thought was the right thing to do, as soon as they admitted it, I knew we were out of the process.

The UFF (Ulster Freedom Fighters) is the UDA by another name and on 23 January, just hours after that group had finally admitted to its involvement in a number of killings, another man was shot dead in North Belfast. The following morning, the paramilitary organisation contacted me at my office to deny any involvement in the murder of Liam Conway. Hours after that phone call, there was another loyalist killing – the victim this time a Catholic taxi driver, John McColgan. It may well be that the UDA had no involvement in these latest shootings, but no one could be sure, and that has been the organisation's problem ever since – its word is not trusted and it has no credibility. Few believed that the smaller splinter group, the Loyalist Volunteer Force, was capable of such a level of activity spread across so many areas. Since the Wright killing, there had been nine other murders and eight of the victims were Catholics – a statistic which made a nonsense of suggestions that this was tit-for-tat.

The killings were creating a huge pressure within republicanism, as were developments within the talks process. Republicans considered a paper that the governments had introduced into the negotiations to be overtly unionist in nature and it was rejected by both Sinn Fein and the IRA – and rejected in a very public way. On Wednesday, 21 January, I met the IRA's spokesman in Belfast and was given a statement from the Army Council:

> The leadership of Oglaigh na hEireann do not regard the 'Propositions on Heads of Agreement' document a basis for a lasting peace settlement. It is a pro-unionist document and has created a crisis in the peace process.
> We have pointed out repeatedly in the past that meaningful inclusive negotiations are crucial to the resolution of the conflict. We have affirmed our willingness

to facilitate such negotiations. We have matched this commitment with deeds in announcing and maintaining a cessation of military operations since 20 July last year.

The British Government have, as yet, refused to face up to their responsibilities in this regard. They have continued with the remilitarisation policy of their predecessors in government. They have stalled on the implementation of any serious or meaningful confidence-building measures. Most significantly of all, in attempting to impose the 'Heads of Agreement' document on the talks process, yet another British Prime Minister has succumbed to the Orange card.

This was against a background of the unionist leadership refusing to meaningfully engage in the talks process and the continuing assassinations by loyalist death squads. Instead of facing up to this pressure the British Government has yielded to it.

The responsibility for undoing the damage done to the prospects for a just and lasting peace settlement rests squarely with the British Government.

P. O'NEILL

This was the IRA speaking in difficult and dangerous times. The loyalists were engaged in a killing spree, republicans believed the talks were proceeding on a unionist agenda, and the IRA was having to manage internal tensions and a situation in which there was still seepage from its ranks following that Convention in County Donegal just a few months earlier. There was no suggestion from republicans that there was any imminent threat to the ceasefire, but this statement was intended as a warning and what it also told us was that the Blair honeymoon period was now over. There may well have been a party-type atmosphere after the general election of the previous year and the renewal of the ceasefire, but now some of the air was getting out of the balloon:

> People were very nervous. There was a widespread fear that Blair was going down the Major road and consequently the critical period of negotiations we were going into was going to be dominated by a unionist agenda and supported by a Labour Government which up to then had appeared to be less stridently pro-unionist.

This is Richard McAuley of Sinn Fein speaking. He is a close aide to Adams and one of the party's most senior figures. He told me that people within the republican community had had a different sense of things up until the governments produced the 'Heads of Agreement' paper: 'They had a sense this wasn't going to be a re-run of Major's term in office.'

But the talks document worried people, and McAuley said they had to make a number of things clear. Republicans had to be assured that Sinn Fein was not involved in the preparation of the talks document that the IRA had so publicly rejected, and the two governments needed to know the paper 'wasn't a runner'.

The full extent of republican concerns can be gleaned from an internal document Sinn Fein was using for briefing purposes around this time. I learned of the paper during my research for this book. It describes the 'Heads of Agreement' document as 'politically loaded and partisan' – a document in which Sinn Fein said the 'effects of unionist and loyalist pressure' could be seen. The briefing paper gave the following assessment of the talks document:

> –It elevates the Six County [Northern Ireland] Assembly proposal;
> –It contains no reference to a singular north–south Body;
> –It relegates north–south arrangements to departmental cooperation as one element in arrangements for the two islands;
> –It proposes the replacement of the Anglo-Irish Agreement in a manner which is clearly dictated by unionism.

The Sinn Fein paper described the 'Heads of Agreement' document as 'a major retreat from the joint position of the two governments contained in the Framework document' – a paper published in February 1995. It did not, according to Sinn Fein, represent 'a neutral starting point' and was therefore unacceptable.

The all-party talks, which had begun in September 1997, had offered up the possibility of something different, but in this fog of killing and quarrelling I found it difficult to see where things were going and how a successful outcome could be achieved. We were still listening out for the chimes of the new beginning, but they were being drowned out by the shooting and the bombing. The IRA now joined in and those dissidents who had broken from the ranks of the mainstream organisation back in October were also about to demonstrate the threat they now posed to the process. This was the most dangerous moment since the negotiations had begun, but, remarkably, by April, George Mitchell had somehow managed to steer the parties to a historic compromise. Before then, in February 1998, the Secretary of State Mo Mowlam was told of the IRA's

Shoulder to shoulder — Adams and McGuinness have moved the IRA from 'armed struggle' to 'arms beyond use'. But in the peace process it has been a case of two steps forward and one step backwards.

Gusty Spence, the author of the 1994 Loyalist
Ceasefire Statement. Like his pipe, however,
much of that ceasefire has gone up in smoke.

Dark clouds over loyalism — Davy Adams and
Gary McMichael were marched onto the political
stage and then marched off it. Their party, the
UDP, folded in November 2001.

Following the leader — wherever the president goes, his aide Richard McAuley follows.

Looking up to Bobby Sands — men who remember the 1981 hunger strike: the IRA jail leader at the time, Brendan McFarlane, Sinn Fein's Jim Gibney and Sands' close friend Séanna Walsh.

Séanna Walsh — one of the first IRA prisoners freed under the Good Friday Agreement.

Brendan McFarlane — IRA jail leader in 1981 during the prison hunger strike.

Sinn Fein's Jim Gibney summed up the decision of the republican leadership to put arms beyond use: 'They turned history on its head and in doing so they turned the IRA upside down as well.'

In the loyalist pipeline — Gusty Spence and David Ervine, architects of the loyalist ceasefire.

David Ervine has moved into the political mainstream but others within loyalism have lost their way.

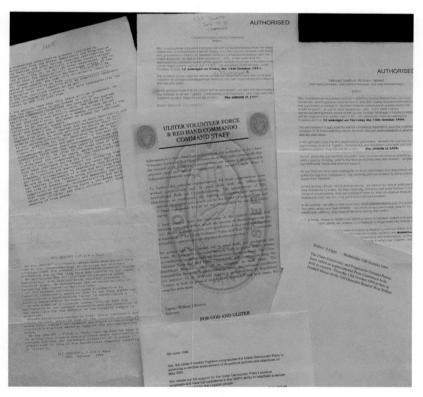

Making peace — from war to ceasefire, some of the key statements that have been issued along the way.

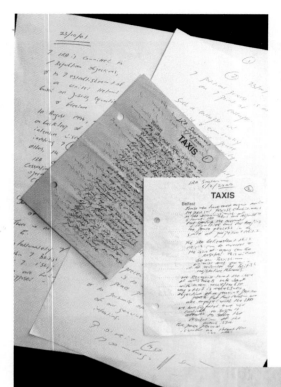

Take a note — Rowan's record of some of his meetings with the IRA's P. O'Neill. An old taxi receipt he had in his pocket was used to log one of the statements in February 2000.

All UDA/UFF L.P.O.W's Maze

We the UDA/UFF volunteers, after much discussion, have come to the conclusion that to continue our military campaign under the present circumstances could be counter productive and in the long term detrimental to our cause.

We appreciate the difficulties in targeting known Republicans, with the increased security presence in loyalist areas. We acknowledge the un-acceptability of targeting non-combative Nationalists.

In the present political climate a cease-fire by Loyalist volunteers, would be seen by our long suffering community as a contributing factor in establishing a lasting peace within Northern Ireland.

In the event of a Loyalist cease-fire, we feel the maintenance of our command structure and the retention of war materials for the defence of the loyalist people is essential.

Should Republicans renege on their peace commitment and return to their genocide against the loyalist peoples. We would fully support our command structure in returning to reactive/pro-active measures against the pan-nationalist front.

We the UDA/UFF L.P.O.W's, Maze, feel we must be seen to be giving this fragile peace process every opportunity to succeed and that our permanent cessation of violence should last as long as the Republicans complete cessation of violence.

All UDA/UFF L.P.O.W's Maze
10th October 1994

Outside-in — the UDA brigadiers go into the Maze to meet their prisoners just days before the 1994 loyalist ceasefire.

ABOVE: Police Chief — Sir Ronnie Flanagan needed all of his powers of persuasion to coax the RUC through a painful period of change.

ABOVE RIGHT: Inside the Maze — the author speaks to Johnny Adair, the loyalist 'Mad Dog' who 'couldn't fit into the peace'. (© BBC Newsline)

RIGHT (2nd from top): On another wing, Rowan with Padraic Wilson (far right), the IRA jail leader in 1998. Seated in the background is the prominent Belfast republican Bobby Storey. (© BBC Newsline)

RIGHT (3rd from top): Moving on — from the table of the IRA Army Council to the seat of government in Belfast, the personal journey of Martin McGuinness.

BOTTOM RIGHT: Changing policing — the new Chief Constable Hugh Orde and, over his shoulder, the man who began the reforms, Sir Ronnie Flanagan.

BOTTOM LEFT: Break-in — Castlereagh, the scene of the St Patrick's Day Special Branch robbery in 2002.

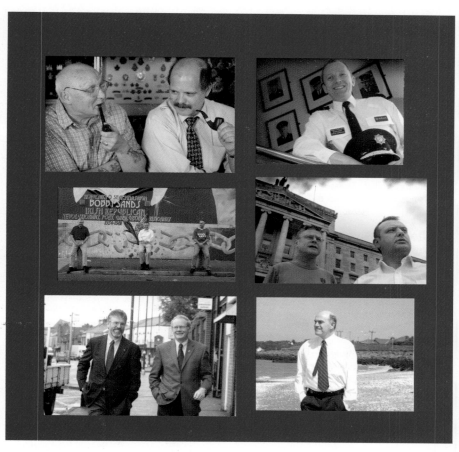

'Provos', 'Prods' and 'Peelers' — faces in the peace.

involvement in two killings and as a consequence Sinn Fein joined the loyalist Ulster Democratic Party in the talks sin bin. In the 24-hour period spanning 9 February into 10 February, the IRA was linked to two killings. Brendan Campbell, a drug dealer, and Bobby Dougan, a loyalist and a member of the UDA, were the latest names to be added to the list of the dead, and a place which by now had hoped to be relaxing to the sound of ceasefire silence was still suffering the noises of war. The Chief Constable Sir Ronnie Flanagan was convinced of the IRA's involvement and he told Mowlam: 'It is my duty and responsibility to brief the Secretary of State as fully and accurately as is possible to do and that's what I did in relation to those two murders.'

In an interview for this book Flanagan said:

> I had no doubt whatever that those two murders were not only executed by members of the IRA but were also planned by the IRA at organisational level. I had no doubt whatever of that and it was my responsibility to brief the Secretary of State in that regard . . . What the Secretary of State does on the basis of that briefing is absolutely a matter for her political judgement and absolutely nothing to do with me.

On Friday, 13 February, Mowlam made public the Chief Constable's assessment and a week later the governments suspended Sinn Fein from the talks. But these negotiations were being run to a tight deadline and the party was told it would be back in by 9 March. The loyalist UDP would return even sooner. If agreement were to be reached, republicans and loyalists would have to be at the talks table.

It was at this point that the new threat to the process became evident – the threat posed by dissident republicans. This was the fall-out from that Convention some months earlier and an indication that those who had raised the rallying flag, which Flanagan described earlier, now felt confident enough and strong enough to show themselves. On 20 February – on the same day that Sinn Fein was suspended from the negotiations – a bomb exploded close to the police station in Moira, in the constituency of the Ulster Unionist MP Jeffrey Donaldson, and just three days later there was another bombing – this time in Portadown, part of the constituency of the Ulster Unionist leader David Trimble. At this time, coinciding with Sinn Fein's suspension from the negotiations, there were those who saw these actions as the work of the IRA and who felt this was the republican organisation venting its spleen. It was too soon for many, particularly on the unionist side, to make a distinction between the mainstream organisation and those who had broken away. The picture was much too blurred to allow for that type of separation, but these bombings were not a breach of the IRA's 'complete cessation of military operations'. They were carried out by those who had learned their trade, if you like, within the organisation, but who were now demonstrating their opposition to the Adams–McGuinness peace strategy.

Within 24 hours of the Portadown bomb, the IRA stepped in to explain its position. I was met in West Belfast by the organisation's spokesman, who had six points to make. These were to be attributed to an IRA source, but this was the leadership of the organisation speaking.

> ● The complete cessation of military operations remains intact.
> ● There is no split in the IRA.
> ● The IRA operates as a single organisation.
> ● It doesn't have satellite organisations or assist other organisations.
> ● There has been an obvious attempt to dictate our agenda, for example using old IRA codes [codewords used to authenticate bomb warnings] and technology.
> ● We will not let anyone determine our agenda. We remain open-minded about who is involved in this and whose agenda they are working.

This was the IRA's way of publicly denying any involvement in the two bombs in the constituencies of Donaldson and Trimble, and of distancing itself from those attacks. The briefing also rejected claims of a split within the IRA, but some significant figures had gone and clearly they had the wherewithal to threaten the process and do so in ways demonstrated in Moira and Portadown. The dissidents included Micky McKevitt – once the IRA's quartermaster general. The IRA's director of engineering had also gone, and these were the 'senior' and 'serious' figures who were rallying others to their cause. Those who left claimed the title Oglaigh na hEireann and they presented themselves as the 'Real' IRA. A new 32-county sovereignty committee, including McKevitt's wife, Bernadette, the sister of the hunger striker Bobby Sands, also emerged in opposition to the Adams and McGuinness strategy. Months later, after the bomb massacre in Omagh, the mainstream IRA would use the threat of its muscle and the mood of public outrage to put the dissidents down.

The negotiations, and more specifically those inside them, were

having to absorb all that was happening on the outside. As I
mentioned earlier, the unionists were having huge difficulty
distinguishing between the IRA and the dissidents. The Portadown
bombing – and the very deliberate targeting of this predominantly
Protestant town – created a climate in which there was all the
potential for a loyalist response. Indeed, I was being told both by
police and UVF sources that that organisation was 'at breaking
point'. As for the talks themselves, Sinn Fein was now on the outside
and not liking what was happening on the inside. So, in February,
this was the dangerous mix of ingredients in the political bowl and
yet somehow George Mitchell would get the parties to the point of
agreement just ten days into the month of April.

In late February, Sinn Fein's Gerry Kelly told a republican rally at
Belfast City Hall that the governments needed to carry out 'a root
and branch examination' of the talks. He said the negotiations had
been allowed to drift aimlessly and that the Ulster Unionist leader
David Trimble had been allowed to impose his will on the agenda.
There was little sympathy for republicans at this time. Senior figures
on the loyalist side were expressing concern at what they considered
to be IRA 'ambivalence' in relation to the bombs in Portadown and
Moira, and there were suspicions too about the timing of the
Dougan shooting in Belfast. It came after the public naming of the
UDA and at a time when there had been a pause in that loyalist
killing spree. So, why then did the IRA strike when it did? Senior
loyalists I spoke to in late February offered two possibilities. They
believed the shooting was either designed to get a loyalist response
or to 'shaft' Adams. Republicans, however, offered an entirely
different explanation. This was a response to that spate of loyalist
murders and to pressure that had been building in the republican
community – a pressure that could no longer be held back.

Right through March and into April, indeed right up to the point
of eventual agreement in the talks, the various dissident factions
remained active and more lives were taken in loyalist and INLA gun
attacks. These included a shooting inside a pub in Poyntzpass,
County Armagh – a gun attack on 3 March 1998 which once again
demonstrated the indiscriminate nature of loyalist violence. Two
men were killed, two friends of different religions – one a Catholic,
the other a Protestant. They were Damien Trainor and Philip Allen.
The Troubles had, by and large, passed this little place by, but here
at a time of supposed peace Poyntzpass was visited by the LVF and
two of its people were gunned down.

This was also a period when dissidents on the republican side
were seen to be particularly active. The INLA – the organisation
which weeks earlier had murdered Billy Wright and triggered that

loyalist killing rage – shot dead a former police officer and a loyalist, and those who left the IRA were increasing their workload and trying to present themselves as an alternative to the mainstream organisation and the strategy it was following. The dissidents were building on Moira and Portadown. We now saw mortar bomb attacks on security bases in Armagh and Forkhill – and in these a further example of knowledge learned within the IRA now being put to use by the dissidents.

Explosives finds in the Republic of Ireland around this time had clearly prevented other attacks that had been planned, but already we were seeing evidence of the serious threat posed to the peace process by those who refused to follow the direction of Adams and McGuinness.

As I mentioned earlier, all of this was creating a fog which blurred my vision in terms of what I thought possible at the talks, but the negotiations produced an agreement – the Good Friday Agreement on 10 April 1998. It was a political compromise that left many of the biggest and most difficult issues unresolved – policing and decommissioning among them. They were put on hold – channelled off to be dealt with by others. There would be an Independent Commission on Policing headed by the former Conservative Party Chairman Chris Patten and the arms issue would remain with the Independent International Commission on Decommissioning. Another controversial issue, that of prisoner releases, would be processed by a Sentence Review Commission, but the time-frame for the releases was settled within the negotiations. The first prisoners were freed in September 1998 and within two years most republicans and loyalists had been released.

It was these issues, prisoners, policing and decommissioning, that Trimble was now most concerned about in terms of trying to sell the agreement to his party, because these were things that touched a raw nerve in the Protestant community. He recalls:

> There was some doubt in my mind on Friday afternoon as to whether the party would endorse it. I knew by Friday morning that, in terms of constitutional issues and in terms of the institutional arrangements here, we'd got the best deal we could have got – a better deal than the one we were trying to make in 1992 . . . So, I was quite sure in my own mind that this was the best deal. Of course, it kicked policing into the long grass – deliberately so. Had policing been made an issue in the talks, we would never have got an agreement and, so, deliberately, the device was taken, hiving off policing, putting it in a commission, leaving it to later.

So, I knew there was going to be a battle to be fought in the
future.

And Trimble told me that he and his senior party colleagues also
believed there was an inevitability about what was going to happen,
even though some of it was being pushed further down the pipe:
' . . . issues such as policing and prisoner releases, these things were
going to happen anyway, because these were how the Government
was going to buy a continuation of the ceasefire'.

The policing change that flowed from the report of the Patten
Commission meant an end to the Royal Ulster Constabulary and its
flag, badge and uniform. There were new special recruitment
arrangements to bring more Catholics into a service that was
predominantly Protestant, and, in terms of accountability, the
various watchdogs were given sharper teeth. So, the policing change,
as part of a process, has been both symbolic and structural, and it is
change that many in the unionist community have struggled with. At
the time of writing, Sinn Fein had not yet endorsed the new policing
arrangements, but were moving closer to doing so.

In the final hours of the Good Friday Agreement negotiations,
the loyalists rejected a Sinn Fein plan for the two sides to jointly
push for the prisoner release period to be reduced to one year. Like
republicans, the loyalists wanted their prisoners out as soon as
possible, but they also knew how this issue was going to play in the
unionist community and how difficult it was going to be for Trimble
to sell an agreement which had prisoner releases as part of it. The
approach inside the talks came from Sinn Fein's Gerry Kelly, but
David Ervine told me it would have been too much to ask of the
unionist community at that time:

> ERVINE: I think we probably could have pushed further and
> potentially broken the Ulster Unionists' back even
> more than the difficulties they did have. It became
> evident to us that the deal on prisoners was as good as
> it gets and frankly, from my own personal point of view,
> as good as it needed to get.
> ROWAN: What did you say to Gerry Kelly?
> ERVINE: I told him I would pass on what he said to me, but
> my sense was it was as good as it got. Of course I was
> met with a crescendo of similar opinions when I
> discussed it with the PUP and the UVF in the
> conference room, and I was able to go back and say to
> him, actually it was Adams I bumped into, and said,
> you're not on, this is as far as it goes . . . I gave Kelly my

> personal answer but then I gave Adams the definitive
> answer – the collective answer was no, this is as good as
> it gets, and, as I say from my own personal perspective,
> as good as it needed to be.
> ROWAN: Had it been negotiated down below two years, how
> much damage do you think would have been done?
> ERVINE: I don't think we could have sustained a peace
> process, I really don't. There is an emotive difficulty
> around the issue of the release of prisoners. I think that
> stems in many ways from the raw emotion of the last 30
> years, but I also think it stems as well from the lack of
> education for a broader public in the issues of conflict
> resolution . . . I think as negotiators we did a bloody
> good job.

The agreement did not break Trimble's back, but it nearly did. He lost Jeffrey Donaldson on the day the deal was done and his Ulster Unionist Party has not been the same since. It has split on pro-agreement/anti-agreement lines and it has been a continuous struggle for Trimble to survive. That weakness has been his strength, for the pace of change – political and security – has been dictated by his needs. Everyone is conscious that without Trimble and those senior members of his party who lined up alongside him there would be no process. The project only works if endorsed by a significant number within unionism and the success of the agreement, therefore, depends on Trimble's survival. To this day there is still a fear that the anti-agreement wolves are closing in on him and that he could be cornered at any time. As I mentioned above, Donaldson was the first to walk before the print had dried on the Good Friday Agreement. He had too many concerns about too many issues, including the IRA's guns:

> Primary amongst the issues was decommissioning. I felt that
> what we had on decommissioning was not precise, it was not
> explicit; in summary it was a fudge. I felt that the linkages that
> we needed between decommissioning and other key aspects
> of the agreement, such as the holding of office in the
> Assembly, had not been clarified in the agreement. The
> linkages were not there and I concluded that
> decommissioning was going to be the Achilles heel of the
> whole process. In addition, I was very, very deeply opposed to
> the early release of the terrorist prisoners and, of course, very
> concerned about the proposals for the reform of the RUC.

The deep divisions within unionism may have been hidden in a referendum result that produced over 71 per cent support for the agreement, but if Trimble had a majority of unionists on his side the gap was wafer thin. This result meant that Paisley was still a significant political force and Trimble has always felt the breath of the DUP leader on his neck. Donaldson, too, has been a constant thorn in his side as unionism has struggled with the new political order. For Trimble, and for some of his senior party colleagues including Sir Reg Empey and Michael McGimpsey, that new order has meant sharing power with Sinn Fein at a time when the IRA was still out there – an IRA still capable of actions which contradict the meaning of ceasefire.

Trimble has a knack of infuriating republicans, but he has worked the agreement, maybe on his own terms and at his own pace, but an easier option for him would have been to do a Donaldson and to walk away. He chose not to do that and, whatever else happens, history will be kind to him for that.

While those issues of prisoners, policing and decommissioning were a problem for unionists, the agreement also posed big questions for republicans. What had been negotiated was well short of 'Brits Out', but Adams saw this as a strategic compromise and something that Sinn Fein should buy into in furtherance of its objectives. Indeed, all that has happened since 1994 should be set in that context. For republicans, this is a long road and a process of transition, and the compromises made as part of the Good Friday Agreement have been part of the journey. Late into Thursday, on the eve of that historic Good Friday, it was by no means certain what Sinn Fein would do. Indeed, there were rumours of a possible walk-out, but moves to dilute the decommissioning section of the agreement and to reduce the prisoner release period from three to two years apparently prevented this from happening.

In David Trimble's opinion:

> I think the prisoner release period was dramatically reduced in the early hours of Friday morning to prevent a Sinn Fein walk-out . . . Knowing that we had got the agreement to way below Sinn Fein's bottom line, I would not have been surprised at a walk-out. I was not surprised that Friday afternoon when Sinn Fein didn't endorse the agreement but reserved their position.

Gerry Adams' close aide, Richard McAuley, was inside Castle Buildings during those critical last hours of the negotiations and he can remember things being 'quite taut'. He further recalls:

I remember we sent Mitchel [McLaughlin] out to do a news
conference and he took a hard line, and I think that's what
stirred the rumours of a walk-out. It was a measure of a very
difficult and critical point in the negotiations. I don't know
that we were ever actually likely to walk out. Things were
very tight, but I don't think we were ever walking away from
it.

Adams did reserve the Sinn Fein position on Good Friday. But he
was going out to sell the agreement and his party would enlist the
help of the African National Congress. There were big issues to be
explained and sold, including Sinn Fein's participation in a Stormont
Assembly and changes to the Irish constitution in relation to its
territorial claim over Northern Ireland, something Adams
acknowledged as being 'emotionally and symbolically' very difficult
for many republicans. In an interview for this book recorded in
December 2001 he said:

> When the Good Friday Agreement was finally concluded,
> while I clearly was putting our leadership on the line, I told
> the assembled meeting of the two governments and the other
> parties that I was going back to Sinn Fein. So, we then went
> and we did all of our heavy lifting at that point. That meant,
> for example, we had to change our constitution in order to
> even come into the institutions at all – to go into a Northern
> Assembly.

All of this would be dealt with at two Sinn Fein conferences and,
separately and secretly, the IRA met in an Army Convention to clear
the way for its members to sit in the Assembly. 'Once we said
publicly that we were going back to our party, that meant we were
going back to our party to try and win the party's support.'
    Again this is Gerry Adams speaking.

> What we had to do was first of all give the party a very
> detailed breakdown. Martin McGuinness gave a very lengthy
> report of all of the negotiations; I did the same. We then
> enlisted the help of the African National Congress, who
> travelled from one part of the country – including into the
> prisons – to the other, reassuring people, drawing on their
> experience . . . This was a big set piece – a huge, big piece of
> negotiation in which we met in the Ard Fheis, gave a report,
> then asked people to go off and think about it. The ANC
> then came and simply argued politically, not for any

particular course of action, but for the need to strategise, for
the need to stay united, for the need to be able to take
decisions in furtherance of objectives and hang together on
the basis that if you make a mistake, then if you stay together
you can recover from the mistake and correct the mistake.

Republicans were hanging together and the Ard Fheis of 10 May –
just a few days after that secret IRA Convention – gave
overwhelming backing to the Sinn Fein leadership and support for a
'yes' vote in the referendums on the Good Friday Agreement. That
support was won in the company of some of the IRA's prisoners,
including the Maze jail leader Padraic Wilson and members of the
Balcombe Street Gang, who had spent long years in prison in
England since the 1970s. They had been given parole to attend this
conference and Adams believes their presence influenced the vote:

> What had a huge effect at the Ard Fheis was the arrival of the
> Balcombe Street prisoners, because these had basically been
> people – I think they had been 24 years in prison – who had
> been entombed. People hadn't seen them. They were myths,
> photographs, old faded photographs, Scotland Yard
> photographs, maybe some old family photographs, more
> recent prison photographs were used, but very few people bar
> maybe their own families had ever seen them in a quarter of
> a century. Now, when they walked into the hall, we didn't
> expect, well, maybe it's wrong to say we didn't expect, we
> knew there'd be a big response, but there was a huge
> response. Now, I think that that gave a false idea, because the
> Ard Fheis then voted hugely – like 90 per cent or whatever it
> was – I forget the exact figure. It was afterwards, I think
> people probably woke up the next morning and said, now
> what have we done. And it was afterwards, when it started to
> settle down, that you got a more critical analysis of where it
> was all at.

Trimble offered very different words to describe this occasion, which
he viewed as an 'obscene display of triumphalism'. He believed
republicans were trying to break the unionists and drive them away
from the agreement:

> I'm quite sure in my own mind that the triumphalism was
> premeditated and it was premeditated for the purpose of
> breaking unionism, because, in the talks, Sinn Fein settled for
> a position way below their bottom line. And the only thing

> that kept them in was the prisoner release scheme that they
> wanted, but, even at that point, after they'd agreed to that,
> they thought that unionism would reject the agreement, and,
> then, when it didn't, they had to look at ways to break
> unionism.

In this comment you see how little trust there was at this time, and
it was in this climate of deep suspicion that the job of building the
new political institutions had to be taken on.

The scenes at the Sinn Fein Ard Fheis were repeated four days
later at the Ulster Hall in Belfast, this time at a loyalist rally and this
time with the spotlight on Michael Stone, who ten years earlier had
been filmed during his killing mission inside Milltown Cemetery.
Stone, on parole from the Maze, was cheered and applauded as he
was marched through the hall and onto the stage, and, within hours,
pictures of him being hero-worshipped were replayed on television.
At a high political level all of this was playing very badly. There was
a rumour that Tony Blair had hit the roof, and the Government
moved to try to limit the damage. The day after the rally, on Friday,
15 May, the Northern Ireland Office told the UDP to ensure that
Stone did no media interviews, but it was too late. A few minutes
before the call reached the party's prisoners' spokesman John White,
Stone had spoken to me about that day in Milltown Cemetery, about
his past and about his hopes for the future. I was still in the building
in East Belfast when White took the call, and the loyalists then
moved to try to prevent the interview from being broadcast. In a
small room in the company of White, Stone and the senior UDA
figure Jim Gray, I was asked for the tape, but I refused to hand it
over. A fax was then sent to the BBC in which we were told that
Stone had now withdrawn his permission for the interview to be
used. Senior UDP figures, including the party leader Gary
McMichael, also contacted the BBC to try to stop the interview
from being broadcast. The referendum on the Good Friday
Agreement was now just a week away and there were huge concerns
that what had happened in Dublin with the Balcombe Street
prisoners and then in Belfast with Stone could feed the 'no' vote.

That afternoon there was a long discussion at the BBC in the
sixth-floor office of the then controller Pat Loughrey. I was
involved, as was our head of news and current affairs Andrew
Colman, and we had a phone link to London and to the BBC's then
director of editorial policy Phil Harding. The outcome of the
discussion was a decision to run the interview. Stone was a member
of the UDA jail leadership, he was big news, particularly in this
period, and he had things to say on prisoner releases, on the Good

Friday Agreement and his own past. He told me his 'war' was over. On decommissioning, he told me the weapons should be allowed to rust in the ground and he believed the agreement could 'give us a lasting peace'. The previous day, I had been contacted by another of the UDA's jail leaders, Sam McCrory, who apologised on behalf of the prisoners to the victims of their violence and I asked Stone was that something he could share:

> *STONE*: I would share in that most definitely. I have said in the past that all deaths are regrettable, be they innocent civilians, members of the security forces, loyalist volunteers and, yes, even members of the republican death squads.
> *ROWAN*: Do you apologise for what you did?
> *STONE*: [pause] Within the context of being a volunteer in a war, no, I don't apologise, but I acknowledge the hurt I've caused.

In this interview, Stone also spoke to me about what he had planned in Milltown Cemetery that day in March 1988, when he opened fire on mourners at the funerals of three IRA members shot dead by the SAS in Gibraltar. He said his 'main targets' were Gerry Adams and Martin McGuinness. Ten years later, Stone, like many others, could see that those two men had moved republicans beyond ceasefire to an endorsement of the Good Friday Agreement. So, was he in anyway 'relieved or glad' that his plan had not worked out?

> With hindsight, and hindsight is a wonderful thing, but, yes, I suppose so. That's a begrudged I suppose so, because, ten years ago, I was willing to sacrifice my life for what I believed in . . . Adams and McGuinness have brought the republican death squads on, seemingly making the transition into a democracy, and, if they believe in that democracy, then majority rules. They've a political mandate, I accept that, and they should have their place at the talks.

Adams and McGuinness survived what Stone intended in 1988 and ten years later the Good Friday Agreement survived what had happened in Dublin at the Sinn Fein Ard Fheis and then those scenes from the Ulster Hall a few days later. Before the referendum, a ceasefire was declared by the Loyalist Volunteer Force and a few months later that organisation became the first group to decommission some of its weapons. These events were driven by self-interest and were designed to secure the early release of the group's prisoners. Without the ceasefire, those prisoners would not have benefited from the arrangements negotiated as part of the Good Friday Agreement.

The organisation's decommissioning was a modest act. Angle grinders hired from a local tool store were used to destroy nine guns – one of them a rifle that would not have looked out of place in the hands of Davy Crockett.

From the referendum, the political process moved on to the elections to the new Assembly in June 1998. Trimble's party won 28 seats; John Hume's SDLP took 24; Paisley's DUP 20; and Sinn Fein had 18 of its candidates elected. David Ervine and Billy Hutchinson of the Progressive Unionist Party also won seats, but the other loyalist party – the UDP – would not be present at the Stormont ball. Gary McMichael (3,725 first preferences in the Lagan Valley constituency) and Davy Adams (1,745 first preferences in South Belfast) failed to get enough votes. It meant that one of the parties which had helped negotiate the Good Friday Agreement was now isolated from the process and there was no political anchor to hold the UDA.

For the four main parties elected to the Assembly, the next step should have been the formation of the power-sharing Executive, but it would take another 18 months or so to get to that point. In between, the debate was dominated by a single issue – by decommissioning. If Trimble's unionists were to sit with Sinn Fein in government, they first wanted to see the colour of the IRA's guns, but Jeffrey Donaldson was right, the agreement had been a 'fudge' and had not secured a republican commitment to disarm. All parties were to use their influence to achieve total disarmament by May 2000, but that target date would pass without even a beginning to IRA decommissioning. Trimble had seemed adamant that without guns there would be no government with Sinn Fein, but he eventually shifted his position, more on a hunch than on a guarantee that the IRA would move. Late into 1999, with a new millennium about to dawn, Trimble took a political leap of faith. He agreed to go to the Executive table with Sinn Fein, but in doing so he set a deadline for decommissioning and in doing that he guaranteed that this period of devolved government in Northern Ireland would be of short duration. The IRA was not going to dance to Trimble's tune.

I will deal with this period in greater detail later, but let us first look at those months immediately after the June elections. At the first meeting of the new Assembly on 1 July, David Trimble and the SDLP's Seamus Mallon were elected First and Deputy First Ministers, but, at this time, there was no way out of the decommissioning maze and therefore no prospect of the power-sharing Executive being formed. The annual Drumcree march was also in the frame and a massive security operation was put in place to block the route of the Orangemen. This year, they would not be allowed to walk on the nationalist Garvaghy Road. In the period of the stand-off, three young Catholic boys – Mark, Richard and Jason Quinn – were killed in a petrol bomb attack on their home at Ballymoney in County Antrim.

Within hours, the Orange Order chaplain in County Armagh, the Reverend William Bingham, called for an end to the Drumcree protest. He contacted me on my mobile phone while I was in Portadown and advised me what he planned to say later that morning. He spoke of no road being worth a life, but three young lives had already been lost. Given the Orange mood and the determination of its members in Portadown to march what they considered to be their traditional route, it was a brave intervention by the Reverend Bingham, but it was too late for the young Quinn boys. A year or so later, the Reverend Bingham issued a statement calling on the then RUC to confirm there was no evidence to link the murders with the Drumcree protests, and in his statement he supported the right of the Portadown Orangemen to walk their traditional route. He added: 'I can assure the Quinn family of my and the Order's absolute commitment to ensuring that justice is done for their family and assure them of our prayers at this time.'

In the summer of 1998, the republican dissidents were also active and this was the build-up to what happened in Omagh on 15 August on that darkest day of the Troubles.

On a busy Saturday afternoon, the 'Real' IRA was responsible for an act of mass murder. A bomb it placed exploded in the market town and took the lives of 29 people – a figure which does not include two unborn babies. The dead included men, women and children, Catholics and Protestants, people from both sides of the border and from outside Ireland. The warning signs had been visible a fortnight earlier in Banbridge in County Down, when 35 people were injured in another dissident bomb explosion and, given the reckless nature of the attacks the 'Real' IRA was engaging in, it was only a matter of time before there were deaths.

Omagh is now remembered as the worst single atrocity of the Troubles. Shamed by their actions, the dissidents retreated and declared an end to their activities. They did so on 8 September 1998 – a week after the IRA had told them to 'disband' and to do so 'sooner rather than later'. Senior dissident figures had been visited and threatened by members of the mainstream IRA. There was also another ceasefire immediately after Omagh – this one declared by the Irish National Liberation Army.

The slaughter in the market town will never be forgotten. President Clinton, Prime Minister Blair and Prince Charles came to offer their sympathy to people who had been visited by unimaginable horror. They were promised that the bombers would be pursued and that 'no stone would be left unturned', but there has been scathing criticism of the murder investigation and some of the relatives of the dead have posed the question: how heavy were the stones? In the aftermath of the explosion, there was so much grieving to be done, so much hurt to heal and so many to bury – both young and old. It all happened when most in Northern Ireland were thinking about peace, but at a time when there were still those intent on war. The dissidents who had broken from the IRA and who had first shown themselves in the bomb explosions in Moira and Portadown in February were now in hiding – swept away in the storm of condemnation that blew up after Omagh. Such was the public desire for peace that an act of political boldness would have been applauded at this time. There was an opportunity to seize the moment, to get on with it, but the process was allowed to stagnate and to continue to be poisoned in a political dogfight over decommissioning.

CHAPTER SIX

Talking to the General

'When you put your hand near the IRA's guns, you're touching a raw nerve.'
Republican source, July 1999

'The IRA is willing to further enhance the peace process and, consequently, following the establishment of the institutions agreed on Good Friday last year, the IRA leadership will appoint a representative to enter into discussions with General John de Chastelain and the IICD.'
P. O'Neill, November 1999

'We all agreed that nobody could do this with the arse hanging out of their trousers. There had to be no humiliation all round.'
Senior Ulster Unionist negotiator, Michael McGimpsey, March 2000

'A blind man on a galloping horse could have seen that the IRA statements did not in anyway match up to the kind of fancy language that Adams and McGuinness were using.'
Ulster Unionist MP Jeffrey Donaldson, March 2000.

TREMONE BAY, COUNTY DONEGAL, 28 AUGUST 1998: On the beach the sun was shining down and I had the rocks and the waves for company. This was Ireland at its most beautiful and at its most peaceful. My kids were playing on the sand, safe with their parents, but in this happy, beautiful, peaceful place, my thoughts were elsewhere. Just 13 days earlier, in the horror of that explosion in Omagh, parents had lost children and children had lost parents. It was the darkest day in a long conflict – so many dead and so many others horribly injured. The cold rage that followed the bombing ensured that the 'Real' IRA was forced into hiding. It had been responsible for mass murder and it now had to hide its face. For now, at least, it was no longer able to function, but the dissidents would re-emerge. The shame of what they did in Omagh was not enough to finish them off and they would kill again.

I was not in Omagh, but then you didn't have to be there to feel and to know the horror of that day. It was there for all to see and you could hear it in the voices of everyone you spoke to. On both sides of the border, people were stunned; they were angry and they feared the potential consequences of the events of that bloody Saturday. What they feared most was what the loyalists might do by way of a response.

I had just started a holiday with my family but in the days immediately after the bombing I spent most of my time talking to my sources at home and trying to answer questions on the radio – questions that were being put to me in a series of special news programmes by my colleagues Noel Thompson, Seamus McKee and Mark Carruthers. The questions for me were about the organisation that had placed the bomb. What did we know about the 'Real' IRA, had it intended to kill and how were the loyalists likely to respond? There were also questions about the speculation of an imminent INLA ceasefire.

It is unlikely that the 'Real' IRA intended what happened in Omagh that day, but just days earlier in Banbridge there had been an indication of what was possible. When you play with bombs in a busy town centre, and when you give warnings which are garbled, then you play with people's lives. That was a risk the 'Real' IRA was prepared to take on 15 August. The loyalists did not respond, but they thought about it. They thought about it long and hard in the hours immediately after the explosion and in an interview for this book a UVF leadership source said: 'The Omagh bombing was almost a nightmare scenario.' He told me: 'There were emergency gatherings that weekend' and he spoke of his organisation burning the midnight oil as it considered its response. There were 'serious, serious, problems,' he said, 'not a going back to war situation', but there were those who wanted 'to burn the fuses again'.

In other words, there were some who wanted to react to Omagh. That was the mood as the UVF leadership gathered on that dark weekend – a mood that could so easily have seen the loyalist organisation add to the horror of that moment. Instead it paused. The decision of its meeting was 'to put it back to the governments' and to tell them that they needed to deal with the republican dissidents. I was told the UVF used a channel it had to communicate this message directly to the Irish Government. The bombers had come from that side of the border. As for the British Government, it would have heard the thoughts of the UVF in conversations with David Ervine and other members of the Progressive Unionist Party.

'Over the next couple of days there was enough coming from the two governments to allow us a breathing space,' the UVF leadership source told me. Certainly there was plenty of tough talking, a promise of new laws to be used against the dissidents, and, as I mentioned earlier, after Omagh, for a while at least, the 'Real' IRA vanished – under threat and under pressure.

What did not disappear, however, was the political problem of how to deal with the issue of illegal arms. Indeed, Omagh had added weight to the arguments for decommissioning and in this climate there was no prospect of removing the obstacle that stood in the way of power-sharing and the new politics promised as part of the Good Friday Agreement. We were heading for more long negotiations and more arguments over guns and government. That decommissioning debate was now playing out in the context of Omagh, with early prisoner releases now imminent and with the Patten Commission on police reform now engaged in its work. All of this was difficult for Trimble, but the IRA still had no intention of moving on the arms issue and made that clear in an interview at the end of August 1998: '. . . some people are using the decommissioning issue in support of their own narrow agendas of subverting or securing a renegotiation of the Good Friday document. This should not be allowed to happen.'

A few days later, Sinn Fein appointed Martin McGuinness to represent the party in talks with General de Chastelain. The terms of the Good Friday Agreement were clear. All parties were obliged to:

> work constructively and in good faith with the Independent Commission, and to use any influence they may have to achieve the decommissioning of all paramilitary arms within two years following endorsement in referendums north and south of the agreement and in the context of the implementation of the overall settlement.

It was out of this that the target date of May 2000 was set for total decommissioning – but the IRA has always stressed that it was not a signatory to the agreement and therefore not bound by this paragraph.

Martin McGuinness may well be one of the most senior and influential figures in the Republican Movement, but in talks with de Chastelain he would be representing Sinn Fein and not the IRA. Indeed, another year would pass before the IRA leadership appointed a representative to talk to the General, and that May 2000 target date set in the Good Friday Agreement for complete decommissioning passed without even a start by the IRA. Deadlines and ultimatums from the unionists had failed to move the organisation.

That said, republicans have had to turn themselves inside out to work the agreement and have had to make considerable compromises. The pre-agreement graffiti had read: 'No return to Stormont', but Stormont was home to the new Assembly and a new place of work for the 18 Sinn Fein members elected to the body, including Adams, McGuinness, Gerry Kelly and Pat Doherty. It was not the old Stormont, but a new place with built-in voting safeguards for nationalists. Nonetheless, this was a big step for republicans, marking as it did the end of their abstentionist policy on northern political institutions. Gerry Adams told me:

> The big strategic compromise was actually to work in the context of trying to build the peace process, to develop a transitional phase towards a level playing field on constitutional, political, institutional, cultural, social, economic issues . . . For Sinn Fein to be involved in institutions in the north was obviously a big move for us.

The party also agreed to a delay in filling the ministerial positions in the new Executive and to an arrangement in which the posts of First and Deputy First Minister would be dealt with first. These were the positions that David Trimble and Seamus Mallon were elected to in July 1998.

'We went along with that,' Gerry Adams told me. 'We were wrong. The argument put at that time was the difficulties within unionism, the Orange marching season etc., etc., etc.' With hindsight, Adams believes Sinn Fein should have insisted that all the ministerial positions – and not just the election of Trimble and Mallon – be dealt with, although, in reality, his party hadn't sufficient numbers in the Assembly to force the issue.

July 1998 became July 1999 and still there was no Executive; still there was no decommissioning. The process needed George Mitchell again and there would be a review of the implementation of the Good Friday Agreement. This began in September 1999 and produced a significant breakthrough two months later.

Earlier in the year, there had been a number of attempts to find a way of ending this protracted political stand-off, but each and every time the process stood still. In this stalemate, all of the focus and all of the attention was on the IRA and its guns, but others also still posed a threat and that was made evident in a loyalist killing in March 1999 – the murder of the Catholic solicitor Rosemary

Nelson. She was well known on Northern Ireland's public stage because she had represented not only the Garvaghy Road Residents' Coalition – which opposed part of the route of the Drumcree Orange march in Portadown – but also the prominent Lurgan republican Colin Duffy. Rosemary Nelson was killed when a bomb, which had been concealed underneath her car, exploded. It was a murder claimed by the Red Hand Defenders, but this was the Loyalist Volunteer Force trying to cover its tracks. That group had announced a ceasefire in May 1998 and, seven months later, had given up some of its guns. There was an attempt to present these actions as significant contributions to peace, but they were not. As I mentioned earlier, this was the loyalist group acting for selfish reasons – to achieve the early release of its prisoners – and the real LVF showed itself in the murder of Rosemary Nelson. That killing in March 1999 was proof that while decommissioning was politically important and important in a confidence-building sense, it was not something that would dent the capability of these organisations to kill.

Some weeks after the killing, I reported that LVF members were linked to the murder and that the device placed underneath Rosemary Nelson's car had been made by a 'freelance' bombmaker. My information had been provided by a number of senior police officers and when I reported their assessment, I predicted that there would be a denial from the LVF. It came within 24 hours. The loyalist organisation called on me to retract what I had said or name the source that had provided the information:

> We maintain the view that only a political imbecile or one intent on causing new levels of mayhem in the country would put forth the statement that Brian Rowan and the BBC have made yesterday.
>
> We therefore call upon both parties to retract the statement or name the source of their so-called intelligence.

I had no intention of retracting what I reported and no intention of naming my sources, and the LVF would have known that. The apologist who wrote that organisation's statement would also have known that the loyalist group was lying. It lied again, some weeks later, when it killed another woman, 59-year-old Elizabeth O'Neill. She picked up a bomb that had been thrown through the window of her home in Portadown. Within hours, there was a statement from the LVF condemning 'without qualification the senseless action taken in the Corcrain area of Portadown last night', but no one believed it. Privately police sources were telling me they had no doubt that the LVF was responsible, and the then Chief Constable, Sir Ronnie Flanagan, hinted at that very strongly when I interviewed him after the denial was issued by the loyalist organisation:

> *FLANAGAN*: While it's too soon to speculate as to which organisation might be behind this, that is not a statement I would take at face value and we're ruling nothing out at this stage in terms of what organisation might be responsible.
>
> *ROWAN*: You would be looking at the LVF as one possibility?
>
> *FLANAGAN*: We would certainly be including them very much in our investigation.

The Rosemary Nelson killing happened just a couple of weeks before Tony Blair and Bertie Ahern came to Hillsborough in the latest search for a formula to end the decommissioning deadlock. Those talks stretched across four days from 29 March to 1 April, and during that period there were two statements from the IRA. Just as Tony Blair was settling in at Hillsborough, I was sitting in a car in Belfast with the spokesman for the IRA leadership. He had a lengthy statement and briefing note to dictate to me – not on decommissioning but on those who had come to be described as the 'disappeared' – people 'executed' and then buried by the IRA in secret graves. Their families had been demanding information and the return of the bodies and, at last, the IRA had responded. It meant that after long years of anguish and waiting, there was now some hope.

IRA STATEMENT DICTATED TO AUTHOR,
29 MARCH 1999:

Eighteen months ago we established a special unit under the command of one of our most senior officers to ascertain the whereabouts of a number of people executed and buried by Oglaigh na hEireann approximately 20 years ago. These burials took place prior to an Army Council directive that the body of anyone killed by Oglaigh na hEireann should be left for burial by their relatives.

This issue has caused incalculable pain and distress to a number of families over a period of many years.

Despite many complicating factors which have both hampered and protracted this investigation, including the lapse in time, changes in leadership and the deaths of both members and former members of Oglaigh na hEireann who were involved, we can now conclude this enquiry.

We believe we have established the whereabouts of the graves of nine people some of whom were members of Oglaigh na hEireann who were executed for activities which put other Oglaigh na hEireann personnel at risk or jeopardised the struggle.

Information regarding the location of these graves is now being processed and will hopefully result in the speedy retrieval of the bodies.

As we have previously stated, we are not responsible for all of those previously listed in the media as having gone missing over the last 30 years. We are responsible for those we have acknowledged today and their families have all been notified.

In initiating this investigation our intention has been to do all within our power to rectify an injustice for which we accept full responsibility and to alleviate the suffering of the families. We are sorry that this has taken so long to resolve and for the prolonged anguish caused to the families.

P. O'NEILL

Before I could report the detail of this statement, something else had to happen and the IRA spokesman listened to a news bulletin on the radio before I left his car. In the Republic, the Irish Government announced plans to give immunity from prosecution to those whose information helped locate the graves of the disappeared. The way was now clear for the IRA statement to be reported and the BBC broke the story across its news outlets at eight o'clock on the evening of 29 March. The names of the nine people were included in a briefing note and the IRA also said why they had been killed. In that briefing note – which was separate from its statement – the republican organisation made the following points:

- This has been dealt with as a humanitarian issue.
- The timing of this development is coincidental.
- We would have sorted this out a year ago had it been possible.
- The investigation is now closed.
- As part of this investigation, we also endeavoured to locate the burial site of British SAS operative Robert Nairac. We were unable to do so.
- Our intention had been to rectify this injustice. We accept responsibility for it and we are sorry it has taken so long to resolve.

'Coincidental', is how the IRA described these latest developments, but many others saw the timing as quite deliberate and an attempt to shift the focus from decommissioning. In searches in the Republic, some but not all of the bodies were later discovered, and for many of the families the anguish is still there and the waiting continues.

With the Hillsborough talks continuing, the IRA spoke again just two days later. On Wednesday morning, 31 March, I travelled into West Belfast for another meeting with the spokesman for the IRA leadership. The organisation had decided to issue its Easter statement early. There was nothing in it to suggest any imminent move on decommissioning, but it was a positive text.

> –The IRA wants to see a permanent peace in this country.
> –IRA guns are silent.
> –We wholeheartedly support the efforts to secure a lasting resolution to the conflict.
> –If the political will exists, the peace process contains the potential to resolve the conflict and deliver a durable peace.

The statement finished with these two paragraphs:

> Injustices which are direct consequences of the conflict must also be addressed. Towards this end we announced, earlier this week, the outcome of our investigation into the location of the burial sites of a number of people executed by Oglaigh na hEireann more than 20 years ago. This was a sincere attempt to do all within our power to rectify an injustice for which we accept full responsibility.
>
> The challenge for everyone, but particularly the British Government, remains the removal of the causes of conflict in our country.
>
> P. O'NEILL

In the absence of decommissioning, the IRA was using these two statements to try to create a positive atmosphere around the Hillsborough negotiations. Others used different tactics to try to move the discussions along and to end the deadlock. The South African President Nelson Mandela spoke by telephone to a number of the key political players, including Adams, Trimble and Seamus Mallon. This was something that had been thought through, and something I was told was going to happen some three weeks or so before the Hillsborough talks. The idea of asking Mandela to use his influence came from Sir Ronnie Flanagan. But this time the magic of Mandela and the efforts of Blair and Ahern failed. The plan the two governments came up with was to dress up decommissioning and call it an 'act of reconciliation'. Not just the IRA but also the loyalists would be expected to contribute, there would be further moves to scale down security and all of this would open the door to the new Executive. It sounded different, but it looked the same and as far as republicans were concerned this was still decommissioning being demanded as a precondition to power-sharing. They saw it as a re-writing of the Good Friday Agreement and they believed they had been ambushed: 'David Trimble didn't get all he wanted but he got too much,' one source told me. 'It's now a matter for the IRA,' he added, 'and the mood I'm picking up is, forget about it. Republicans need now to sit down and work it out and they haven't got it worked out.'

It would not take them long and, within a week of the Hillsborough talks, we would know not only the IRA's thinking but the position of the UVF leadership as well. For Blair and Ahern and their officials, it was back to the drawing board.

On Thursday, 8 April, at around three o'clock, I met two members of the UVF's Brigade Staff in the heart of the loyalist Shankill Road. They knew what the Hillsborough Declaration was all about. Its main purpose was to create the circumstances that would allow the power-sharing Executive to be formed. Loyalists were being asked to give up guns to accommodate their republican enemy – to help Martin McGuinness and Bairbre de Brun into government. How likely was all of that? On the Shankill Road that Thursday afternoon in April, I got the answer I expected: 'The focus of the document is for a difficulty that Sinn Fein have. It has taken the spotlight off Sinn Fein and put the floodlights on both of us.'

I was told the UVF would not hand over guns 'to get Sinn Fein into office'. The sources said this was not about snubbing the notion of a day of reconciliation and they pointed to past statements by the Combined Loyalist Military Command – to the expression of 'remorse' that came with the 1994 ceasefire and to the 'no first strike' position outlined a year later. They told me they still wanted to hear the IRA say 'the war is over'.

By teatime that evening, I was running the details of this briefing – details which were picked up by all of the other major news outlets, and the following day I met again with the spokesman for the IRA leadership. It was in this meeting that I heard that organisation's response to the Hillsborough Declaration. In three short sentences, it was dismissed and another decommissioning initiative had failed. I was told the IRA was 'unimpressed' by the draft declaration; it had 'represented a failure by both governments to confront the unionist veto' and it had caused anger among republicans. The IRA spokesman put an embargo on the briefing and I was unable to report its detail until one o'clock on Saturday, 10 April. So, in the space of a couple of days, first the UVF and then the IRA had ruled out any move to put arms beyond use, no matter how it was dressed up and no matter what it was called. There would be no collective act of reconciliation and no guns still meant no government.

By mid-May, the talking had moved to Downing Street, and, for a few hours, there was some speculation that a deal could be done – that at last a breakthrough was possible, but this was another of those moments in the process which promised much and delivered very little.

On Friday, 14 May, there was a long session of negotiations in London, involving Blair and Ahern, the Ulster Unionists, Sinn Fein and the SDLP. Gerry Adams also chose this day to state publicly that he believed the UDA and the LVF ceasefires were over. His assessment was based on the Rosemary Nelson murder and a series of other attacks that had been linked to the UDA. As a result of the political logjam, the main focus was on the IRA's guns, so Adams was pointing elsewhere and putting the arms question into a wider context. After the talking in London on Friday, the rumour in Belfast on Saturday morning pointed to possible progress. Indeed, Sinn Fein would disclose in a document in July that it believed there was agreement in Downing Street between the parties and the governments that the procedures to form the Executive would be triggered on Thursday, 20 May. On the previous Saturday, hours after the London talks, there was certainly a hint that something was moving: 'We'll know better this afternoon,' a Government source told me. 'We may have a way of moving the process forward.'

'It's up to the unionists,' a senior SDLP figure in Belfast told me.

Everything, it seemed, hinged on a meeting of the Ulster Unionist Assembly Party, where Trimble was briefing his colleagues on the Downing Street talks. Some believed he was going to sell a text that had been drawn up in London, but nothing was sold and nothing was bought. By early evening on that Saturday, I had obtained the unpublished words. They were read to me by a political contact in Belfast and in the text I could see how republicans would be comfortable, but wondered how anyone had thought that Trimble could deliver his party based on this:

> All parties agree to the full implementation of all aspects of the agreement including the objective of achieving total disarmament and the complete withdrawal of all weapons from politics in Ireland.

They accept the issue of arms must be finally and satisfactorily settled and will do what they can to achieve decommissioning of all paramilitary arms within the time-frame set down in the agreement in the context of the implementation of the overall settlement.

The International Commission on Decommissioning will now begin a procedure of intensive discussion with all parties and report back on progress before 30 June.

In light of that report all parties anticipate, without prejudice to their clear positions on this issue, achieving full devolution of power by 30 June.

Decommissioning was still an objective and not something that was guaranteed, the parties would do what they could to achieve it, but still there was no firm commitment from the IRA, and this latest Downing Street text had all the ingredients of the political fudge. Republicans had retaken ground since Hillsborough, and the arms issue was once more firmly set in its Good Friday Agreement context.

In the period between the Hillsborough and Downing Street negotiations, a senior IRA figure had spoken to me and had made clear that organisation's position on decommissioning as a precondition to the Executive being formed. It was not going to happen pre-power-sharing, simultaneously with the formation of the Executive or in some sequenced move after the formation of the Executive. In other words, the IRA was not discussing decommissioning as a means to achieving the political institutions agreed as part of the Good Friday Agreement. The IRA source could not have been clearer when he spoke to me, and another republican I was in contact with throughout that Saturday after the Downing Street talks was dismissing any suggestion of imminent decommissioning.

In one of our conversations, he referred me back to something that Gerry Adams had said a few weeks earlier: 'When he says it would destroy the IRA, he means it. It's not going to happen.'

My source placed that comment in the context of the 'here and now' and, in the here and now of May 1999, there was no immediate way out of the guns and government deadlock. On the arms issue, Trimble needed something more substantial than a statement that Sinn Fein and the other parties would do what they could to achieve decommissioning. That was not available now but, six months down the line, he would get enough to allow him to move things forward.

This was a hugely difficult period for the process, not just because the negotiations were not making progress, but also because the paramilitaries were back at play. There were the killings of Rosemary Nelson and Elizabeth O'Neill, both of which were linked to the LVF, two other murders in May and then in early June for which the IRA was blamed, and in Belfast, the UDA was active again and a senior figure in its leadership told me we were 'a click of the fingers away from a major incident'. In the two killings the IRA was linked to, the victims were drug dealers, and the UDA activity was sparked by a shooting incident at a concert in Belfast in which Johnny Adair was slightly wounded. His associate John White blamed the IRA. There was no evidence to suggest that this was true, but making such a claim probably suited the UDA's purpose at this time. Whoever was behind the Adair shooting, and whatever it was about, it was used by the loyalist group as an excuse for a number of attacks. The Secretary of State Mo Mowlam expressed her 'gravest concern' but said her judgement, for now at least, was that 'the ceasefires are holding'.

Mowlam was between a rock and a hard place. The Rosemary Nelson and Elizabeth O'Neill murders were sectarian killings and in clear breach of the LVF's May 1998 ceasefire. The IRA would not consider the shootings it was linked to – those in which two drug dealers were killed – to have breached the specific terms of its cessation of military operations, but the Government could not make that distinction. If Mowlam moved against the Loyalist Volunteer Force, she would have to move against the IRA also, and then there was the whole question of what the UDA was up to. The decision at this time was to issue a warning to all the paramilitary organisations and not to take any specific action against any one group. The process was standing on shaky ground and soon its foundations would be further weakened.

Before then there would be another attempt to crack the decommissioning nut. The talking moved to Castle Buildings on the Stormont estate, where at the end of June and the start of July there were five long days of negotiations. Just a couple of weeks before the beginning of these talks there was another indication of Sinn Fein's growth, when the party came close to winning the third Northern Ireland seat in the European elections. Paisley just topped the poll ahead of Hume, and the Ulster Unionist Jim Nicholson scraped through in third – less than 2,000 votes ahead of Sinn Fein's Mitchel McLaughlin. His party's share of the vote was a little over 17 per cent, and it was another indication that decommissioning – or more accurately the absence of it – was not damaging the republican vote.

In the Castle Buildings talks, there was a new Sinn Fein initiative – 'Breaking the Impasse'. If Trimble established the political institutions by 30 June, Adams would make a declaration on behalf of his party using more positive language on decommissioning and this in turn would have allowed the de Chastelain Commission to report progress.

The impasse continued. Adams was offering new words. Trimble needed weapons. The republican initiative was progress, but the unionists wanted product in the shape of actual disarmament. This was not on offer and so the political freeze continued with the decommissioning ice unbroken. Adams believed that had the power-sharing Executive been formed, then the parties to the Good Friday Agreement 'acting in good faith, could succeed in persuading those with arms to decommission them in accordance with the agreement'. The Sinn Fein declaration would also state:

> We agree that this should be in a manner set down by the Independent Commission on Decommissioning within the terms of the Good Friday Agreement.
>   This reflects our conviction that through the overall implementation of the Good Friday Agreement we are working to remove the causes of conflict. Conflict must be finished forever – it must be for all of us a thing of the past.

All of this was Sinn Fein offering a context in which it believed the arms question could be addressed, but there were no guarantees from the IRA that decommissioning would begin, never mind be completed, by May 2000, and we were looking at another failed initiative. Adams thought he had a deal with Trimble in Downing Street in May, and Sinn Fein believed it had further stretched republicans to put the party's declaration on the table in these talks, but the unionists did not bite. In the end, there was a joint statement by the two governments and they published their proposals in a document headed 'The Way Forward'. The parties to the Good Friday Agreement would reaffirm three principles: an inclusive Executive exercising devolved power; decommissioning of all paramilitary arms by May 2000; and decommissioning to be carried out in a manner determined by the International Commission on Decommissioning.

At no stage had anyone on the republican side suggested to me that actual decommissioning was possible before May 2000 and, based on many conversations with a number of sources, I had always believed that it would take more time to resolve this issue. The governments now proposed that on 15 July ministers would be nominated for positions within the power-sharing Executive and that the de Chastelain Commission would hold urgent talks with its contacts:

> The Commission will specify that actual decommissioning is to start within a specified time. They will report progress in September and December 1999 and in May 2000.

The document also included a 'fail-safe' clause:

> The governments undertake that, in accordance with the review provisions of the agreement, if commitments under the agreement are not met, either in relation to decommissioning or to devolution, they will automatically, and with immediate effect, suspend the operation of the institutions set up by the agreement.
>
> In relation to decommissioning, this action will be taken on receipt of a report at any time that the commitments now being entered into or steps which are subsequently laid down by the Commission are not fulfilled in accordance with the Good Friday Agreement. The British Government will legislate to this effect.

After all that had failed at Hillsborough, in Downing Street and now in Castle Buildings, this was the governments trying to force the issue. A decommissioning fudge may have been necessary to achieve the Good Friday Agreement in April 1998, but in July 1999 the consequence of that fudge and that ambiguity was political stalemate. Adams, through the use of positive language, was reaching out to Trimble and the unionists, but he also had to be conscious of his own constituency. These latest proposals from the governments had changed what was an objective of the Good Friday Agreement into a must, and the ground that republicans had recovered after the Hillsborough talks had been lost again. The IRA was not yet ready for any big decommissioning gesture. In these latest negotiations, Adams had failed to move the unionists and the proposals from the governments would not move the IRA – an IRA that would soon be under a political spotlight because of gun-running from America and murder in Belfast.

Before then, the move to establish the power-sharing Executive on 15 July provided a moment of political farce. Trimble and his Assembly colleagues stayed away from Stormont. The nominations for the ten ministerial posts came from the SDLP and Sinn Fein.

Mark Durkan, Bairbre de Brun, Sean Farren, Martin McGuinness, Brid Rodgers, Pat Doherty, Joe Hendron, Denis Haughey, Mary Nellis and Alban Magennis were nominated by their party leaders John Hume and Gerry Adams. Adams has often complained that there are unionists who 'don't want a fenian about the place', but on that day someone wryly quipped that 'the fenians were running the place'. The appointments were quickly undone, the Executive was not representative of both sides of the community and the agreement was heading for a period of review.

The following day, 16 July, I met the IRA's spokesman in Belfast. This was not a formal briefing, but we discussed recent events and I knew I was getting an informed analysis. On decommissioning, he told me the position of the governments was 'out of sync with reality'. He believed the independence of General de Chastelain had been undermined and that the legislation that the British Government was planning was about 'boxing the IRA into a position'. On what the governments now wanted to happen on decommissioning, he said the IRA would not be responding to their demands, and he told me there was anger about 'the unionist veto and Blair feeding it'. Soon, this thinking would appear in a formal IRA statement – a statement delivered by P. O'Neill in an angry tone:

> –The agreement has failed to deliver tangible progress and its potential for doing so has substantially diminished in recent months.
> –The credibility and motivation of unionist leaders who signed up to the agreement is now clearly open to question.
> –Recent events at Stormont cannot obscure the fact that the primary responsibility for the developing political crisis rests squarely with the British Government. They have once again demonstrated a lack of political will to confront the unionist veto.
> –Over the past five years, we have called and maintained two prolonged cessations of military operations to enhance the peace process and underline our definitive commitment to its success. We have contributed in a meaningful way to the creation of a climate which would facilitate the search for a durable settlement.
> –The first of these cessations foundered on the demand by the Conservative Government for an IRA surrender. Those who demand the decommissioning of IRA weapons lend themselves, in the current political context, inadvertently or otherwise, to the failed agenda which seeks the defeat of the IRA.

—Responsibility for repairing the damage to the argument
that the present political process can deliver real change rests
primarily with the British Government.

The above is an edited version of the IRA statement issued on 21
July, and it was against this background of the IRA questioning the
worth of the political process and the commitment of others to it,
that its ceasefire began to be doubted. A gun-running operation
from Florida was exposed and then the IRA was linked to the murder
of a Belfast man, Charles Bennett, whose body was discovered with
a bullet wound to the head. Unionists demanded a ruling on the IRA
ceasefire. Mowlam was in another tight political corner, but the
Government managed to wriggle out of it. At just after midday, on
Friday, 6 August 1999 – a week after the Charles Bennett killing –
the IRA issued a brief statement.

IRA LEADERSHIP STATEMENT DICTATED TO
AUTHOR, BELFAST, 6 AUGUST 1999:
Following recent media reports of an alleged IRA arms
importation operation from the USA, a preliminary
investigation has been concluded by Oglaigh na hEireann.
The Army Council has not sanctioned any arms importation
operation.
    There has also been speculation about the recent killing of
Charles Bennett. Let us emphasise that there have been no
breaches of the IRA cessation, which remains intact.
                                                        P. O'NEILL

This was a carefully worded statement from the IRA, in which it
denied nothing and admitted nothing. The IRA's 'complete cessation
of military operations' meant no attacks on the security forces, on
loyalists or against so-called economic targets. Charles Bennett was
a Catholic – a Catholic who somehow had sinned, if you like, against
the IRA. What his 'crime' was I don't know, but clearly the IRA did
not view his execution to have breached its ceasefire. On the other
issue of gun-running, all the IRA said was that its Army Council had
not sanctioned any arms importation operation. If Mowlam was
looking for help to get out of the corner, she would not have found
it in this statement, and her position became even more
uncomfortable when, on 25 August, the then Chief Constable Sir
Ronnie Flanagan publicly linked the IRA to the Charles Bennett
murder.
    This was on the eve of Mowlam's ceasefire ruling – a ruling that
was of the 'deeply concerned' variety. Sinn Fein got a rap over the

knuckles and the IRA got another chance, but Mowlam said she wanted to make 'entirely clear' that she had come 'very close to judging that the IRA's ceasefire is no longer for real'. Her statement said:

> . . . the Chief Constable has said that there is no doubt that the IRA were involved in the Bennett murder. Information is also clear in relation to the arms importation. Both are utterly deplorable and incompatible with the society that all are striving to develop under the Good Friday Agreement . . . although the situation in relation to the IRA is deeply worrying, I do not believe that there is a sufficient basis to conclude that the IRA ceasefire has broken down. Nor do I believe that it is disintegrating, or that these recent events represent a decision by the organisation to return to violence . . . The peace we have now is imperfect, but better than none. If violence continues, the political process – which depends on confidence and trust – will be increasingly at risk.

Mowlam was right. The IRA ceasefire was not 'disintegrating', but that organisation had been involved in the Bennett killing and the gun-running from the United States, and these were activities that many would view to be in violation of the cessation of military operations. Other actions since then, in Northern Ireland and elsewhere, have clearly contradicted what others would expect a ceasefire to mean, and in 2002 the British Government produced new commandments and a few more 'thou shalt nots' for the IRA and the loyalists. Back in 1999, however, there had been three big pushes to move things forward at Hillsborough, in Downing Street and then in Castle Buildings; so far, all had failed. It would once more take the magic of George Mitchell to change things, and, before the year was out, the IRA and de Chastelain would meet for the first time. This was the beginning of the dialogue between the Army Council and the Canadian General which would lead to some of the IRA's arms being put beyond use.

During this period there was also a change at the Northern Ireland Office. Mowlam had moved on and had been replaced by Peter Mandelson. The Mitchell Review of the implementation of the Good Friday Agreement stretched across a period from early September to mid-November 1999 and what he achieved was a more direct dialogue between the unionists and Sinn Fein. He put them face-to-face, switched the venue for the talks, took them out of Northern Ireland for a while and steered this review process towards a carefully choreographed sequence of statements. At long last it brought about the formation of the power-sharing Executive and it put the IRA – at the level of a leadership representative – into direct contact with de Chastelain. These were big steps both for the unionists and for the IRA. The breakthrough, in the run-up to Christmas and close to the new millennium, meant a ministerial position for the Ulster Unionist Michael McGimpsey and in an interview for this book in March 2000 we discussed the Mitchell Review and the events leading up to it:

> I think you've got to think back to Hillsborough and also Downing Street to an extent, but also the Way Forward [discussions] and the suggestions during the Way Forward about seismic shifts and so on. At that stage, the two prime ministers were doing most of the bargaining with Sinn Fein, the republicans, and it was all about decommissioning – getting a start made to decommissioning someway or another – to allow unionists, to allow us all, to go forward. Basically republicans [were] saying decommissioning is surrender and unionists [were] saying, well, without decommissioning or movement on this, you're asking unionists to surrender . . . and it was trying to find a way forward here, where neither of us surrendered and we had been very interested the previous March when Gerry Adams talked about stretching constituencies and jumping together . . . They [republicans] had it put up to them by the prime ministers at Hillsborough. We thought that was daft. The timing was all wrong at Easter. We then had Downing Street and that was basically a suggestion that seemed that the pendulum swings one way and then the other. Blair and Ahern had pushed them and got nowhere – didn't do the business at Hillsborough. So, they came back – pushed us a wee bit at Downing Street. That didn't work, and then you come through to the Way Forward in July and, instead of pushing us a little bit, they pushed us really hard . . . We didn't believe in seismic shifts. We had meetings and, indeed, it may have been the first time we sat down in a room together with Adams and McGuinness on our own, without prime ministers or without the other parties being present. It was myself, Trimble, Donaldson, Empey, Jim Wilson and Ken Maginnis [on one side] and Martin McGuinness and Gerry Adams on the other [side], and they went through it, saying to us what they'd just said to the prime ministers, that they believed they could achieve decommissioning, but threw in the, 'of course, we may not succeed'.

So, Mitchell's task was to create the circumstances which would make possible that act of republicans and unionists jumping together – to find the compromise that would bring movement on both decommissioning and devolution, and which would mean that neither side had surrendered or caved in. He managed to talk them through it. At this time there was all kinds of speculation about what the IRA might do – speculation about internal republican briefings and about when decommissioning would begin and end.

Personally I found this a very difficult period, because, in my reporting, I was swimming against that tide of speculation. Republicans were telling me that decommissioning was not imminent and, given whom I was speaking to, I knew this was information and guidance I could rely on, but others were trying to tell me something else. By 9 November, I knew that an IRA statement, or a formulation of words that could be developed into an IRA statement, was being discussed in the review, but, on that same day, a senior republican source told me: 'If there is a deal, Trimble is jumping without guns.'

On our television news programme that evening, I was interviewed by Noel Thompson, who asked whether it was possible that the IRA would appoint a go-between to the de Chastelain commission. I said that I was not going to pretend to know what was in the text that was being considered, but that the possibility of a go-between being appointed was not being dismissed in the same way that actual decommissioning was being rejected. There was the possibility that the IRA would appoint an 'interlocutor', but I said this was not just a negotiation about unionist requirements, it was about what republicans needed as well. I made the point again that they were saying that decommissioning could split the Republican Movement; it would be seen as surrender – as the stuff of the white flag. And I emphasised the point that I had heard nothing to suggest that the IRA was about to give up any of its guns.

The speculation about imminent decommissioning continued through to the Sunday newspapers on 14 November, but republicans – republicans in the highest tier of the Movement – were advising me not to change my line: 'If I were in your shoes, I would keep my nerve.' This advice was offered by a member of the IRA Army Council and on that Sunday, 14 November, I travelled to the border with Eamonn Mallie for a meeting with a senior republican.

We met in a hotel. Tea and biscuits were ordered and we discussed the decommissioning issue. That nothing was imminent could not have been clearer, but our source was not ruling out the possibility of something happening 'up the road'. He pointed us to the terms of the Good Friday Agreement and said they would be 'rigidly adhered to'. Achieving decommissioning was a collective responsibility – all parties using their influence – and he said it was up to the politicians to make politics work. Decommissioning could not be imposed.

On the basis of that discussion in the border hotel I was sticking to my guns, if you like. The following morning, in an interview on the BBC's *Good Morning Ulster*, I was asked about speculation that the IRA would begin decommissioning in January and complete the process within four months. I dismissed it and said if all we were reading was true, then the IRA was about to jump over the moon. Over the next couple of days I was called several times by someone at the Northern Ireland Office. The calls came after radio interviews I had done and I was told I had got things wrong, that I was overstating my knowledge and that I should suspend judgement. The man from the NIO knew better than I just how jittery the unionists were, just how difficult a selling job Trimble would have, and clearly my rather bleak analysis on the early prospects for decommissioning was not helping. I think he also believed there was a logic and an inevitability about the process that the IRA was about to involve itself in – that if the power-sharing Executive was to survive, then decommissioning had to happen soon, and I think this is where the NIO and some unionists got the Mitchell Review wrong. They read too much into what the IRA was offering. I was confident of my line not only because of what I was hearing from republicans but also because of what I was being told by security sources and, indeed, by some on the unionist side.

At the time of the Mitchell Review, Ken Maginnis – one of the party's senior negotiators – was by no means convinced that decommissioning was going to occur. He acknowledged that progress was being made within the review and that things were happening that were 'more encouraging than on previous occasions', but he also knew there was no definite commitment from the IRA to decommission.

The unionists had to be massaged quite a bit to get them through this and on Thursday, 11 November, the review came close to collapse. Trimble was in trouble trying to sell what was on offer from the republican side and the deal on the table appeared to have been rejected. Mandelson had to step in. He spoke directly to the Ulster Unionist Assembly Party. Privately, Government sources were making clear that if the IRA did not deliver on decommissioning there would be consequences. Trimble would not be left on his own – the Government would suspend the institutions. The review was adjourned to Monday, 15 November, and in that breathing space things seemed to settle and get back on track. That weekend, Gerry

Adams addressed a Sinn Fein women's conference in Dublin and spoke there of his hopes for the Mitchell Review:

> I am bitterly disappointed at Thursday's rejection by the UUP of efforts to end the crisis in the peace process. The Review should have been over. It was to be short, sharp and focused. It wasn't, but we stuck with it. We made strenuous efforts. We took initiatives; we planned our way forward. We encouraged others to move. We stretched ourselves and our constituency to the limit in a serious and genuine effort to end the difficulties. But, when it came down to it, all of our efforts were rejected in just 20 minutes on Thursday afternoon.
>
> Maybe the UUP were only negotiating. Maybe they just don't know when to stop saying no. Maybe it is too big a jump for them to take. Maybe the real and genuine difficulties which they face cannot be overcome. Maybe they aren't up to it. It is hard to know. During this review we did have better discussions. We did listen and they did listen. We did come to understand each other's positions better.
>
> So for all these reasons on Thursday when our hearts would have told us that enough was enough our heads told us that rather than knee-jerk to the UUP rejection this was now the time to allow unionism the space to reflect . . .
>
> We want a just and lasting peace. So, come Monday, hopefully, the conclusion of that review will be a positive one. Come Monday, hopefully, the reflections by unionism will have led them to the only possible conclusion if they really want this process to work. And that is that the only way forward is to work with the rest of us in shaping a new future and a new beginning for all sections of our people.
>
> Come Monday, hopefully, progressive unionism, new liberal unionism will emerge to tell us all that the time to do this is now.

In the days that followed, the detail of the review emerged piece by piece and the jigsaw began to take shape. What began to roll out, in terms of statements from Mitchell, de Chastelain, Trimble, Adams and the IRA had been sequenced. The order of events and the words had been agreed in the negotiations. General de Chastelain wanted the IRA to appoint a representative to talk to his commission and, if that organisation responded positively, Trimble would form the power-sharing Executive. He had not achieved his goal of guns before government, but there had been some progress: the IRA had moved and in that movement there had been another step towards putting arms beyond use.

There was a lot in the Adams statement which came at midday on Tuesday, 16 November:

> IRA guns are silent and the Sinn Fein leadership is confident that the IRA remains committed to the objective of a permanent peace . . .
>
> Sinn Fein accepts that decommissioning is an essential part of the peace process. We believe that the issue of arms will be finally and satisfactorily settled under the aegis of the de Chastelain commission as set out in the agreement. All parties to the agreement have an obligation to help bring decommissioning about. Sinn Fein is committed to discharging our responsibilities in this regard . . .
>
> Sinn Fein has a total and absolute commitment to pursue our objectives by exclusively peaceful and democratic means in accordance with the Good Friday Agreement. For this reason we are totally opposed to any use of force or threat of force by others for any political purpose . . .
>
> We are totally opposed to punishment attacks . . .
>
> We reiterate our total commitment to doing everything in our power to maintain the peace process and to removing the gun forever from the politics of our country.

These were the highlights, the bits that jumped out of a detailed statement. In the planned sequence, the IRA would speak 24 hours later, but I got hold of its text early, not from republicans but from another source with knowledge of the Mitchell Review.

On the evening of 16 November, I ran the following report on our radio news bulletins:

> The next development in a carefully choreographed sequence of events is expected to be a statement from the IRA.
>
> Sources are suggesting it will be brief and will confirm that the IRA leadership is appointing a representative to enter into discussions with the Canadian General John de Chastelain and his Decommissioning Body.
>
> The IRA statement will not respond to the unionist demand for it to say that the war is over, but don't be surprised if it states a strong commitment to freedom, justice and peace. The IRA is expected to put on record its support for Sinn Fein, probably acknowledging the leadership the party has given during the peace process.

In the past the IRA has described the Good Friday Agreement as a significant development. That is likely to be repeated, with the IRA possibly adding that its full implementation will contribute to a lasting peace.

Today, Sinn Fein spoke of the IRA's guns being silent. They will have to remain so if David Trimble is to have any chance of selling the deal on offer.

At just after noon the following day, I met the IRA's spokesman in West Belfast. He handed me a brief statement, but told me I was the last person who needed one. His few words were confirmation that the report I had run the previous evening was accurate, and the piece of paper I now had in my hand confirmed this:

> IRA LEADERSHIP STATEMENT PASSED TO
> AUTHOR, BELFAST, 17 NOVEMBER 1999:
> The IRA is committed unequivocally to the search for freedom, justice and peace in Ireland. In our view the Good Friday Agreement is a significant development and we believe its full implementation will contribute to the achievement of lasting peace. We acknowledge the leadership given by Sinn Fein throughout this process.
>
> The IRA is willing to further enhance the peace process and consequently, following the establishment of the institutions agreed on Good Friday last year, the IRA leadership will appoint a representative to enter into discussions with General John de Chastelain and the IICD.
>
> P. O'NEILL

The unionist response to the IRA statement came from one of the party's negotiators in the Mitchell Review, Michael McGimpsey. He believed the IRA's acknowledgement of the Sinn Fein leadership was a 'direct endorsement' of the statement Gerry Adams had made the previous day, and he read a lot into the IRA's decision to begin talks with de Chastelain:

> An IRA representative entering into discussions with General de Chastelain on modalities, i.e. the amounts, types, locations of weapons and timetable for their destruction, is a major development. The statements from IRA/Sinn Fein move us closer to achieving our party's twin objectives of securing devolution and total decommissioning.

The unionist demand had been no guns – no government. That had not been achieved and the statement from the IRA leadership made clear that no government would mean no contact with de Chastelain.

Trimble had to jump first and he had no guarantee that the IRA would deliver actual decommissioning. There was nothing in the IRA statement to suggest it was about to discuss methods for decommissioning, the locations of its arms dumps or a timetable for their destruction. The unionist assessment of the statement was an overly optimistic one, and events and time would confirm this. It was not until August 2001 that the IRA proposed a method for putting arms beyond use and the first act of decommissioning occurred two months later.

The Ulster Unionist Council met on 27 November 1999 and, here, the Mitchell deal was re-written, in that Trimble added a decommissioning deadline – something he probably had to do to get through this day and to get into the Executive. What had been achieved in the review was already beginning to unravel.

Trimble was moving forward into the Executive but only for a matter of weeks. He and his UUP colleagues in the Executive would lodge post-dated resignation letters with the party president, the Ulster Unionist Council would be re-convened in February 2000 and if the IRA had not moved by then, the political institutions would come tumbling down. The decommissioning deadline was the end of January and this approach won 58 per cent backing at the Unionist Council. Trimble told Adams the unionists had done their bit: 'We've jumped; you follow.'

Michael McGimpsey, who would join Trimble in the Executive, told me that while the Mitchell Review had not produced any promises on arms, there was a very clear understanding of what was needed. Neither side should be left to feel humiliated:

> We all agreed that nobody could do this with the arse hanging out of their trousers. There had to be no humiliation all round. There was never any promises given but there were what we have described as clear understandings – clear understandings being that if we would jump first, if by the end of January there had been no reciprocation from Sinn Fein and republicans in terms of decommissioning, that we could not sustain the Executive devolution and that was the clear understanding. It was also clearly understood that de Chastelain would report at the end of January and he would give a progress report. That progress report would be the determining factor on whether anything had happened on decommissioning or not, and if he reported that nothing had

happened we could not sustain devolution. We could not
guarantee to republicans that we could deliver and jump first.
We had to go to the Council. They could not guarantee
decommissioning to us. They had their constituency, the
Army Council, whatever, to address. So, there were no
guarantees. There were clear understandings . . . and we
made appeals, publicly and privately, look, don't go into this
unless you're certain you can do it.

The IRA was not about to jump on the terms dictated by Trimble at
that party council meeting and on that Saturday Adams struggled
out of his sick bed to respond to the Ulster Unionist leader. He
welcomed the decision to establish the institutions, but he was
disappointed by the setting of this new deadline. In reality he is more
likely to have been bloody furious. He accused Trimble of stepping
outside the Mitchell Review and the Good Friday Agreement by
'unilaterally introducing a new element, a new deadline, which seeks
to dictate and totally undermines and contradicts the agreed role of
the Independent International Commission on Decommissioning'.

Trimble is someone who wears his problems on his sleeve; Adams
is not. Trimble may have needed a deadline to get him through the
meeting of the Ulster Unionist Council, but it would be wrong to
assume that Adams delivered the Sinn Fein and IRA statements in
the Mitchell Review without difficulty. He was stretching his people
– particularly the IRA – and taking them, as one source put it, into
positions and places where they did not want to go. Another
republican source said people had been 'unsettled' and were asking
the questions: 'What is it leading to? What's the next shock we are
going to have to take?'

The source told me:

There's a raw nerve being exposed . . . particularly Army
[IRA] people. It seems to me that the context for resolving
the arms question is beginning to change. When are you
going to see some evidence of the arms question being
resolved in this context? I don't know.

Republicans were still playing the long game as regards the arms
issue, but Trimble needed short-term results. The republican
context was put into this nutshell by a source I spoke to in
November 1999: 'There is a long-term reality about a process,
bedded in, which sees an end to a range of armed groups and then
whatever they do to sort the materials.'

This was thinking ahead – looking into the future – but Trimble had been hanging around for a long time and was already tired of waiting, and the republican leadership now had to manage a new situation which had a new unionist deadline built into it. After the Mitchell Review, there was the prospect of the process having some rhythm, but now it was starting to stutter again – stymied by an old demand which, for now at least, could not be met.

The unionists having jumped in November 1999 were now waiting for the IRA to respond, and one senior party source told me there would be a lot of 'bed wetting' between then and Christmas. Michael McGimpsey believed the IRA's 'window of opportunity' was in the period Christmas Eve to New Year's Day – 'new year, new century, new millennium, new Northern Ireland, new dispensation, all of that' – but, even before that meeting of the Ulster Unionist Council and the subsequent move into the power-sharing Executive, doubts were creeping in. At around the same time that the Mitchell sequence was triggered, two senior republicans – Martin Ferris and Pat Doherty – were in the United States and comments attributed to them while they were there clearly suggested that imminent decommissioning was highly unlikely, to put it at its best. The following comments were attributed to Ferris, now a member of the Irish parliament: 'If IRA guns are silent, the Executive is up and doing business, the Assembly is up and doing business, why on earth would Blair collapse all of that over the non-decommissioning of guns that are silent anyway?'

Doherty, now the MP for West Tyrone, was reported to have been asked in a taped interview for a Boston newspaper if he believed voluntary decommissioning would begin after Sinn Fein was admitted to the Executive. He apparently replied by saying 'no' three times. In an interview for this book, recorded in March 2000, Michael McGimpsey told me:

> We also read that what Ferris and Doherty were saying was the true position of the Army Council. So, we decided at that point that it was probably, almost certainly in fact – and we all shared this view – that they were going to play us false, but, nevertheless, we were determined to test this.
>
> We'd invested so much in this entire agreement, the process, we were determined to test this to its destruction.

One of McGimpsey's party colleagues, Jeffrey Donaldson – the man who walked away on the day of the Good Friday Agreement – was not prepared to give the IRA the benefit of the doubt, and in the Ulster Unionist Council meeting he was one of those who opposed Trimble's decision to go into government with Sinn Fein, however

conditional that decision was. I also interviewed him for this book in
March 2000:

> I noted always the differences for example in the spin that
> Gerry Adams would apply as compared with statements that
> were emanating from the IRA itself. A blind man on a
> galloping horse could have seen that the IRA statements did
> not in any way match up to the kind of fancy language that
> Adams and McGuinness were using, and in those
> circumstances I was not convinced, and I could not
> understand why colleagues were convinced, that the IRA
> were going to deliver decommissioning in the circumstances
> and in the form that we'd envisaged.

The Executive was elected on Monday, 29 November, with Trimble
and Mallon as First and Deputy First Ministers. The other Ulster
Unionists were McGimpsey, Sir Reg Empey and Sam Foster, the
SDLP nominated Mark Durkan, Sean Farren and Brid Rodgers,
Sinn Fein Martin McGuinness and Bairbre de Brun and the DUP
Peter Robinson and Nigel Dodds, although they would refuse to sit
at the Executive table with republicans. Jeffrey Donaldson watched
in disbelief:

> I think perhaps more than anything else connected with the
> agreement, the shudder which went down the spine of
> unionism when Martin McGuinness was appointed Minister
> of Education and Bairbre de Brun the Minister of Health was
> unparalleled. I think people just couldn't begin to come to
> terms with a situation where a man who was the former chief
> of staff of the Provisional IRA, for all we know perhaps a
> member of the IRA Army Council to this day, would become
> the Minister of Education in the government of Northern
> Ireland without a single bullet having been decommissioned.

I think a shudder probably went down the republican spine after that
November meeting of the Ulster Unionist Council and the decision
by Trimble to set his decommissioning deadline, and in the period
immediately after the formation of the Executive, the IRA began to
address that issue. On Tuesday, 30 November, in West Belfast, I was
briefed by the spokesman for the IRA leadership. He told me the
IRA had been persuaded to appoint a representative to enter into
discussions with de Chastelain on the basis that it would enhance the
peace process, and then he made the following points:

• The context in which the IRA agreed to this was a clear understanding that the announcement and appointment would be part of a series of events which would move the political process beyond the impasse in which it has been stuck for the past 18 months.

• The subsequent setting of preconditions for future progress towards the full implementation of the Good Friday Agreement by David Trimble was not part of this context and in our view represents a clear departure from the terms of the Mitchell Review.

• The IRA will take its own counsel on the implications of this development.

• As agreed by the IRA leadership, the appointment of a representative to meet with the IICD will go ahead.

I was told this was the IRA acting in good faith, while at the same time it was giving serious consideration to the implications of the Trimble deadline and the threat that posed to the political institutions. The IRA statement, which came as part of the Mitchell sequence, was very precise. The organisation was entering into discussions with de Chastelain. There had been no secret deal on actual decommissioning, and my source dismissed newspaper reports suggesting there had been as 'crap'.

A couple of days later on 2 December, when I again met my IRA contact, the organisation confirmed the appointment of its representative.

> IRA LEADERSHIP STATEMENT DICTATED TO
> AUTHOR, BELFAST, 2 DECEMBER 1999:
> On Wednesday, 17 November, the IRA leadership announced that following the establishment of the institutions agreed on Good Friday last year they would appoint a representative to enter into discussions with General de Chastelain and the IICD.
>
> We have since expressed our concerns at the conditional way the UUP have agreed to the establishment of the institutions. The implications of this serious development are being carefully considered. Despite this, we will honour our commitment.
>
> We confirm that a representative has been appointed to enter into discussions with the IICD.
>
> P. O'NEILL

Confirmation of a first meeting came that weekend. The IRA,

through its leadership representative, was now talking to the General, but another crisis in the peace process was just around the corner.

The new year, new century, new millennium, and new dispensation did not move the IRA to where Trimble needed it to go and soon Mandelson would suspend the political institutions – the first of a number of times this would happen in that clash between guns and government in Northern Ireland.

CHAPTER SEVEN

The Cupboard is Bare

'The IRA have never entered into any agreement, undertaking or understanding at anytime, with anyone on any aspect of decommissioning. We have not broken any commitments or betrayed anyone.'

IRA leadership, February 2000

'. . . the IRA leadership has agreed to put in place within weeks a confidence-building measure to confirm that our weapons remain secure.'

IRA leadership, May 2000

'If the process was dependent on British or unionist initiatives it would have died a long time ago.'

Sinn Fein's Gerry Kelly, October 2000

'In a recent meeting with the commission, the IRA representative proposed a method for putting IRA arms completely and verifiably beyond use.'

Independent International Commission on Decommissioning report, August 2001

JANUARY 2000: There was now an inevitability about things. General de Chastelain's decommissioning cupboard was bare, Trimble's patience exhausted and, for now at least, the IRA had gone as far as it was going. So, had republicans miscalculated, had they misread Mandelson and the unionists and had they really believed that if the Executive was functioning and the guns were silent the institutions would not be suspended? If they had thought that, then they were wrong, but others had also misunderstood them. The Government and unionist fortune-tellers had read far too much into the IRA's tea leaves and their anticipated decommissioning dream was once more turning into a no-guns nightmare. As the Trimble deadline approached, there was a late flurry of activity – IRA briefings and statements, and signals from Mandelson that he was getting ready to move. In a report in December 1999, the de Chastelain commission gave a positive assessment that decommissioning would occur, but they did not say when.

There was progress in that they had had their first meetings with the authorised representatives of the IRA and the UDA, but, as far as the unionists were concerned, there was only one question that mattered: had any weapons been destroyed? General de Chastelain and his team had only a few short weeks to try to persuade republicans to move some more, but it was too soon for them and too late for the process. The decommissioning window of opportunity was closing.

A few days before Christmas, I bumped into a senior republican in Belfast – someone who I knew was in a position to know the mind of the IRA leadership and in a position to know the detail of the Mitchell Review and what had been agreed. We chatted in a quiet corner and I asked him why some unionists appeared so confident that decommissioning was going to happen in January. His answer was brief: 'I don't know. It's not, and they know that.'

There was no attempt to dress it up. It was a simple, straightforward: it was not going to happen. 'Any chance we had of sorting this out was killed off by Trimble,' he told me.

Christmas passed and, on the decommissioning calendar, the days of January were being ticked off one by one. By now you could sense that the unionists and those on the Government side were becoming increasingly anxious. Time was running out, there was no sense of republicans increasing the decommissioning pace and, privately, people began to concede that the IRA was not going to deliver.

Soon it would be there for all to read in the reports of the International Independent Commission on Decommissioning, but even before then within unionism and at the Northern Ireland Office there was a mood of let-down. A senior unionist I spoke to on 22 January 2000 said it would be viewed as IRA 'bad faith'.

He told me, 'They broke their word', and he said they had wasted unionist time. He said republicans would have to 'face the consequences of that' and he now expected that Mandelson would pre-empt unionist resignations from the Executive by suspending the institutions. The blame game had begun.

That same day, I spoke to a source at the Northern Ireland Office. He told me if de Chastelain reported 'default', the Government would suspend: 'That is the option. We are not saying that in any hardball way.'

On the question of blame, he said: 'The finger is pointing in one direction.'

What he meant by default was no decommissioning, and however positively the de Chastelain report of 31 January was presented, that was its message. In the early hours of 1 February, a commission source told me the report was now with the British and Irish governments. It had been delivered just before midnight. Days earlier, Gerry Adams had twice warned of the consequences of suspending the institutions. He believed the IRA would withdraw from its talks with de Chastelain. He appealed to unionists not to 'hardball' on this issue and not 'to take it down to the wire'. The governments would not publish de Chastelain's findings for some days yet, which was another indication of a negative result, but on 1 February Trimble said the commission had reported that no decommissioning had occurred and he predicted suspension.

I was at the Trimble news conference and spent several hours that day at Stormont. Indeed, it was while I was there that I took a call from the IRA. At the time, Eamonn Mallie was standing beside me and we were waiting for another news conference to hear what Gerry Adams had to say. The call meant we had to leave and we made a quick journey from the east to the west of the city.

This time we were met by two representatives from the IRA. The man who had been dealing with us was moving on and he introduced us to a new contact. This was a briefing and the IRA had a number of points to make:

> The IRA were persuaded to enter into discussions with the IICD to help move the situation out of the political vacuum in which it had been stuck for the previous 18 months. We did so in good faith and constructively.
>
> Our representative met with the IICD on three occasions and, as late as last night, we were in contact with the IICD.
>
> Our representative stressed that we are totally committed to the peace process; that the IRA wants a permanent peace; that the declaration and maintenance of the cessation, which is now entering its fifth year, is evidence of that; that IRA guns are silent; that there is no threat to the peace process from the IRA.

This briefing gave us a flavour of those early discussions between the IRA and de Chastelain. They were not about the nuts and bolts – or bombs and bullets – of decommissioning. This was a discussion in which the organisation was stressing its commitment to its ceasefire and to the peace process. Its guns were silent, but there was nothing here to suggest that the fine detail of decommissioning was being discussed – nothing to suggest that the IRA was proposing methods for decommissioning or discussing timetables for the destruction of its arms.

Mandelson knew this and on 3 February he began to prepare the ground for the suspension of the political institutions. Speaking in parliament, he pointed to the positive aspects in the report of the IICD on 31 January, but the main purpose of his commentary was to highlight the gap that still remained:

> With the appointment of contact persons by the IRA and UFF in December 1999, all the main paramilitary groups on ceasefire are now engaged with the commission – a significant advance.
>
> The commission's report points to a number of other positive factors.
>
> The ceasefires remain in place. The fact the guns are silent, and the unequivocal support of the IRA and the other paramilitary groups for the political process, has played a vital part in recent political advances. The assurance repeated this week that there is no threat to the peace process from the IRA is important and will be welcomed.
>
> However, the report also stated that there has not yet been any decommissioning of arms by a major paramilitary group.
>
> This is totally unacceptable. Notably in the case of the IRA, it has to be clear that decommissioning is going to happen.

The Secretary of State said the commission needed 'definite information about when decommissioning will actually start'. As he spoke, there were intensive contacts going on in the background, Adams would soon confirm he was talking to the IRA and Mandelson said:

> Even at this very late stage, it is right that we and all the parties continue to see if there is a basis on which the institutions can continue to operate and decommissioning start . . . But if it becomes clear that because of the loss of confidence the institutions cannot be sustained, the Government has to be ready to put a hold on the operation of the institutions.

It was the signal for suspension and Adams and the IRA reacted angrily to Mandelson and to a comment in which he accused the paramilitaries of betraying the people by not engaging adequately with de Chastelain. Soon, there would be another statement, another meeting with the IRA and more angry words.

Whatever was going on in the background, it was not going to be enough to save the power-sharing Executive, and in the league of British political hate figures republicans now ranked Mandelson alongside the previous secretaries of state Roy Mason and Patrick Mayhew. Adams accused him of caving into unionist demands: 'This is no way to build confidence among nationalists and republicans and it is a slap in the face to the Sinn Fein leadership, who are engaged at this time in trying to save the very same institutions.'

It was too late for that – new IRA words and a second de Chastelain report were not enough. Before those developments, Mallie and I again met the IRA in Belfast – this time on Saturday, 5 February.

This was the IRA's way of joining in and contributing to the public debate on guns and government, and its statement that day was the organisation's response to Mandelson and to the unionists. I copied it onto two taxi receipts I had in my pocket.

IRA LEADERSHIP STATEMENT DICTATED TO
AUTHOR, BELFAST, 5 FEBRUARY 2000:

The British Secretary of State has accused the IRA of betrayal over the issue of decommissioning. Similar allegations have been made by others.

The British Secretary of State has now used this in threatening to collapse the political institutions.

We totally reject these accusations. The IRA have never entered into any agreement, undertaking or understanding at any time with anyone on any aspect of decommissioning.

We have not broken any commitments or betrayed anyone.

It was the IRA who took the first step to remove the guns from Irish politics by silencing our weapons. By so doing we created the space for the development of the peace process and for politicians to make politics work.

Those who have once again made the political process conditional on the decommissioning of silenced IRA arms are responsible for creating the current difficulties and for keeping the peace process in a state of perpetual crisis.

The IRA believes that this crisis can be averted and the issue of arms can be resolved. This will not be on British or unionist terms, nor will it be advanced by British legislative threats.

We recognise that the issue of arms needs to be dealt with

in an acceptable way and this is a necessary objective of a
genuine peace process. For that reason we are engaged with
the IICD.

We have supported and we will continue to support efforts
to secure the resolution of the arms issue. The peace process
is under no threat from the IRA.

P. O'NEILL

The unionists who had spoken after the Mitchell Review of a 'clear
understanding' of when decommissioning would have to occur now
had their answer. The IRA statement could not have been any more
frank – no agreement, undertaking or understanding at anytime,
with anyone, on any aspect of decommissioning. There was the
positive language that 'the issue of arms can be resolved', but
Trimble was equally clear that words would not be enough. It all
looked pretty bleak, but the IRA had moved forward when it entered
into those discussions with de Chastelain. It was that move back in
November 1999 which prompted a republican source to tell me that
the context for resolving the arms issue was beginning to change. It
was. It may not have been all that evident under those clouds of crisis
back in February 2000, but the IRA man I spoke to that day is the
same man who delivered the 'arms beyond use' statement in October
2001. Republicans were not running at a pace dictated by unionist
deadlines, but, slowly, carefully, they were moving their own people.
What Adams and McGuinness were working on with the IRA in the
background became clear on 11 February 2000, but it was too late to
stop Mandelson from pulling the political plug and suspending the
institutions. Trimble was becoming increasingly anxious and the
unionist resignation letters were about to be opened. The
Government had to move quickly to prevent this. Such was the pro-
agreement/anti-agreement unionist arithmetic there would be no
certainty that if Trimble, McGimpsey, Empey and Foster resigned
that they would be re-elected. So, the Government saw the freezing
or suspension of the institutions as a better option. Adams and the
IRA did not.

Suspension came on that Friday, 11 February. Three days earlier,
Adams had thought out loud about where things were going and
what his future role would be:

No process can limp from crisis to crisis the way this one
has. I don't intend to spend the rest of my life trying to
shore up a process that is going to be in perpetual crisis . . .
If we do not do this, if the institutions are collapsed, if we
go into review, then this party and this party leader are

> going to sit back and reflect in a very contemplative way
> what role I have to play as a messenger who continuously
> gets shot.

Adams was clearly angered. After the detail of the latest IRA
initiative emerged on 11 February, I too found myself on the
receiving end of some republican sharp tongue. I had suggested, in
a television interview, that what we were looking at was more
context and no 'semtext'.

Adams and others, tired from long discussions, were not amused.
The new line in the de Chastelain report which came on suspension
Friday was this: 'The representative indicated to us today the context
in which the IRA will initiate a comprehensive process to put arms
beyond use, in such a manner as to ensure maximum public
confidence.'

The context was the full implementation of the Good Friday
Agreement and the removal of the causes of conflict. It was better
than before, but not good enough for the unionists: 'The Republican
Movement totally misread the mood of unionism – listened to what
we said, but didn't hear it,' said Michael McGimpsey in an interview
for this book. 'They suddenly worked out that they were in a game
here – that they had to deliver, this had to be addressed, and there
was a last-minute panic, and, in fact, they came through with
something to de Chastelain but missed the last post.'

Adams knew what the IRA would do if Mandelson suspended the
political institutions and had publicly predicted the course of events.
So, it was now a question of waiting for another call. It would not
take long and, on Tuesday, 15 February, I was again in the company
of the IRA's spokesman. We met at about half past four. He had a
statement from P. O'Neill – a statement from the organisation's
leadership which signalled the IRA's withdrawal from the de
Chastelain talks.

IRA LEADERSHIP STATEMENT DICTATED TO
AUTHOR, BELFAST, 15 FEBRUARY 2000:
On 17 November, the leadership of the IRA agreed to
appoint a representative to enter into discussions with the
IICD. This was on the basis that it would be part of a series
of events including, and in particular, the establishment of the
political institutions set out in the Good Friday Agreement.

This was designed to move the situation out of an 18-month
impasse. This impasse was created and maintained by unionist
intransigence and a failure by the British Government to
advance the implementation of the Good Friday Agreement.

The British Secretary of State has re-introduced the unionist veto by suspending the political institutions.

This has changed the context in which we appointed a representative to meet with the IICD and has created a deeper crisis.

Both the British Government and the leadership of the Ulster Unionist Party have rejected the propositions put to the IICD by our representative. They obviously have no desire to deal with the issue of arms except on their own terms.

Those who seek a military victory in this way need to understand that this cannot and will not happen. Those who made the political process conditional on the decommissioning of silenced IRA guns are responsible for the current crisis in the peace process.

In the light of these changed circumstances, the leadership of the IRA have decided to end our engagement with the IICD. We are also withdrawing all propositions put to the IICD by our representative since November.

P. O'NEILL

Back at the office, David Lynas was the duty editor on our radio desk and I called him from West Belfast to alert him to the breaking news story. I knew it would travel outside Northern Ireland and I told him to round up our colleagues from BBC national news. The IRA statement was embargoed till five o'clock – the institutions had been frozen, and, for now, the IRA was ending its dialogue with de Chastelain. Now he had lost the IRA's context for decommissioning and his cupboard was once again bare. It was the beginning of a kind of hokey-cokey-type relationship. The IRA would put its representative in and take its representative out, put its proposals in and take its proposals out, and, I suppose, that was the way things were going to be until the right political balance was found. After the fall-out over the 'context and semtext' remark, I decided to keep my hokey-cokey theory to myself – that is until now.

On a more serious note, dissident republicans used the cover of this latest crisis to sneak out of the shadows, and in this period we saw a resumption of 'Real' IRA activity. They had been in hiding since the shame of Omagh, but gradually they re-emerged and a pattern developed. At times when the peace process has been at its most vulnerable, the dissidents have been at their most active. Their way of getting noticed has been through their attacks aimed mainly at security targets, but in 2002 they murdered a civilian worker at a Territorial Army centre in Derry. It was their first killing since Omagh.

So, at the time of suspension back in February 2000, there was a new
dissident republican threat and also a very volatile situation within
loyalism. The UVF and LVF were still locked in a feud and that
infighting within loyalism would develop and bring in the largest of
the organisations, the UDA. This will be dealt with in more detail
later, but back in February 2000 things were not looking particularly
good. On top of the feuding within loyalism and that dissident
threat, there was a political fight over policing. The report by the
Patten Commission meant major structural and symbolic change,
including the scrapping of the RUC title, and for unionists this was
another piece of the new Northern Ireland that they did not like.
With no decommissioning to report, unionists demanded an end to
prisoner releases. It was a demand that was dismissed, and it was in
the middle of this mess that political efforts to rebuild and restore
the institutions got underway. Once more, this would be achieved
without decommissioning.

As things were developing, the IRA was re-writing the
decommissioning process – stretching it out, playing it long and
taking it beyond May 2000 – the target of the Good Friday
Agreement for complete disarmament. Power-sharing would be
restored, not after actual decommissioning, but as a result of an IRA
confidence-building measure. It was not part of the envisaged de
Chastelain process, but something new.

In its initial contacts with de Chastelain, the IRA was stressing its
commitment to the peace process – a commitment underscored by
the duration of its ceasefire – and it stressed too the silence of its
guns. It moved from there to providing the commission with the
political context in which it would consider putting arms beyond
use. That context would emerge publicly in a statement in May
2000, and there was something else – the confidence-building
measure. A number of arms dumps would be examined by
international inspectors to confirm that IRA weapons remained
secure.

This came right out of the blue. There had been no hints, no
whispers, nothing – nothing until I met the man from the IRA on
Saturday, 6 May. This is a big date in running, remembered because
Roger Bannister ran the first sub-four minute mile at Oxford on 6
May 1954, and, here, on that same date many years later, the IRA
was breaking new ground, changing the arms context and setting
new challenges for Trimble. This was decommissioning's equivalent
of the first sub-four minute mile – so important because of how
emotive this issue is for the IRA. It sees itself as an army that has
been to war, and no army with an intention of continuing war allows
anyone, no matter how trustworthy, near its weapons.

There have been subsequent events that would appear to contradict this analysis – security assessments suggesting all sorts of IRA activities, but there has been nothing which has pointed to any imminent threat to its ceasefire. The IRA's army mentality means it will function until it is stood down, and it was those security assessments pointing to continuing activities which prompted the British Government in 2002 to demand more of the ceasefires. There would have to be an end to training, targeting and the acquisition and development of weaponry – the new ceasefire commandments I referred to earlier.

The IRA's May 2000 statement came out of another of those long negotiations which culminated in another gathering of the key political players at Hillsborough, including the British and Irish prime ministers Tony Blair and Bertie Ahern. From inside those talks, late on Friday night, 5 May, a source gave me the first hint that something was taking shape. The Government would make a statement, it would call on the paramilitaries to respond and a date would be set on which the political institutions would be restored. I called my colleague Mark Simpson, who was at Hillsborough, to tell him what was happening and I spoke, also, to the BBC's head of news and current affairs in Belfast, Andrew Colman. These developments would mean special news programmes early the next morning and the preparations began.

Within hours, I was going much further in my reports on the BBC News 24 channel, on Radio 5 and Radio 4 and on BBC Radio Ulster. I was predicting there would be an IRA statement soon, resumed contact with de Chastelain and a positive IRA response to a call from the governments that weapons should be put 'completely and verifiably beyond use'. My source withheld the jewel of the confidence-building measure. That would have to wait for my meeting with the IRA – a meeting that happened just after midday on Saturday.

Overnight and through to the early-morning news bulletins on 6 May, I was running the following report across the BBC's output:

> Sources are suggesting there will be an IRA statement soon – possibly within the next 24 hours. It is expected to confirm that the republican group will renew its talks with General John de Chastelain's Decommissioning Body.
>
> Last night's joint statement from the governments called on paramilitaries to state that they will put their arms completely and verifiably beyond use. My understanding is that the governments have grounds to believe that the IRA

will respond in a way that meets that requirement. The de Chastelain commission will then discuss with the representatives of the paramilitaries the next steps.

There are two important questions: what exactly does putting weapons beyond use mean and who will verify that this has happened?

A letter being sent to party leaders will deal with the implementation of other aspects of the Good Friday Agreement and, according to one source, will make commitments and set dates.

This latest deal allowed more time for decommissioning. The May 2000 deadline was discarded and June 2001 set as a new target. The IICD was also given space to explore possible new methods for putting arms beyond use – another example of how the decommissioning process was being reworked.

The negotiations were not just about weapons. There was a timetable for the implementation of the outstanding elements of the Good Friday Agreement covering a range of issues including policing, criminal justice, prisoners and victims, and, most important as far as republicans were concerned, there was a commitment from the governments to rebuild the institutions. All of this meant that Trimble had another selling job to do and, for a second time, there would be government before guns.

Next, came my meeting with the man from the IRA, in a leisure centre just after noon. He placed a typed statement on the table and I read it before we discussed its detail. There was the confirmation that the IRA would resume contact with de Chastelain and a context in which the organisation would completely and verifiably put arms beyond use. The context was something of a mouthful:

> The full implementation, on a progressive and irreversible basis, by the two governments, especially the British Government, of what they have agreed will provide a political context, in an enduring political process, with the potential to remove the causes of conflict and in which Irish republicans and unionists can, as equals, pursue our respective political objectives peacefully.
>
> In that new context the IRA leadership will initiate a process that will completely and verifiably put IRA arms beyond use. We will do it in such a way as to avoid risk to the public and misappropriation by others and ensure maximum public confidence.

The gem was in the last three paragraphs:

> We look to the two governments and especially the British
> Government to fulfil their commitments under the Good
> Friday Agreement and the joint statement to facilitate the
> speedy and full implementation of the Good Friday
> Agreement. Our arms are silent and secure. There is no
> threat to the peace process from the IRA.
>
> In this context, the IRA leadership has agreed to put in
> place within weeks a confidence-building measure to confirm
> that our weapons remain secure. The contents of a number of
> arms dumps will be inspected by agreed third parties who will
> report that they have done so to the International
> Independent Commission on Decommissioning.
>
> The dumps will be re-inspected regularly to ensure that
> the weapons have remained secure.

There was no direct role in this for the IICD. The commission
would not provide the inspectors. They would be brought in from
elsewhere and de Chastelain would simply be told when inspections
occurred. The agreed third parties were Cyril Ramaphosa, a former
secretary general of the African National Congress, and Martti
Ahtisaari, the former Finnish president. That de Chastelain was by-
passed was another example of how the IRA was managing to change
the arms context and managing to move the unionists with new
initiatives that fell short of actual decommissioning. The IRA, by
going at its own pace, was also managing to bring the republican
base with it. For six years, the IRA had been changing things,
moving things and getting around the demands for guns before
talks, guns during discussions and then guns before government.
The stuff of the exploratory dialogue which had followed the
original ceasefires in 1994 – the Mayhew demands and then the
Mitchell compromise of talks and decommissioning in parallel –
were the things of a distant past.

Twice Trimble jumped and took his unionist colleagues into the
Executive before a single bullet had been destroyed. He did it after
the Mitchell Review and he was about to do it again. The
confidence-building measure and that convoluted context for
weapons to be put completely and verifiably beyond use had done
the trick. This was the IRA's best offer – better than anything before.
In March, Trimble had seen off a leadership challenge from the anti-
agreement MP and prominent Orangeman Martin Smyth – the gap
57 per cent to 43 per cent. But the vote at the Ulster Unionist

Council in May to return to government with Sinn Fein was much closer – this time 53 per cent to 47 per cent. Trimble was skating on very thin unionist ice and republicans had bought themselves some more time.

David Ervine has watched the IRA change and has watched how it has 'incrementally' moved its people. He in no way underestimates the significance of the arms initiatives, and when we spoke for this book he described them as 'absolutely huge'. He accepts that the only way the IRA could deal with this issue was by 're-inventing' decommissioning and he believes that it would have taken time for the republican leadership 'to pluck up the courage' to discuss it internally: 'Some of what the Provos did looked quite masterful, but others had no choice,' he told me.

What he meant by that was that the IRA had control of the accelerator – that republicans were dictating the speed of movement and the more the IRA was able to reduce unionist demands, the easier 'the internal management' would be. The unionist demand for total disarmament was unrealistic: 'If one side gets what it wants, you don't have a process,' Ervine told me. 'The Provos needed space and the unionists needed something.'

That something would be delivered – maybe not the decommissioning that unionists had wanted – but certainly something more than the 'not a bullet, not an ounce' had once suggested. Ervine believes Trimble has moved the IRA and has achieved much more than Paisley could ever hope for.

The initiative involving Ahtisaari and Ramaphosa was another example of the IRA lowering the unionist bar while at the same time raising the bar internally. Remember, the IRA set out from that position of 'not a bullet, not an ounce', but it then appointed a representative to talk to the IICD and now it was about to allow arms inspections. These are things which will have come as a shock to the republican system. So, while it succeeded in changing the arms context, I am not suggesting that internally the IRA was getting things easy. As Gerry Adams himself commented in an interview for this book in December 2001:

> *ADAMS*: There is a kind of merit in the thought that if there had been a total and absolute iron-clad point, that there would be no movement from the IRA at all, that that may have been a better position. That is a criticism which is made within republicanism of the position which the Sinn Fein leadership took up and it is also, ironically, a criticism made by some more enlightened elements of loyalism.

ROWAN: You mean, had they just said clear off . . .
ADAMS: Yeah.
ROWAN: It's not happening.
ADAMS: Yeah. Now, against that, against that, you have to say
          . . . and I accept that that is a valid position. So, I'm not
          even going to argue in defence of any alternative
          position, but the Sinn Fein position has consistently
          been that the gun has to be taken out of Irish politics
          and that that is an objective of a peace process. Now,
          what you then do, and you can see it once you start to
          engage in the issue, you end up trying to convince
          people that the overall republican strategic objectives
          are best served by keeping the process moving.

In keeping it moving, in keeping the process alive, many republicans
will not have been comfortable with the things that had to happen
and had to be done, and there were occasions when the IRA moved
even though it believed the Blair Government had not honoured its
commitments – its side of the Hillsborough bargain.
Demilitarisation is one of the big Sinn Fein demands and while there
have been significant security adjustments, these have not been
nearly enough for republicans.

The May 2000 initiative did not, however, mean that the IRA was
opening up all of its arms dumps to inspection. Only a small number,
thought to be two, would be examined, and what the IRA has by way
of arms and explosives tells only part of the story in terms of its
capability. In January 2000, I was given this police Special Branch
'guesstimate' of what the IRA held in its armoury:

- 1,700 weapons, over one thousand of them long arms –
  nearly all rifles
- 500–550 handguns
- 50 heavy and general purpose machine guns
- Two and a third metric tonnes of the explosive Semtex, and
  a huge quantity of ammunition

The security assessment also emphasised the IRA's ability to
manufacture weapons and explosives. So, when you put all of that
together, you see that the IRA was not exposing anything like its
entire armoury to inspection, and, to go back to that David Ervine
observation, the less it did, the easier the internal management.

The first hint that the first inspections had happened came late on
Sunday, 25 June 2000 – seven weeks or so after the IRA had first

suggested the confidence-building measure. Through London sources, my colleague Denis Murray had been told that Ahtisaari and Ramaphosa were due in Downing Street the following day to brief Blair. If that was happening, I knew the events of that day would be choreographed and before long I would be contacted with arrangements for a meeting with the IRA.

Eamonn Mallie and I would meet our contact in Belfast early the next morning. There was now enough to run with a speculative report and before that meeting with the IRA the BBC ran details of the expected Downing Street talks and suggested the first inspections may have taken place.

Confirmation of that came when the man from the IRA joined Mallie and me at 7.15 on Monday morning. Again he brought with him a statement from the IRA leadership:

> On 6 May the leadership of the IRA announced an unprecedented initiative which had the effect of breaking the impasse at that time in the peace process.
>
> In our statement we made it clear that our initiative was in the context of a series of commitments made by the two governments, especially the British Government. We announced that we would resume contact with the IICD and put in place a confidence-building measure.
>
> We now wish to confirm that we have re-established contact with the IICD and that a number of arms dumps have been examined by the two agreed third parties. These dumps contained a substantial amount of material including weapons, explosives and other equipment.
>
> The leadership of the IRA have consistently sought to enhance the peace process. This initiative demonstrates once more our commitment to securing a just and lasting peace.
>
> P. O'NEILL

Ahtisaari and Ramaphosa reported positively, stating that the arms dumps they examined held a substantial amount of military material; the weapons and explosives were safely and adequately stored; the inspectors had ensured that the weapons and explosives could not be used without their detection; the dumps would be re-inspected on a regular basis; and that they believed this was a genuine effort by the IRA to advance the peace process.

This was the first of three inspections and what happened in June 2000 gave the process a little breathing space, but the IRA was not out of the decommissioning woods and Trimble was far from satisfied. More unionist sanctions were coming.

At this time, the IRA's promised resumed contact with the IICD amounted to very little – not an engagement on the detail of putting arms beyond use, but a phone call. By early October, I was aware that there had been no contact between the IRA and de Chastelain since June, and by April 2001 the Commission had still not been told what the IRA meant by 'arms beyond use' and what its role would be in that process. By this stage, however, direct contact had been re-established between the IRA and the International Commission. So, what was holding things up? The IRA would spell its position out in late October 2000, but before then a republican source summarised the situation with the following thoughts.

He said the British had 'made a deal with the IRA' but had not kept their side of it. In slowing things down, the IRA was 'protecting the integrity of the Movement', and he also made this observation about pro-agreement unionists: 'Yes, unionism appears so weak, whatever you would do for them wouldn't be good enough.'

At this time there were mixed signals on the possibility of a second IRA arms inspection, with one source talking down the likelihood of it happening and another hinting that it could go ahead. The issue was cleared up when the IRA spoke a few weeks later, but before then Sinn Fein's Gerry Kelly, who in this process has been an important figure in his party's negotiating team, put the situation into the following context.

- He was confident that the IRA would honour its commitments.
- The real question was about the British Government's commitment to its joint letter and statement with the Irish Government on 5 May.
- He described the first of the IRA arms inspections as a 'historic and unprecedented' initiative.
- It had taken place despite the British Government failing to keep its May commitments on policing and demilitarisation.
- If the process was dependent on British or unionist initiatives it would have died a long time ago.

> Both governments are also expressing concern about the future of David Trimble's leadership of the UUP. While Sinn Fein also is concerned to do whatever we can to consolidate the pro-agreement section of unionism this cannot be at the cost of changing the Good Friday Agreement. The British Government has already made that mistake.
>
> Nor can Sinn Fein shoe-horn the IRA to take initiatives within deadlines which are being set by those within

unionism who are against the Good Friday Agreement and the changes it involves.

For my part I remain confident that the IRA will honour its commitments. The history of the process shows that it will do so on its own time-frame – not in response to deadlines from others who have failed to keep their commitments.

The Kelly statement then directly addressed the British Government:

> Peter Mandelson says he expects the IRA to repeat its confidence-building measure now. Mr Mandelson knows the context for the IRA initiative. This is contained in the 5 May joint letter and statement from the two governments. He also knows that Gerry Adams met with him and the British Prime Minister during the summer to warn against London dragging out the delivery of its commitments until now. He and Mr Blair and their advisers will recall that Gerry Adams pointed out the difficulties for everyone if the British failed to deliver their commitments or were slow to do so.
>
> In my view, if the British Government had kept its side of the May agreement the confidence-building measure would have been repeated by now and the re-engagement with de Chastelain would have proceeded. It remains my view that these developments will occur . . . Unionists should listen to the IRA when it says that it is no threat to the peace process. The IRA keeps its commitments. That is one of the certainties of this process.

At this time, this was an important statement from Gerry Kelly, because it set out not just the position of the Sinn Fein leadership, but also set the context that would be necessary for the IRA to move further.

That organisation would soon speak for itself, would confirm its intention to allow a second arms inspection, but, on the more important issue of decommissioning talks with de Chastelain, it made clear that these would only happen when the IRA judged the timing was right. Its arms proposals had been set in that very clear context of other commitments made by the British Government and in a statement on 25 October 2000 it accused the Government of not honouring its undertakings: 'Despite this the IRA leadership has decided that the re-inspection of a number of arms dumps will be repeated to confirm that our weapons remain secure.'

In this statement, the IRA also said it would resume talks with the

IICD, but only when it was satisfied that the peace process would be advanced by those discussions:

> . . . the British Government has yet to honour its commitments. The IRA are doing our best to enhance the peace process. This is not our responsibility alone. Others also must play their part. The political responsibility for advancing the current situation and making progress rests with the two governments, especially the British Government.

At around lunch-time the following day, 26 October 2000, there was confirmation that the arms dumps had been re-inspected. Tony Blair was in town and Trimble was preparing for a weekend meeting of the Ulster Unionist Council.

There was also a report from de Chastelain and his commission – a report which confirmed that his decommissioning cupboard was still bare:

> –The commission has not been able to engage with the IRA representative since the re-opening of contact in June.
> –The commission will continue its efforts to meet with the IRA representative to determine whether 'putting arms beyond use' meets the commission's mandate for arms destruction and when that process will begin.
> –The commission cannot report progress on actual decommissioning during the period following the IRA's renewal of contact in June.

In its contacts with politicians, the IICD said the commission had been told of republican concerns over the implementation of the Patten Report on policing and on the issues of demilitarisation and OTRs – republicans on the run and still wanted by the authorities.

For Trimble, with a party council meeting in 48 hours, this would not have made pleasant reading, and another confrontation with Sinn Fein was now inevitable.

This was another of those periods in the process when there was a particular focus on the IRA's guns, even though loyalist weapons were in use – at this time as part of a bloody internal feud. In the months spanning August to November 2000, there were seven killings – four by the UVF and three by the UDA – as well as many other attacks. The convicted UDA leader Johnny Adair, who was released early as part of the Good Friday Agreement, was re-arrested and returned to jail. I deal with this in detail in the next chapter, but had all of this been linked to republicans and to the IRA, the political roof would have caved in.

The infighting within loyalism was not the only violence. Republican dissidents, having re-emerged slowly earlier in the year, were now fully active again and had been behind a whole range of attacks – in Northern Ireland on security bases and on the railway lines, and in London there had been attacks on Hammersmith Bridge and at the Headquarters of MI6. Many other planned actions had been prevented by the security forces and in October 2000 the mainstream IRA was linked to the murder of a leading dissident republican in Belfast, Joseph O'Connor. The 'Real' IRA threatened a response, but did nothing: 'At a time and place of our choosing, those guilty of this offence will be dealt with accordingly. This is not an idle threat and should not be treated as such.'

The IRA said it was not involved in the killing, and said threats directed against it would do nothing but 'exacerbate the situation . . . The IRA leadership will not be deflected from our current strategy.'

Security sources were not taking this IRA statement at face value. Their assessment of IRA involvement was 'pretty firm', but they believed the IRA was confident that evidentially the shooting could not be traced back to the organisation. So, with another arms crisis looming and Trimble getting ready to do battle again with his anti-agreement opponents on 28 October, this was the picture at the time: loyalists killing each other, increased dissident republican activity and the IRA not yet ready to discuss decommissioning with de Chastelain.

Jeffrey Donaldson had never been of the view that the IRA would deliver on decommissioning before the original May 2000 target and in the run-up to that date he thought out loud on the possibility of the process collapsing – a process in which he believed unionists had given a lot for little return. The unionist MP was speaking to me in an interview for this book:

> Internally, the party is deeply divided and it is going to take some time to heal those divisions, and healed they must be if unionism is to recover from this process . . . if the process collapses, what has unionism got to show for its participation in this process, for the concessions that have been made, for the compromises that we've made in terms of our own long-held positions – a change to articles two and three [of the Republic's Constitution] and the ending of the Anglo-Irish Agreement, but to be replaced by what, another Anglo-Irish

Agreement mark two. When, I think, the history of this
period is written, whilst it is clear that there will be
admiration for the risks that were taken by some in the
leadership of the Ulster Unionist Party, I think that future
generations will wonder at the wisdom of some of the
decisions that have been taken, they will wonder whether
unionism has emerged from this process in a stronger or
weaker position, and I think without being premature, it is
certainly the case at the moment that unionism is in a weaker
position given the deep divisions that exist, the uncertainty
and the lack of confidence.

The IRA's confidence-building measure – the inspection of a
number of its arms dumps – and the context it had set for putting
weapons beyond use, had prevented the collapse of the process in
the summer of 2000, but clearly it had not been enough to settle
unionism. In October, Trimble was having to fight again. The ring
for this political battle would once more be a meeting of the Ulster
Unionist Council and once more his challenger on unionist policy
would be Donaldson. To find a way through, Trimble had to impose
some immediate sanctions and threaten others. Republicans were
not moving fast enough for the unionists and the Government was
not moving fast enough for the IRA. This all meant the process was
once again caught in a political traffic jam.

The unionist move at this stage was not to force the suspension of
the Executive, but to sanction its Sinn Fein members Martin
McGuinness and Bairbre de Brun. It was the first of six proposals
that Trimble put to the Ulster Unionist Council:

> In view of the failure of the IRA to re-engage with the IICD,
> as from today Sinn Fein ministers will not be nominated to
> attend any North–South Ministerial Council meeting.
>   This sanction to be lifted when there is substantial
> engagement by the IRA with the IICD and to be re-imposed
> in the event of such engagement not making reasonable
> progress on decommissioning.

This, as part of a package of proposals, carried Trimble through this
latest party council meeting with a 71-vote majority, and the sanction
would remain in place for about a year – until the IRA moved to put
some of its arms beyond use. In a conversation for this book, in August
2002, Jeffrey Donaldson told me he believed the Trimble wing of the
Ulster Unionist Party had been prepared to compromise the 'guns
and government' principle to protect devolution, which they saw as

important for Northern Ireland, and he told me they were determined to retain the Assembly 'virtually at any cost':

> I think the IRA and their Sinn Fein political representatives have managed the process much better than unionists, and at every stage they have been successful in extracting maximum concessions from both the Government and unionists in return for giving the absolute minimum in order to secure those concessions.
>
> Undoubtedly there has been resistance within the Republican Movement to some of these moves, but the Sinn Fein leadership has managed that unease very successfully and that is largely due to the minimalist approach that has been adopted, which has seen concessions made by republicans on a drip, drip basis.

Donaldson dismisses the IRA's arms moves as minimalist, but republicans put them in an entirely different context. They see their initiatives as 'historic' and 'unprecedented' and delivered against a background of the Government not honouring commitments on key issues such as policing and demilitarisation. In the 12 months between the Ulster Unionist Council meeting and the October 2001 arms breakthrough, there would be many more political twists and turns. Mandelson would be replaced at the Northern Ireland Office by the Scot John Reid, there would be periods of intense negotiations, Trimble would resign once more from the position of First Minister and the institutions would twice be suspended. On decommissioning, progress would be slow and in that year stretching from October 2000 to October 2001 I would have many meetings with the IRA. I now want to set out in summary form how things developed on the arms question:

8 March 2001: IRA statement says its leadership has decided to enter into further discussions with the IICD. 'This will be on the basis of the IRA leadership's commitment to resolving the issue as contained in our statement of 6 May 2000, and on no other basis.'

8 March 2001: Second IRA statement says there has been contact with IICD to make it aware 'of our intention to enter into further discussions'.

8 March 2001: Statement from British and Irish governments says those discussions should start promptly and 'lead to agreement on the ways in which arms will be put completely and verifiably beyond use . . . We look forward to early and positive reports from the IICD about progress made.'

14 March 2001: IRA confirms meeting with IICD and says its representative 'set out the basis for discussions'.

This is the first meeting between the IRA and the commission since February 2000.

22 March 2001: IICD welcomes re-engagement with IRA, which it considers to be in 'good faith . . . We will build on it at future such meetings, which we expect will occur soon.'

22 March 2001: Secretary of State John Reid says re-engagement 'allows us to move from talking about whether decommissioning will take place, to how'.

18 April 2001: On decommissioning, Trimble tells the *Financial Times*: 'Unless there is movement there is going to be a crisis and that crisis could come before the general election. I can't see how we can get through June if republicans have not moved.'

Trimble would move soon to try to force progress on decommissioning. In moving, the crisis he spoke of began to take shape. In a statement to the Assembly on 8 May, he told members he had lodged a resignation letter with the Speaker. If by 1 July the IRA had not moved on decommissioning, Trimble would resign as First Minister. This development came around the anniversary of the IRA's May 2000 statement and with the new target date of June 2001 for the full implementation of the Good Friday Agreement fast approaching:

> Sunday, 6 May 2001 marked the anniversary of the IRA statement that led to the decision of the Ulster Unionist Party to resume participation in the Northern Ireland Executive. In that statement the IRA promised to 'initiate a process that will completely and verifiably put IRA arms beyond use in such a way as to avoid risk to the public and misappropriation by others and ensure maximum public confidence'. As we made clear at the time, it was on the basis of that clear promise and in the expectation of its fulfilment that I and my party agreed to the restoration of devolution on an inclusive basis. Members will recall that this represented a second chance for the Republican Movement following its failure to fulfil the expectations it created during the Mitchell Review . . . Today I am making it clear that the promise made a year ago must be kept and that failure to keep that promise will have consequences.
>
> In taking this step I believe I will have broad support from the people of Northern Ireland. I know that, like me, they are proud of these institutions and relish the prospect of a

peaceful Northern Ireland at ease with itself. They know it
will not be achieved without effort and risk. I believe they
have supported me in the past when I have taken risks, not
with the agreement, but for the agreement. I believe they will
understand and support the step I have taken today.

Trimble left something out of that statement – the detailed
paragraph and the complicated context in which the IRA said it
would put arms beyond use. If there had been any prospect of the
IRA moving before 1 July, it had now gone. The First Minister had
set another deadline; this in republican eyes was yet another
unionist ultimatum and while talks with de Chastelain continued
and there was a third arms inspection by Ahtisaari and Ramaphosa,
the IRA did not do what Trimble had demanded and he followed
through with his resignation. On Saturday, 12 May – four days
after the First Minister's resignation letter had been lodged – I ran
the following report on BBC Radio Ulster and, given my source
for this, I knew the IRA was not going to deliver on Trimble's
timescale:

> After the election it's expected that negotiations will resume
> on a range of issues. But one source has told me that the 1 July
> deadline set by David Trimble for arms beyond use is not
> possible. Republicans are still referring back to negotiations
> that took place at Hillsborough a year ago – and are still
> claiming that the Government failed to honour a deal made
> with the IRA on policing and demilitarisation.
>
> The post-election negotiations will return to those issues
> and, to quote one source, republicans will want to see the
> colour of the Government's money before any decisions are
> taken on what happens to the IRA's arms.
>
> A year ago, the IRA set out its terms for putting weapons
> beyond use – a context in which policing and demilitarisation
> were key issues. My sources are stressing that the process will
> take time, will require further discussions within the IRA and
> more talks between that group and the de Chastelain
> commission, all of which suggests a further extension to the
> decommissioning target date.

That new target date as part of the full implementation of the Good
Friday Agreement was June 2001, and while Trimble unquestionably
viewed decommissioning as something the IRA was required to do,
that is not how republicans saw things. Their assessment of the
Good Friday Agreement put the arms issue in the context of an

objective of the peace process – it was aspirational. That is what Sinn Fein says it signed up to and nothing more.

In the course of my research for this book, I was made aware of an 'internal' Sinn Fein assessment of the decommissioning section of the Good Friday Agreement. The third of the agreement's five paragraphs on the arms issue is the important one:

> All participants accordingly reaffirm their commitment to the total disarmament of all paramilitary organisations. They also confirm their intention to continue to work constructively and in good faith with the Independent Commission, and to use any influence they may have to achieve the decommissioning of all paramilitary arms within two years following endorsement in referendums North and South of the agreement and in the context of the implementation of the overall settlement.

The internal Sinn Fein assessment of this paragraph highlighted the reference to 'all participants' in the opening sentence and stated that 'no action commitment' was attached to the sentence: 'It states the objective to which the participants are committed, but as none of the participants are in possession of weapons, then none of them can directly bring it about.'

On the second sentence, the Sinn Fein assessment read:

> No action commitments are attached to this sentence – to work constructively and in good faith with the IICD – to use any influence the participant may have to achieve decommissioning by May 2000.
>
> Importantly, this is set in the context of the implementation of the overall settlement. The action commitment is a collective obligation. It doesn't fall to one party.

The Sinn Fein document also included the following observations:

> –The decommissioning section of the Good Friday Agreement is a stand-alone section.
> –It is explicitly set in the context of the implementation of the overall settlement.
> –The terms of the agreement make no requirement or obligation for decommissioning to happen ever, let alone by May 2000, because none of the parties to the agreement could give such an undertaking, because none of them are in possession of weapons.

–Sinn Fein could not and would not in good faith have signed
up to such a commitment.

–We would not and could not undertake an action
commitment which is not directly in our gift.

So, while unionists make little or no distinction between Sinn Fein
and the IRA, this internal republican document was making it
absolutely clear that there was no IRA commitment to
decommission as part of the Good Friday Agreement – something
the IRA itself stated publicly just before the suspension of the
political institutions in February 2000. The only commitment Sinn
Fein had given was to be part of a collective approach to try to
influence the paramilitaries to disarm. The IRA's attitude to June
2001 was the same as its attitude to May 2000. These were not
decommissioning deadlines in terms of any commitments given by
the republican organisation. So, despite the Trimble resignation
threat, the IRA continued to progress at its own pace and progress
to the point where it agreed with de Chastelain a method for putting
arms beyond use. Before then there were more statements, more
reports, more talks and two elections – elections in which the Sinn
Fein vote grew significantly and it overtook Hume's SDLP to
become the largest nationalist party:

30 May 2001: Ahtisaari and Ramaphosa report they have carried out
a third inspection of IRA arms.

30 May 2001: IICD reports continuing talks with IRA representative
in pursuit of Commission's mandate.

31 May 2001: IRA statement confirms inspections and ongoing
discussions with IICD. There have been four meetings since 8
March:

'This continuing dialogue and the inspections represent clear
and irrefutable evidence of the IRA's commitment to a just and
equitable peace settlement. The IRA leadership has honoured
every commitment we have made and we will continue to do so.
Others should do likewise.'

8 June 2001: Sinn Fein's Gerry Adams, Martin McGuinness, Pat
Doherty and Michelle Gildernew win seats in British general
election. With almost 176,000 votes, Sinn Fein becomes largest
nationalist party.

12 June 2001: In local council elections, Sinn Fein has a 20.66 per
cent share of poll – the SDLP 19.42 per cent.

On 20 June 2001, the IRA gave the following briefing:

• All IRA commitments are a matter of public record.
• It's now seven years since the first IRA cessation of August 1994.
• We've had a series of meetings with the IICD.
• We have put in place a confidence-building measure which saw three inspections of a number of our arms dumps.
• Every commitment we have entered into we have honoured.
• On the other side, last year, the British Government entered into an agreement on two of the major aspects of this agreement – policing and demilitarisation. They have reneged.
• We re-state our belief that the issue of arms can be resolved, but it will not be resolved by unionist ultimatums or on British terms.
• The IRA poses no threat to the peace process.

This was the last time the IRA spoke before the Trimble resignation date and again the organisation made clear that it would not be moved by unionist ultimatums. The date of 1 July came and passed without decommissioning, and Trimble's resignation was now part of the political mix.

A de Chastelain report to the two governments on resignation day spoke of lengthy meetings between the commission and the IRA's representative – including recent talks in the days leading up to this latest IICD statement. The commission had been assured of the IRA's commitment to put its arms beyond use 'but only in the context of its statement of 6 May 2000'. There were two vital pieces of information still missing – how the IRA intended to do it and, more importantly, when. The how was settled at a meeting on Sunday, 5 August, when the IRA's representative Brian Keenan put his organisation's proposed method to de Chastelain and his commission colleague Andrew Sens. The when was 23 October 2001 – confirmed that day in a report by the IICD and a statement from the IRA leadership. The first of these developments was not enough for Trimble and not enough to prevent another suspension of the political institutions, and this led to another of those 'hokey-cokey-type' moments between the IRA and de Chastelain. Having only just put its arms proposal in, the IRA was about to take it back out again.

In the eyes of de Chastelain and his colleagues, the IRA's proposal represented significant progress, and the commission's report said it viewed this development as the beginning of a process that would put IRA arms completely and verifiably beyond use. Republicans also saw it as big stuff; to quote Danny Morrison, it was a bigger development than any republican had contemplated at the time of the original ceasefire in 1994: 'It's the first time in 30 years that the IRA has really entered into a process – they're in a process now of putting the guns beyond use', and, according to Morrison, this was a process in which the IRA was 'retiring from the scene'.

The Secretary of State John Reid believed the republican organisation had taken a highly significant and important step, and the Taoiseach Bertie Ahern called it 'an historic breakthrough'. There is no doubt that the IRA had jumped – that, internally, it had once again raised the bar as it had when it first appointed a representative to talk to the IICD and then when it allowed Ahtisaari and Ramaphosa to come and inspect its arms. The bar, however, was still below the height set by Trimble.

I had interviewed Danny Morrison on 9 August – the day the IRA confirmed the detail of the IICD report, confirmed it had agreed a method with de Chastelain for putting arms beyond use and told us of eight meetings with the commission since the beginning of this latest dialogue on 8 March 2001: 'We note the ongoing attempts in some quarters to prevent progress. They should not be permitted to succeed. Our representative will continue to meet with the IICD. The IRA leadership will continue to monitor political developments.'

The IRA had moved – a significant distance as far as republicans were concerned, but not far enough for the unionists. Based on what was on offer in August, Trimble was not prepared to return as First Minister and that left the Secretary of State with a choice to make: to suspend the political institutions for a short period – a technical move that would buy a further six weeks to try to end the guns and government stalemate; or he could call fresh elections in Northern Ireland. Reid saw suspension as the 'common-sense option' and by 10 August everyone knew that was the road he was travelling:

> In these circumstances, at a delicate moment in the political process when discussions are still continuing and the parties are still digesting the two governments' proposals, I have concluded that it would be against the interests of the peace process to plunge Northern Ireland immediately into an election campaign and into the more polarised political atmosphere that would inevitably result from such an election campaign.

The proposals that Reid referred to emerged out of the latest talks –

this time at Weston Park in July – talks which again covered the familiar ground of policing, demilitarisation, decommissioning and the future of the political institutions. The negotiations did not produce the big political breakthrough, but they did make progress, and in the grand setting of Weston Park new light began to shine out from old windows.

The area in which most was achieved in this period was policing. Sinn Fein was not yet ready to embrace the new arrangements. Republicans believed the British Government had stripped out important elements of the Patten Report and had pulled its teeth in the key area of accountability. As part of the Weston Park discussions, the British Government promised a review of the implementation of Patten's proposals and legislation to 'reflect more fully' the report's recommendations. Sinn Fein would wait to see that, but Hume's SDLP was now prepared to encourage young nationalists to join the Police Service of Northern Ireland and senior party members, Alex Attwood, the MP Eddie McGrady and Joe Byrne, would take seats on the new Policing Board. These were significant steps in the process of policing change – a process which would seek to correct the religious imbalance there had been in the ranks of the RUC. At the time of the Patten Report, 92 per cent of the Force's members were Protestant.

It was after Weston Park that the IRA proposed its method for putting arms beyond use. The package to emerge from the negotiations also included specific commitments on demilitarisation and the governments promised proposals soon to resolve the issue which had come to be described as OTRs – republicans on the run. An international judge would also investigate allegations of security force collusion in a number of killings, including the murders of the solicitors Pat Finucane and Rosemary Nelson and the loyalist Billy Wright. In the proposals the two governments made after Weston Park, there was also a paragraph on decommissioning – probably the least specific in the document:

> In respect of the issue of putting arms beyond use, the two governments repeat their view that this is an indispensable part of implementing the Good Friday Agreement. All parties to the agreement recognise that; and that, under the agreement, this issue must be resolved in a manner acceptable to and verified by the Independent International Commission on Decommissioning in accordance with its basic mandate in law.

There was nothing new in this paragraph – no demands, no dates, no detail, just a repeat that the two governments wanted it to happen and in a way acceptable to de Chastelain.

He had refused to respond to unionist demands for a decommissioning timetable – a calendar drawn up by his commission, and had resisted doing it because he knew it would not work. Decommissioning was supposed to be a voluntary process. It would happen at a time and in a way of the IRA's choosing. That is what the organisation had meant when it said it would not be delivered to unionist ultimatums or on British terms. So, on 5 August when de Chastelain and Andrew Sens met the IRA's representative, they heard for the first time the organisation's proposed method for putting its arms beyond use. At last in their talks they were getting down to the nitty-gritty – the business of how to get rid of the guns, but five or so weeks after the Trimble resignation there was still no product and, as I mentioned earlier, he was not yet willing to return to the post of First Minister.

This is when Reid stepped in to suspend the institutions and to buy some more time. He saw this as a 'common-sense' approach, but republicans viewed it entirely differently. Martin McGuinness said it was the second time in 18 months that the British Government had 'capitulated' to the unionists. Within days, the IRA would speak through a statement, but on Friday, 10 August – suspension day – I was briefed on the probability of that organisation withdrawing its arms proposal. I knew this was the mind of senior IRA leaders who had met that Friday, but others had yet to be consulted. Remember, in its statement of 9 August, the IRA leadership had said it would continue to monitor political developments. I had read this as meaning one of two things: if there was more political development towards meeting the context that the IRA had set for putting arms beyond use, then more progress on the weapons issue was possible; but there was also a reminder here of what had happened in February 2000, when Mandelson suspended the political institutions. Back then, the IRA withdrew from the de Chastelain talks. This time in August 2001, the organisation took back its proposed method for putting arms beyond use. It was no longer on the de Chastelain table, and the day of the next step – the biggest step – the actual doing of decommissioning, was being further delayed. This was P. O'Neill retaliating following Reid's decision to suspend the power-sharing Executive.

At about 7.30 on the morning of Tuesday, 14 August, I was wakened by a telephone call. On the other end of the line was the spokesman for the IRA leadership. He had a statement to dictate to me. It was embargoed to nine and it confirmed what I had been told four days earlier – that the IRA's arms proposal was now off the de Chastelain table. This is part of the text of the IRA statement:

> Our initiative was a result of lengthy discussions with the IICD over a protracted period. This was an unprecedented development which involved a very difficult decision by us and problems for our organisation.
>
> While mindful of these concerns, our decision was aimed at enhancing the peace process.
>
> We recognise the very broad welcome which the IICD statement [of 6 August] received. However, the outright rejection of the IICD statement by the UUP leadership, compounded by the setting of preconditions, is totally unacceptable. The subsequent actions of the British Government, including their failure to fulfil their commitments, is also totally unacceptable. The conditions therefore do not exist for progressing our proposition. We are withdrawing our proposal.
>
> The IRA leadership will continue to monitor developments.
>
> Peace keeping is a collective effort.
>
> P. O'NEILL

Twenty-four hours before that statement was released, three Irishmen – three republicans, one of them an official Sinn Fein representative – were arrested in Colombia and subsequently charged with travelling on false documents and with training FARC guerrillas. In these developments, the unionists were given another stick with which to beat Adams and McGuinness. Others, including significant political figures in Washington, wanted to know what was going on. Whatever it was, the timing of these arrests, right in the middle of another arms crisis in the Irish peace process, was disastrous for Sinn Fein, and the party stuttered and struggled and stammered in an unconvincing effort to provide credible answers. This was not a confident Sinn Fein performing to usual standards.

Weeks later, on 11 September, came the shocking events in New York and Washington – the terrorist attacks in the United States which left nearly 3,000 dead. Bush and Blair launched their war on terrorism. This was the big world picture and in its wide frame there would be little tolerance for any armed groups. McGuinness and Adams needed to get Irish republicans to the right side of the lines. In an earlier chapter, I said I did not believe that Colombia and the events in the United States were the only factors in moving the IRA, but they were part of the context. Certainly the pace seemed to quicken. Eight days after the attacks on the World Trade Center and the Pentagon, there were new words from the IRA – a detailed statement covering Colombia, decommissioning and the events in the United States.

The opening sentence of this statement addressed the events of 11 September. The IRA extended its sympathy to the people of the United States and described the attacks as 'deplorable'. On the Colombian arrests, the IRA said there had been 'a lot of ill-founded and mischievous speculation' and 'some ill-considered and aggressive comment directed at our organisation'.

> We wish to make it clear that the Army Council sent no one to Colombia to train or to engage in any military cooperation with any group.
>
> The IRA has not interfered in the internal affairs of Colombia and will not do so.
>
> The IRA is not a threat to the peace process in Ireland or in Colombia.
>
> The three men have asserted their support for the process and we accept that.

This would not be enough to make the Colombian story go away and questions would continue to be asked long after this IRA statement of 19 September 2001. Thirty-six days had passed since the IRA had taken its arms proposal off the table, but now that organisation was going to 'intensify' its engagement with the IICD. Something had made the IRA change its mind, and Colombia and 11 September had to be a part of that. On the new de Chastelain talks, this is what the IRA had to say:

> This dialogue is within the context of our commitment to deal satisfactorily with the question of arms. It is with a view to accelerating progress towards a comprehensive resolution of this issue.
>
> Progress will be directly influenced by the attitude of the other parties to the peace process, including and especially, the British Government.
>
> The IRA's commitment is without question.

The next time the IRA would speak would be on 23 October to confirm that some of its weapons had been put beyond use. In between its 19 September statement and then there had been more unionist resignations from the Executive, another Reid suspension of the political institutions and long hours of background discussions in which Adams and McGuinness were the key republican players.

The IRA had not responded to the May 2000 decommissioning deadline set in the Good Friday Agreement, or to the new target date of June 2001, but had stretched things out to October. There was now a beginning to the arms process, and on that October day, as I mentioned in an earlier chapter, there was a sense that crisis could, for now at least, be replaced by the stuff of once upon a time and happily ever after. Certainly Martin McGuinness saw this as an opportunity for a new beginning – for a fresh start and he believed the IRA had broken the logjam in the peace process and had done so by moving on this most difficult of all issues for republicans:

> It meant everything to me, and also as an Irish republican with all the emotions that the republican grassroots and base had gone through, I went through that journey maybe long before they did, and as they were going through the journey after the announcement, I was still going through it. So, there was a lot of pain and emotion in it for me and for everybody who was connected to me within republicanism, but it was a journey that had to be travelled and it was a journey that hopefully is going to lead us to a whole new situation on this island.

The IRA's arms move made things better for a while, but not for long. Within a year of October 2001, the process was in its deepest crisis, and Tony Blair moved to set new standards and new rules.

In October 2001, the vast majority of republicans were prepared to travel with McGuinness and Adams, but others were not – others such as Tommy Gorman, a former IRA member, who escaped from the prison ship *Maidstone* in 1972. He is now opposed to the use of violence, but he has been openly critical of the strategy of the republican leadership and, for him, decommissioning was another step too far:

> For republicans to focus on IRA weapons in that sort of way criminalises those weapons and criminalises therefore the struggle which had gone 30 years hence. What republicans are asking themselves is a very stark question: is the weapon that Francie Hughes used, the dead hunger striker from South Derry, is his weapon, which he used to engage the SAS, less legal than the weapons used by the paratroopers in Derry on Bloody Sunday? And to me it is a sign of surrender. An undefeated army does not give up its weapons.

Speaking to me for this book, the loyalist David Ervine accepted that decommissioning – or putting arms beyond use – had not been easy for republicans. He has sat in private talks – talks in which Gerry Adams, apparently close to tears, has explained just how difficult a decision this was for the IRA, and Ervine believes him. 'He was moved in his explanation of just how serious and difficult it had been to achieve,' Ervine told me. 'It was clear that they had put themselves through hoops, but the public perception is different.'

Not just the public perception, but the unionist political perception also. The start to decommissioning put something into de Chastelain's cupboard, put the political Humpty-Dumpty – which has been power-sharing at Stormont – back together again, but it did not stabilise the process for long. Colombia would come back to haunt it, and the Saint Patrick's Day robbery at Castlereagh and then the allegations of intelligence gathering inside the Northern Ireland Office put the IRA ceasefire under another security and political spotlight. There was a strong belief that that organisation had gone behind enemy lines into the heart of the Special Branch and into the heart of the British Government in Northern Ireland, and it was this thinking and these allegations which plunged the process into its deepest crisis yet. I will come to all of this in my final chapter, but what about the loyalists, what about their guns, their ceasefire and their commitment to the peace process? Let us now turn those pages.

CHAPTER EIGHT

Mad Dogs and Ulstermen

'They have actively stirred up sectarian hatred, they have systematically breached their ceasefire and I believe the patience of the people of Northern Ireland has run out.'

Secretary of State John Reid, on UDA ceasefire, October 2001

'The UDA was in the gutter and it was John White and Johnny Adair who put us there.'

Member of UDA Inner Council, May 2003

'From the outset we knew that White and Adair were both trying to undermine the peace process.'

Billy Hutchinson, Progressive Unionist Party, May 2003

AUGUST 2000: Adair's phone was 'on' and Special Branch were listening as the loyalist known as 'Mad Dog' gave the command, 'Shoot him fucking now.' Everything he said as he barked out his orders to another senior UDA figure in the Shankill was heard and recorded, and everything he said was ignored by the man at the other end of the line. This was typical Johnny Adair – typical spur of the moment stuff and typical of the man whose own boasting and bragging some years earlier had led to his conviction on charges of directing terrorism.

A senior loyalist paramilitary who spoke to me for this book described Adair as a mixture of ego and adrenalin – someone who had to be 'it' and would never settle for being 'part of it'. His release from jail in September 1999 was a response to the peace process and part of the Good Friday Agreement, but Adair never changed. He remained a man of war, driven by sectarian hatred and greed. To use the words of one of those who sat with him at the table of the paramilitary leadership, 'he couldn't fit into the peace'.

Adair is not loyal to the Crown, but is one of those in the UDA leadership whose motivation was self-interest and self-gain. Many believe he was the puppet on the end of a string controlled by his close associate John White – a man who had been jailed for life for his part in the gruesome murders of a Catholic politician and a woman friend in 1973.

According to an intelligence source, the man Adair wanted shot as he ranted on his phone was Billy Hutchinson – himself a former life sentence prisoner and now a member of the Progressive Unionist Party, which is aligned to the other major force in loyalism, the UVF. In August 2000 Adair had sparked a bloody feud within loyalism. Hutchinson was now his enemy, and Adair was watching him on television.

In an interview for this book in May 2003, Billy Hutchinson told me, 'From the outset we knew that White and Adair were both trying to undermine the peace process.' Hutchinson believes that the 'drive' in Adair 'was to destroy the UVF', and that he left that organisation with no option but to fight back.

> I think that Johnny and John actually had an agenda . . . they thought that if they were able to destroy the UVF in the Shankill it would actually give them some sort of kudos . . . Their attempt was either to discredit or destroy the UVF.

Hutchinson told me that as the events of 19 August 2000 developed, 'the anger turned to hatred'. That Saturday, Adair staged a massive UDA march on the Shankill Road – a parade in which he allowed the flag of the Loyalist Volunteer Force to be displayed. He did so against the wishes of the UVF and many in the leadership of his own organisation. In the fragmented world of loyalism, the LVF is a splinter of the UVF and the two are enemies. By this gesture at his parade, Adair was taking sides. The flag incident sparked an inevitable confrontation, the guns came out, hundreds of people were driven from their homes and over a period of some weeks seven men were killed – four by the UVF and three by the UDA. This was war within loyalism and the man who had started the fight was Adair.

One of the first homes attacked belonged to Gusty Spence – the veteran UVF figure and the man who, six years earlier, had delivered the words of the Combined Loyalist Military Command ceasefire. John White had also been at the top table on that occasion. It had been a time of great hope and great expectation within loyalism. This was their new beginning, but it did not last long. As people such as Hutchinson and David Ervine of the Progressive Unionist Party prospered in the new politics of Northern Ireland, others such as White and his colleagues in the Ulster Democratic Party were left behind, allowing petty jealousies and rivalries to open up within loyalism. What Adair triggered was the violent manifestation of all of these feelings, and, hours into the feud, he was warned by a leader in his own organisation that he had left the UVF with no option but to kill him.

The public Johnny Adair was a man who spoke of peace, but out of sight of watchful eyes he practised something entirely different. One of those who sat with him on the UDA Inner Council – that organisation's six-member leadership – likened him to the moth near the flame. He just couldn't stay away from trouble.

Just weeks before that feud flared on the Shankill, I had spoken to him in the car park of the Maze Prison. This was on 28 July 2000 – the last big day of releases as part of the Good Friday Agreement – and Adair was there to greet those who were getting out. The jail was now virtually empty and its closure was inevitable. I asked Adair for his thoughts:

> Well, first and foremost, my friends and my comrades are home with their loved ones. Some of them have been in there a long, long time as a result of the conflict, and what it means to me, I hope, is that this is the end of the conflict, and that is the end of the Maze, and there'll be no more suffering, no more hurt, no more pain and no more young men having to go back to jail.

This was the public Johnny saying all of the right things, but those who operate in the intelligence world were seeing and hearing something else – and seeing and hearing it long before the loyalist feud blew up in August. Adair had spent the summer weeks stirring up trouble on the sectarian interfaces of Belfast, at the so-called peacelines which divide Catholic and Protestant communities, and he had made a number of menacing appearances in Portadown during the period of the controversial Drumcree Orange march. This was the stuff of the moth and the flame.

He was being watched and listened to throughout this period, however, and he was given a public warning by the then Chief Constable Sir Ronnie Flanagan. But Adair ignored it all and turned the Shankill Road into a type of Dodge City – a place where the sound of the gun was loud, a place where boundaries were drawn and territory claimed by the UVF and the UDA. Adair and his men in the so-called 'C Company' held the lower Shankill, but they were vulnerable. This was a fight that the rest of the UDA organisation wanted nothing to do with and this was the beginning of that organisation creating distance between itself and Adair and White.

Within 48 hours of the UDA march the UVF had murdered one of Adair's associates and shot up an office used by John White – an office that later would be destroyed in a bomb explosion. If Adair had calculated that the UVF would roll over, then he had been wrong, and this move by him to rule the loyalist roost would fail.

Secretary of State Peter Mandelson had seen enough by then, both in terms of what was happening on the streets and what he was reading in secret intelligence reports. On 22 August 2000, he suspended Adair's early release licence and the Shankill loyalist was returned to jail.

The following day, over lunch in a Chinese restaurant not far from the BBC building in Belfast, I was shown the intelligence report which had prompted Mandelson to act. The document was placed on the table and I was allowed to take notes – notes which I used to guide my news reports on radio and television later that evening. The intelligence information was assessed 'high-grade, reliable and accurate' and it logged the activities of John James Adair – DOB 27/10/63 – since his release from prison in September 1999. It was a report that exposed Adair for what he was, and in its commentary there was no hiding place for the Shankill loyalist. His claims to be a supporter of the peace were shown to be fraudulent:

> DETAILS OF INTELLIGENCE REPORT SHOWN TO
> AUTHOR, 23 AUGUST 2000:
> The following intelligence summarises Adair's involvement in the preparation, instigation and commission of terrorist activity.
>
> Since his release from prison, he has been involved in the acquisition of a number of firearms and munitions. These transactions have involved other leading loyalist terrorist organisations.
>
> During Drumcree 2000, Adair gave his unequivocal support to members of the LVF. He encouraged public disorder and he was involved in the exchange of weapons.
>
> The report logged comments Adair was alleged to have made in Portadown on 3 July, which included: '. . . the instruments of war were available for those who wished to use them'.
>
> Adair has demonstrated considerable military influence within the UDA/UFF.
>
> Adair was involved in the instigation and orchestration of

sectarian tension on the interfaces of North and West Belfast
during July and August 2000 and actively encouraged attacks
on these interfaces.

Adair was the major driving force behind the UDA/UFF
Shankill parade on 19 August 2000.

Adair has now established a substantial drugs empire. His
activities in this field continue to amass a vast amount of
money, some of which he uses in the pursuit of his terrorist
ideals.

At Stormont and at police headquarters, there was concern that the
BBC had obtained details of such a sensitive intelligence report and
a leaks inquiry was considered, but, in the end, a decision was taken
to let the matter rest.

Based on the content of that leaked report, Adair was back in jail,
but it would take several more months to bring the feuding within
loyalism to a close and during that time others were killed by the UVF
and the UDA. The most intense period of violence was 28 October to
1 November 2000 – a period in which there were four more killings.
The feud had now spread beyond the Shankill into North Belfast and
to Newtownabbey on the outskirts of the city. Within days, however,
the three main organisations – the UDA, the UVF and the Red Hand
Commando – were involved in truce talks, and by early December we
were told these were at an advanced stage. This statement followed
the killing of a Protestant taxi driver, Trevor Kell, in Belfast on 5
December – a killing linked to rogue republicans, but not to the IRA.
In a phone call, I was told that the three major loyalist paramilitary
organisations were 'investigating' the murder: 'We are convinced that
Mr Kell's death has nothing to do with the so-called loyalist feud.
Talks between the three groups are at an advanced stage and the hope
is that there will be an early resolution to our differences.'

Talk of an investigation was nonsense. Within a couple of hours of
that statement, the UDA had murdered a Catholic man and wounded
another. The man who was killed was Gary Moore, shot while
working at a house at Monkstown in Newtownabbey. The UDA's
South-east Antrim brigade, under the command of the loyalist leader
John 'Grugg' Gregg, was blamed for this shooting – the first of a
number of sectarian murders it would be linked to in a period of
several months. Gregg had a big reputation within loyalism, earned
because of his part in a shooting in 1984 in which Gerry Adams was
wounded. The prominent loyalist was released from prison before the
1994 ceasefire and later, after one of the 'doves' in the organisation's
leadership was pushed to one side, he took command of one of the
UDA's six brigade areas.

A statement bringing an end to the UDA–UVF feud of 2000 was released on 15 December. Billy Hutchinson, when he spoke to me for this book, said he could see the 'sense of relief' on the faces of people of the Shankill Road that day. Another senior loyalist I interviewed – the same man who told Adair that he had left the UVF with no option but to kill him – had this to say on the feud and the role of the so-called 'Mad Dog': 'He did more damage in those few months than the Provos did in 30 years on the Shankill. It was a total disgrace.'

By mid-December 2000, things had been patched up, for now at least, but there was more trouble down the road – more infighting within loyalism and more sectarian murder as the UDA abandoned its ceasefire, turned its back on the Good Friday Agreement and then dumped its political representatives in the Ulster Democratic Party. This was the paramilitary organisation's retreat onto familiar ground, it was taking backwards steps and it began to show its old face. In all that was happening, Gary McMichael was being undermined, and we watched as the UDA drifted slowly back to its past. Adair was in jail, but those he left behind in the lower Shankill – including his close associate Gary Smith – were now pulling the UDA in another direction and so too was Gregg. These men had no interest in peace and that was obvious in the events that were unfolding: the attacks on vulnerable nationalist communities, acts of sectarian murder and the UDA's involvement in a protest which blocked a road used by young Catholic kids to get to school. The loyalist organisation brought its muscle and its bombs onto a stage in North Belfast – a stage on which the young girls of the Holy Cross primary school were terrorised in the most shameful display of paramilitary intimidation and bullying imaginable. This was the UDA at its sectarian worst, and Adair's Shankill associate Gary Smith was a major player in all that was going on.

From the earliest months of 2001 it was obvious in which direction the UDA was now travelling, but the paramilitary organisation tried to hide behind the flimsy cover of the Red Hand Defenders. This was its flag of convenience – its pathetic attempt to disguise its activities. On Wednesday, 14 February 2001, I was among a number of journalists invited to the Shankill Road for a UDA briefing – at which a number of that organisation's most senior figures were present. Smith and another prominent Shankill loyalist William 'Winkie' Dodds were there along with Gregg and the group's brigadiers in South Belfast and Londonderry. John White was also in the room. Just weeks earlier, a Catholic builder, Gary Moore, had been murdered by Gregg's men, and there had been a whole spate of pipebomb attacks on the homes of Catholics in towns including Larne. The UDA still insisted, though, that its ceasefire was 'intact', that it was still 'committed to peace' and that it also wanted to state 'categorically' that it was not involved in the pipebomb attacks.

I told the men in the room they wouldn't be believed, and in news reports and in interviews afterwards I made it clear that I had not bought their line. The then Chief Constable Sir Ronnie Flanagan, his Assistant Chief Constable in Belfast at the time, Alan McQuillan, and the Security Minister in this period, Adam Ingram, had all linked members and elements of the UDA to activities which that organisation was now trying to deny.

In the briefing the paramilitary group also spelt out its position on the Good Friday Agreement. We were told that the organisation had signed up to it to 'give it a chance' but that it had had 'reservations'. It now viewed the agreement as an 'appeasement' process from which republicans were benefiting, and we were told that most of the organisation now opposed the Good Friday deal. This shift in the UDA's position in the early part of 2001 was the beginning of the end for the Ulster Democratic Party and for people such as McMichael and Davy Adams, who had played a part in the Good Friday negotiations.

That said, not all within loyalism view the Good Friday Agreement in the same way as the UDA. David Ervine once told me that the public perception within the unionist community was that Trimble had made the biggest compromise, but he believed that Adams and republicans had moved the most:

> The momentous circumstances of Sinn Fein – the political expression of the IRA – accepting a partitionist circumstance is incredible . . . It is one of the most significant decisions that has ever been taken on the island of Ireland . . . Whatever we might think of Adams and McGuinness and the leadership of Sinn Fein, it has negotiated what is a treacherous and difficult journey – quite amazing – and I don't think you could have anything other than a degree of respect for that. It doesn't necessarily mean we respect them as people. We don't know them as people. Maybe that will come at a later date.

This was Ervine speaking just a few weeks after the Good Friday Agreement – but his view of it has not changed: 'The agreement hasn't failed,' he told me in May 2003. 'Whatever its flaws, it was a magnificent creation. At fault are the politicians.'

Ervine and those around him in the leadership of the Progressive

Unionist Party and the UVF went into the Good Friday Agreement negotiations with their eyes wide open and well aware of the likely outcome of those talks. Inside this part of the loyalist family, you will find the more progressive voices, and while the UDA ceasefire has been a sham, the UVF's has been much more disciplined. This is what Gusty Spence – mentor to Ervine and Hutchinson – told me in October 1997, months before the Good Friday Agreement and just a few weeks into the all-party talks:

> We are cognisant of the fact that at least 40 per cent of the people of Northern Ireland are not unionist. So, there has to be a manifestation of their identity, of their culture, of equality, of plurality, of all those things which sadly have been lacking in Northern Ireland society for so long . . . I think we all have difficult decisions to make, and Sinn Fein are no different from anyone else. We have to tackle the realities of society in Northern Ireland. We can no longer run away from all the abnormalities . . . but, for the first time ever, we have an opportunity to build a society, and if there is an agreement reached it would be as near as damned perfect – it may even become a paragon for other societies – because, at long last, nationalism and unionism will have sat down and agreed a way forward.

Over a period of years, the PUP and the UVF had thought things through and clearly had prepared themselves and those around them for the likely outcomes. They were better placed than the UDA to deal with the developing situation and this has become obvious in the course of the process. You can read in the comments of Gusty Spence in October 1997 that he believed a compromise deal was possible and that any agreement would re-shape Northern Ireland society.

Spence and those closest to him had been watching republicans over a long period of time. As far back as 1988 they believed that their 'enemy' was moving beyond the rhetoric of 'Brits Out' and 'Unite Ireland'. This observation coincided with the SDLP–Sinn Fein talks of that period, and within the UVF and the PUP a small 'think tank' was created. Spence and Ervine were part of it, so too was Jim McDonald – another of those who had a seat at the top table on the day of the loyalist ceasefire announcement in 1994 – and the group also included two senior UVF figures. It would take six years to work things through to 1994 and to the declaration of a cessation of 'operational hostilities', but the roots of the loyalist ceasefire can be found in this 'think tank' and in the talking that went on within it.

This process was driven from within the UVF and by those within loyalism who, in the new Northern Ireland, have demonstrated a political awareness and an ability to move in changing times. This is why Hutchinson and Ervine have found a place on the new political stage.

When the talking in the 'think tank' began in 1988, political and peaceful outcomes were by no means guaranteed. One of the paramilitary figures involved told me the possibility of 'all-out war' was considered: 'Hit the streets, winner takes all,' was how he described it.

Another source put it differently. He said the thinking was that to end the war it would first have to be escalated. That happened in the early 1990s, when the loyalists first matched and then exceeded the killing rate of the IRA. As I mentioned, the loyalist truce of 1991 prepared the way for the 1994 ceasefire, but before it was announced the UVF leadership engaged in a detailed consultation with its membership across Northern Ireland. By then the leadership had satisfied itself that no secret deal had been done to secure the IRA ceasefire of August 1994 and its decision was 'to give peace a chance – to give the people and the politicians breathing space' and to see what developed out of that. In its discussions with its membership, the UVF leadership stressed that the ceasefire was not about getting prisoners out of jail. Indeed, it made the point that if the peace process failed, the jails could fill rather than empty.

Here, I believe, there is a significant difference between how the UVF and the UDA handled things. In its decision-making, the UDA relied too heavily on its prisoners. Their agreement was allowed to be a prerequisite to any ceasefire announcement and the organisation later allowed them to unilaterally withdraw their support for the peace process both in 1996 and again in 1998. As I mentioned earlier, this was designed – however it was dressed up and presented – to force the issue of early releases, and within a year of those releases being secured the UDA withdrew its support for the Good Friday Agreement, abandoned its ceasefire and created a situation in which its political wing was forced off the stage. This has left the PUP and people such as Ervine and Hutchinson swimming against the tide in terms of the mood within their community and the position that community has now taken up in relation to the agreement.

The UDA formalised its position on the Good Friday deal in a statement released on 10 July 2001 – a statement in which it said the vast majority of the loyalist community had grown to despise the agreement.

Whilst our ceasefire remains intact, the UFF from today have withdrawn our support for the Good Friday Agreement.

We can no longer remain silent in our criticisms of an agreement which our membership have continuously voiced their opposition to and which the vast number of the loyalist community have grown to despise.

We find it intolerable that Sinn Fein have gained concession after concession yet there is still a growing erosion of our culture and our heritage. This has to stop. We cannot allow this to go any further. There can be no more concessions to nationalism while the fabric of our loyalist community is torn asunder.

In trying to put this statement into context, there are several things that need to be said. The UFF is the UDA by another name. So, this was the largest of the loyalist paramilitary organisations speaking out against the Good Friday Agreement. On its claim that its ceasefire was intact, this was as much a nonsense on this day as it had been on that day back in February when the paramilitary group had briefed a number of journalists including myself.

For Gary McMichael and Davy Adams – the most public of the pro-agreement figures inside the Ulster Democratic Party – this was the end of their political road. The politicians in the UDP were being dumped by the paramilitaries in the UDA and McMichael responded within 48 hours. His position as the political leader in this particular loyalist household had been undermined for the last time, and when I interviewed him on 12 July, he accepted that his party could no longer represent the UDA on matters relating to the Good Friday Agreement: 'I think that our role in that respect is now over. I don't think that we can speak for the UDA in that respect because they have made their position clear and it is at odds with the UDP's position.' It was now just a case of formalising the separation and that would come in a few months' time.

In the lead-up to the UDA's July statement, and in the period immediately afterwards, there was ample evidence of that organisation's move away from its ceasefire – and evidence, too, of its attempt to hide behind the cover of the Red Hand Defenders. On Monday, 25 June, Gary Smith – the prominent Shankill UDA figure and associate of Adair – became the second loyalist and the second member of this organisation to have his early release licence suspended, this time by the Secretary of State John Reid.

As in the case of Adair, an intelligence report had been prepared on Smith and this was the basis for his arrest. Reid had made his mind up the previous Friday after briefings with the then Chief Constable Sir Ronnie Flanagan and having assessed the intelligence information that was available. The timing of the decision was during the period of the Holy Cross blockade in North Belfast in which the UDA and Smith were active. The intelligence report detailed his involvement in riots in this part of the city and his pivotal role in sectarian paramilitary activity, including instigating and orchestrating pipebomb attacks and shootings. Reid was told that Smith was still someone of influence within the UDA, that he had links to another paramilitary organisation – the LVF – and, like Adair, he was involved in drugs crime. The report on this one individual made a nonsense of the UDA's claim that its ceasefire was intact.

On his arrest, Smith also faced an additional charge of making a telephone call to a television station to warn of a bomb at the Holy Cross school. That warning was given in the name of the Red Hand Defenders and was made by one of the most senior figures in the UDA organisation. He was subsequently given a three-year jail sentence.

Smith's arrest came before that 10 July statement from the UDA, but it was what developed after that organisation's decision to withdraw its support for the Good Friday Agreement that caused the greatest concern. On 20 July, once again behind the cover of the Red Hand Defenders, the UDA threatened to escalate its campaign, and in the most sectarian of statements it labelled all nationalists as 'hostile' and branded them 'legitimate targets'. Nine days later, John Gregg's men murdered a young Protestant teenager – Gavin Brett – in the mistaken belief that he was a Catholic. Their latest victim was only 19 and his life was taken in the most indiscriminate of shootings. Were we really expected to believe that Ulster was being defended by those who murdered Gavin Brett? He had been about 12 when the loyalists declared their cessation of 'operational hostilities' in 1994, and the UDA had allowed him little time to live in Northern Ireland's peace.

Within 24 hours of the shooting, Gerry Adams blamed the UDA for this killing and for other attacks. He said the refusal of the British Government to 'face up to this' was 'totally unacceptable' and that the refusal of the RUC to 'declare this' was also unacceptable.

Reid and Flanagan knew that the UDA was up to its neck in what was going on, but the question was what to do about it. The Secretary of State had the authority to 'specify' the organisation – which would mean the Government no longer recognised its ceasefire, but there was no penalty, no sanction, to go along with this, and there were fears that such a move would simply trigger even more attacks by the UDA. A source at the Northern Ireland Office said a move to specify the UDA would be 'a grand gesture, but a gesture that could cost people their lives'. This was the Government's dilemma, but the UDA was pushing it into a position from which it had no choice but to act.

At the start of the new school year in September 2001 the situation in North Belfast deteriorated and an incident captured on camera shocked even those who had become hardened by 30 years of war in Northern Ireland. As the kids of the Holy Cross walked the road to their school, a pipebomb was thrown in their direction and exploded at police lines injuring a number of officers. This place – this road – had become a theatre of hatred and fear and the cameras saw it all: screaming, terrified children clinging to their parents, running for their young lives and running to escape this moment of absolute madness. It was a shocking image, viewed on television screens across the world, and this was the UDA at play – playing with bombs, playing behind the cover of the Red Hand Defenders and preying on children, many of whom were experiencing their first days of school. This was bigotry and sectarianism of the worst kind. For its target the paramilitary organisation had selected a group of young children between the ages of four and eleven. Those who live on the loyalist side of this peaceline in North Belfast may have had genuine grievances, but their voices were drowned out by the sound of that bomb and by the screams of the children. What had begun as a protest had been hijacked by the paramilitaries.

On 6 September – 24 hours after the incident – the Secretary of State said there was 'increasing evidence' that elements of the UDA were 'on anything but ceasefire'. It was an indication that John Reid was moving closer to declaring that ceasefire a sham.

He almost made the move in late September – on the 28th to be precise – but paused at the last minute on the advice of Sir Ronnie Flanagan and issued a final warning to the UDA. That night, another of the loyalist organisations – the LVF – murdered the Sunday newspaper journalist Martin O'Hagan and when Reid finally moved against the UDA on 12 October, he also specified the LVF.

Two ceasefires had been erased – two ceasefires which long before now had been stripped of all credibility and of any meaning. The straw that finally broke Reid's back was a night of rioting on 11 October in the lower Shankill – the home of Adair's so-called 'C Company'. A few weeks later, on 28 November, came the decision to wind up the Ulster Democratic Party and to shut down the pro-agreement politics of people such as Gary McMichael and Davy Adams. They had come onto the political stage with such strong and confident voices, but they left it

without as much as a whisper. The end of the UDP came in a
statement of just four sentences:

> During the past months, intensive discussions have taken
> place within the Ulster Democratic Party regarding the
> future electoral and representative viability of the party.
>
> These discussions are now at an end and it has been
> decided that, from this date, the UDP should be dissolved
> and therefore cease to exist as a political party.
>
> Former colleagues within the UDP, having reached this
> decision without rancour or ill will, wish to make it clear that
> they part on perfectly amicable terms.
>
> There will be no media comment on this matter by the
> former leadership of the UDP as further comment would
> serve no useful purpose.

In local council elections six months before this decision,
McMichael and Adams polled just over 500 votes each. Adams lost
his seat and McMichael was elected on the eighth count. It was
obvious then that the party was going down the political drain and
this statement of November 2001 had become an inevitability.
McMichael and his party had been destroyed by the UDA. The
paramilitary organisation went on to take more lives, to pollute its
own community with drugs and, then, as it went to war with itself,
it looked as if it was about to self-destruct. In this battle, Adair and
his associate John White were the obvious losers, and it was a fight
in which John Gregg was to lose his life.

In terms of the way the UDA describes itself, John 'Grugg' Gregg
was a brigadier and a member of that organisation's Inner Council.
In death, loyalists attempted to reinvent him as a man of peace, but
that was far from the truth. He and his men had terrorised
vulnerable nationalist communities. He was someone whom a senior
security figure once described as being driven by 'pure and absolute
bigotry' and he was one of those who destabilised the UDA and
pulled it away from its ceasefire and from the Good Friday
Agreement.

Whatever is now said about him, and however he is described
within the UDA, that was the reality of his reign in the paramilitary
leadership. Indeed, one loyalist source, far from persuaded by the
new description of Gregg, told me: 'Grugg would have been in his
element in the SS in Germany.' Given the position he held, he has
been the most senior casualty in all of the in-fighting within
loyalism. Gregg was murdered along with another man – Rab

Carson – on 1 February 2003, when the car they were travelling in was ambushed by Adair's men not far from Belfast city centre. They had just returned from Scotland, where Gregg had been to watch Rangers play. It was this shooting which led to the purge of the so-called 'C Company', when Adair and White found themselves on the wrong side of the loyalist lines.

There had been a build-up to all of this – a period in which the loyalists had been responsible for other sectarian murders. Adair was first released and then returned to jail, but emerged once more to turn the loyalists against each other. The feuding first involved the UDA and the LVF, and then there was that battle inside the UDA itself. 'I think Johnny had it in his head that he was going to be the head of the UDA and the LVF,' said a member of the UDA Inner Council in an interview for this book. 'He was going to bring them all together, but he was going to be the boss.'

Before the in-fighting began again, the UDA and Gregg's unit – his so-called South-east Antrim brigade – killed again. This time it picked out another young victim. Danny McColgan was a Catholic postman. He was 20 but looked much younger. For his job, he had to travel into the sprawling loyalist estate of Rathcoole, where, in the early morning of Saturday, 12 January 2002, he was shot dead in the street. He was the softest of targets and he was killed purely and simply because of his religion. The murder was first claimed by the Red Hand Defenders, but then Gregg's UDA put its name to the killing. The shooting of Danny McColgan sent a political and community chill wind in the direction of the loyalist organisation. The trade unions organised protests, people made a stand and the UDA was shamed into pulling back. It was all too late for Danny McColgan, for his partner and their young child, but there was now a very bright spotlight on the UDA and that group was desperately trying to escape its attention. For that reason it chose to speak to me and another journalist – Ivan Little of Ulster Television – and speak to us from behind its balaclavas, but there was nothing of value or truth in what the UDA had to say. It was just another lie told from behind its masks.

That meeting would happen on Tuesday, 15 January 2002, and I was contacted about it as I arrived at Hillsborough Castle with my wife, Val, for a reception that was being hosted by the Secretary of State John Reid. I would not be able to enjoy the reception for long, however. The phone call I took as I arrived was one of two. In the second, I was given instructions to go to the lane leading to Fernhill House, at Glencairn, which sits above the Shankill Road. I would be met there just before nine.

In the story of the peace process, Fernhill House is remembered for what happened there on 13 October 1994 – the date of the Combined Loyalist Military Command ceasefire, which was announced inside the building by Gusty Spence. That statement included an apology to the families of the 'innocent victims' and spoke of 'abject and true remorse', but there had been many 'innocent' victims since – the latest being young Danny McColgan.

At the rendezvous point, on that dark lane leading to Fernhill House, a car with two loyalists inside moved off first. Ivan Little of Ulster Television followed and I was in a third car with my South African cameraman Tony Davis. We were heading back towards the Shankill Road and to a loyalist drinking club where the masked and armed men of the UDA would appear before us. They were summoned into the room by a senior paramilitary figure and then a statement was read from behind a balaclava. In it, the UDA ordered the Red Hand Defenders to stand down. It was a statement full of threat and muscle. There would be no more warnings, individuals using the title of the Red Hand Defenders were ordered to desist, they were undermining loyalism and they had 14 days to stand down.

This was nonsense. The UDA *was* the Red Hand Defenders. In this latest stunt, it was talking to itself and fooling no one else. I wondered whether the balaclavas were needed because those involved could not have kept their faces straight as this statement was read. In my news coverage the following morning I suggested that those involved in what had happened the night before should repeat a hundred times: 'I must not be a Red Hand Defender.' I was not trivialising things. A young man was dead and others felt threatened, but I was not going to allow myself, or the BBC and the people listening into our coverage, to be conned by this nonsense. The men in the balaclavas who had stood before us the night before were members of the UDA – the organisation responsible for the killing of Danny McColgan and the organisation which for months had been using the title of the Red Hand Defenders as a shield. They were standing themselves down.

The statement was full of lies and hypocrisy. The UDA – the organisation which had been so heavily involved in what went on at the Holy Cross, and the organisation which had owned up to the killing of Danny McColgan – now 'condemned unreservedly' threats to schoolteachers and to post-office workers. Had it not been so serious, it would have been laughable. The UDA was showing its two faces and nothing it was saying could be believed. This was the UDA leadership twisting and turning and trying to escape the spotlight that was now fixed on its organisation. This was an organisation which had now openly declared its opposition to the Good Friday Agreement and an organisation no longer on ceasefire. It backed off for a while, but soon it would kill again.

To try to understand what was going on, you have to know the structure within which the UDA operates. While it has a six-man Inner Council, it is not an organisation which functions under central control. Six brigadiers sit on that Inner Council representing six areas – North, South, East and West Belfast, South-east Antrim and North Antrim–Londonderry. Within those six areas, the brigadiers have autonomy to do as they choose, and for some that meant directing sectarian violence and trying to disguise their involvement by hiding behind the paper-thin cover of the Red Hand Defenders. The entire organisation was not involved, but a major part of it was, and senior and significant figures in the UDA stood back and let it happen.

Adair's release from prison was now close and the UDA was about to be torn apart in a struggle for power within its ranks. On 15 May 2002 – the day he was freed from Maghaberry jail – the UDA put on a show of happy families. The Inner Council went to greet him at the gates of the prison. Gregg was there along with William 'Mo' Courtney from the Shankill, Jackie McDonald from South Belfast, Jim Gray from the east of the city, Billy McFarland, who is the organisation's brigadier in Londonderry, and Jim 'Jimbo' Simpson, who at the time was the UDA leader in North Belfast. 'We tried to put the arm round him and tried to get him settled down because of what he had done in the past,' said a member of the UDA leadership in an interview for this book, and in his reference to the past here he meant the period before the 1994 republican and loyalist ceasefires.

> Since the Troubles started, there has been a niche there for somebody. It went from maybe John McMichael or Billy Wright or whoever, but the niche arrived at the same time as Johnny, when the violence escalated and he took it to a new level and he was respected for it . . . It was the increase in violence that brought about the ceasefires . . . I have to give him that. It's the same as Michael Stone in the graveyard. You give him that, because whether people say it's right or wrong, it took a lot of balls to do it, but then after that, when the violence wasn't there, he couldn't fit in. The niche was gone . . . He couldn't fit into the peace . . . I said to him, Johnny, fair play to you for what you did, but those days are gone – those circumstances aren't the same any more.

Within four months of Adair's release, the battle for control of the UDA had begun, and intelligence officers, working on information provided by one of their informants, believe the Shankill loyalist planned to wipe out the Inner Council. 'He was going to shoot them all,' a Special Branch source told me, and this is something that the UDA leadership itself suspected. A member of that Inner Council told me: 'I would say that that was definitely on his mind – definitely on his mind.'

There was no real calm before the September storm and the next feud within loyalism. Throughout the summer months, there was trouble on the sectarian interfaces of North and East Belfast and in this period David Ervine warned that another of the loyalist organisations – the UVF – had reached 'a crossroads' on the Good Friday Agreement. He also said the group's attitude to decommissioning remained 'not a bullet – not a stick [of explosives]'. That organisation and the IRA were linked by Belfast's most senior police officer at the time, Alan McQuillan, to the violence in the east of the city, where in June five men were shot and wounded – hit by gunfire which came from the republican side. The following month in North Belfast a young Catholic, Gerard Lawlor, was murdered by the UDA when it went on a killing mission after a Protestant teenager was wounded by a shot fired from Ardoyne – an incident later attributed to the Irish National Liberation Army. Just a few weeks before the Gerard Lawlor killing, the Secretary of State John Reid had met members of the Loyalist Commission in East Belfast. That commission has at its table churchmen, community workers, politicians and representatives of the three main loyalist paramilitary organisations – the UDA, the UVF and the Red Hand Commando (not to be confused with the Red Hand Defenders). Adair was at the meeting but did not speak. He arrived with John White, 'Mo' Courtney and the UDA's new leader in North Belfast Andre Shoukri. Some considered Shoukri to be close to Adair, but, when September came, he stood on the opposite side of the loyalist lines.

Before the meeting, which went on for about two and a half hours, Reid had made his position clear. He had this message for the loyalists:

> If you want to work for a constructive political resolution to our problems and a better Northern Ireland, I will work with you.
>
> If you're wedded to the old ways and you are stuck to the path of violence, I will oppose you by every means at my disposal.

Adair had no interest in a new Northern Ireland and no interest in peace, and that would become obvious in the weeks ahead. His interest was power, and soon he would move to try to take control of the UDA. Again, however, he miscalculated and he and his closest associates would be the losers in this next battle.

A murder on Friday, 13 September, was the spark for this latest feud. A senior figure in the Loyalist Volunteer Force, Stephen Warnock, was shot from close range as he sat in his car at Newtownards in County Down. The current assessment of his murder is that he was probably killed by members of the Red Hand Commando – an organisation with close links to the UVF, and this was probably a revenge attack – the Commando group hitting back and reacting to a bomb incident in which one of its members had been targeted and seriously hurt. In this place, the paramilitaries have long memories and the Red Hand organisation eventually caught up with Warnock. At the time, however, the finger of suspicion for Warnock's murder was pointing at the UDA in East Belfast. In the crazy, mixed-up, fragmented world of loyalism, someone, somewhere, planted that seed and Warnock's associates believed it. In response they shot and wounded Jim Gray – one of the most senior UDA figures in the east of the city – and in doing so they declared war on the Inner Council. Here the plot thickens and Adair comes into play.

Although a senior figure in the UDA leadership, Adair had always been close to the LVF, and those who sat with him on the Inner Council suspected he had some involvement in the Gray shooting and that he may even have 'orchestrated it'. Adair's days in the UDA would soon be over, but there were other developments before then. The organisation's brigadier in North Belfast, Andre Shoukri, was arrested on Saturday, 21 September, and charged with possession of a firearm with intent to endanger life. Four days later, the Inner Council expelled Adair and 48 hours after that – on Friday, 27 September – his close associate John White was also shown the door. So, in the space of two weeks – in those 14 days spanning 13 to 27 September – the UDA had been turned upside down. This is the story so far:

13 September 2002: Senior LVF member Stephen Warnock murdered. Red Hand Commando group now suspected, but at the time suspicion fell on UDA figures in East Belfast.

16 September 2002: LVF shoot and wound UDA Inner Council member Jim Gray.

21 September 2002: UDA North Belfast brigadier Andre Shoukri arrested and charged with possession of a firearm. (In July 2003,

Shoukri was jailed for six years for having the gun, but was cleared
of the more serious charge of possession with intent to endanger
life.)

25 September 2002: UDA Inner Council meets in East Belfast. Adair
expelled.

26 September 2002: Statement issued by Red Hand Defenders, cover
name used by Adair's so-called 'C Company'. It orders Jim Gray,
Jackie McDonald and John Gregg to publicly stand down from
their positions as UDA brigadiers 'otherwise direct military
action will take place'.

27 September 2002: UDA Inner Council issues statement. John White
is expelled.

Before the UDA and the LVF ended their feud, there were two more
murders, but by early November – after a series of meetings
involving leaders in both groups – the two organisations said they
had 'resolved any differences which may have existed'. In a hotel
outside Belfast, some of the most senior figures in these two groups
had met and agreed a joint statement, which was dictated to me over
the phone on the afternoon of Tuesday, 5 November 2002:

> It has now become obvious that erroneous information was
> being furnished to both organisations which resulted in this
> unfortunate conflict.
>
> The LVF now accept totally that East Belfast brigade
> UDA had no involvement – directly or indirectly – in the
> murder of Stephen Warnock.
>
> Both organisations have therefore now resolved any
> differences which may have existed and have initiated a policy
> whereby intermediaries have been set up to prevent any
> further recurrence of this sort of conflict.

With this feud settled, the UDA believed the 'noose was tightening'
on Adair, and when the move was made against his so-called 'C
Company' in the lower Shankill, the LVF stood up with the UDA
against Adair and his associates. They were gradually being isolated
within loyalism. They had nowhere to hide, and when all of this
came to a head their only option was to run. It would be a
humiliating end for Adair and White and for those closest to them.

When it ended its feud with the LVF, the UDA moved quickly to
try to further isolate Adair. His powerbase was the lower Shankill,
but his authority stretched beyond there. He was also the UDA's
West Belfast brigadier, and what the organisation's leadership sought
to do was to persuade the 'A' and 'B' companies in the upper Shankill

to abandon Adair and his men – to take action 'to distance themselves from these individuals'. This would take a little more time, a little more patience on the part of the UDA leadership, but it would happen, and when it did, Adair's 'C Company' knew it was finished. The end came in early February 2003, but for weeks before then this paramilitary organisation was at war with itself, and it was clear that the main target, as far as Adair was concerned, was John Gregg – the UDA's brigadier in South-east Antrim.

On 8 December, Gregg discovered a bomb underneath his car and a couple of weeks later another device was found close to his home. The Inner Council moved and warned Adair and White that it would not tolerate 'this blatant attempt to overthrow the leadership of the UDA', and it also made public that it had knowledge of an imminent plan to murder a senior loyalist. The Inner Council again warned those close to Adair and White that they 'should distance themselves forthwith'. This was a war of words, bullets and bombs – a feud which led to two murders in December 2002 and January 2003 – and a battle in which Adair's role was so obvious that it could only be a matter of time before he was killed or thrown back into jail.

By now, the Secretary of State Paul Murphy, who had replaced John Reid at the Northern Ireland Office back in October, had seen more than enough. On 10 January 2003, Adair was arrested and returned to jail. This was the second time his early release licence had been revoked and 24 hours later the reasons for his arrest were detailed in a letter given to him inside Maghaberry jail. It was a senior loyalist who told me that Adair could not 'fit into the peace', and the letter he was given described a man of war:

> You are hereby advised that your licence was revoked by the Secretary of State because it appeared to him that your continued liberty would present a risk to the safety of others and that you were likely to commit further offences.
>
> In reaching that decision, the Secretary of State had regard to information available to him to the effect that you had since May 2002 in Belfast, County Londonderry, in mid-Ulster and elsewhere in Northern Ireland engaged in unlawful activity including: directing the activities of an organisation concerned in the commission of acts of terrorism; the procurement, distribution and possession of illegal firearms and munitions; threatening acts of violence and inciting and conspiring with others to carry out acts of violence; dealing in illegal drugs; extortion; membership of a proscribed organisation – namely the UDA; soliciting,

inviting support and recruiting for that organisation; being concerned in arrangements whereby the retention and control of terrorist funds was facilitated; money laundering; supporting proscribed organisations – namely the UDA and LVF; and the absence of any credible information to indicate that you would not persist in such illegal activity if you remained on licence.

The book had been thrown at Adair and, on the basis of this information, he could be held in jail until January 2005 without any further charges being put to him. He had been removed from the lower Shankill and removed from the feud, but the UDA leadership knew that the danger had not yet passed. Adair's associates still posed a serious threat to the Inner Council and within weeks that threat would be seen in the murder of John Gregg.

Before then, one of Adair's most senior associates, William 'Mo' Courtney, defected. He sided with the mainstream organisation and claimed to have uncovered a plot by 'Adair and his cohorts' to murder him. Courtney was a senior and influential figure within the UDA and is understood to have held the position of 'military commander'. This was, therefore, a significant defection and within days he would play a key part in the final moves to purge Adair's 'C Company'.

That push came in early February just days after the murder of John Gregg. Adair's men had killed a 'brigadier' and the weight of the UDA organisation was about to come down on top of them. The 'A' and 'B' companies in the upper Shankill were now ready to move and stated publicly that they no longer recognised Adair's leadership. Next, the LVF made clear that it wanted no part in this fight. Adair was losing long-time friends and associates and his 'C Company' was about to lose the war. His downfall was being choreographed and next to speak was the UDA leadership – its Inner Council. It issued an ultimatum – a final warning in which Adair's men were given until midnight on Thursday to choose sides. They were warned that if they stayed loyal to him they would be treated the same 'as the enemies of Ulster'. Before that deadline was reached, the battle was won and lost.

Before midnight on Wednesday, on the eve of Gregg's funeral, dozens of Adair's men deserted him, and his wife Gina, his close associate John White and the men who held leadership positions in his 'C Company' fled the lower Shankill. The UDA came looking for them; they were outflanked, outnumbered and they had to run. For Adair in jail and for his closest associate John White, this was a humiliating defeat and an embarrassing end. They had wanted to rule the loyalist roost and had considered themselves to be untouchable. Now, in terms of having any influence within loyalism, they were finished. Adair was in prison and White was in hiding, and for both of them there is no way back.

The senior loyalist who likened Adair to the moth drawn to the flame – the man who said he would never fit into the peace – also knew that this day was coming. Adair was always going to test authority and eventually he was going to push people too far: 'I think he was in awe of Michael Stone. He hated Michael Stone for this graveyard thing, because that image will always be there, but there'll be no one, specific image of Johnny Adair and he can't get past that.'

After the feud, the UDA began to rebuild, but there are those in leadership positions inside this organisation who know it has a mountain to climb. The UDA has no credibility and no reputation. It became an enemy of the peace process and then an enemy of its own community, and at the level of its Inner Council that is accepted. One of the UDA's 'brigadiers' told me in an interview for this book: 'There's no doubt that loyalism was in the gutter, especially the UDA was in the gutter, and it was John White and Johnny Adair who put us there.'

Rebuilding has meant a new ceasefire – or to describe it accurately a '12-month period of military inactivity', which was declared in February 2003. It has also meant renewed contact with the de Chastelain arms commission and the organisation has spoken out against drugs. But the UDA is steeped in drugs crime and some in its leadership are involved. If it is to have a new beginning, if it is to be taken seriously, then it knows that actions – or inaction – will speak so much louder than its words.

The Ulster Democratic Party has been replaced with an Ulster Political Research Group (UPRG), but its political rehabilitation will also be a slow process, and that too is accepted: 'We have to make sure that nobody ever comes along or tries to dictate or has the same influence as Johnny Adair and John White had.'

These words were spoken by one of the UDA's most senior figures and they suggest that the organisation is trying to learn from its past mistakes. The man they call 'Mad Dog' did so much damage to this group and to the wider peace process, and inside that process loyalism has struggled. The Prime Minister Tony Blair is now trying to push the IRA towards 'acts of completion', but there are still huge questions about the UDA, about wider loyalism and about its place within this process. There are big questions too about drugs, about criminality and about the money which is now such a big part of everyday life in these communities – communities which have been abandoned in this process and left to the control of mafia-like figures. This is not the loyalism that stepped onto the ceasefire stage in 1994, and Johnny Adair is not the only one to blame. Somewhere along the way, things went terribly wrong, and this situation will now have to be addressed if the process is to work again. David Ervine, who has been the most progressive and consistent voice within loyalism since the ceasefires, says fixing what went wrong is the journey that now has to be taken on: 'Paramilitarism has done so much damage to itself, and it can't swim against the tide, especially if that tide is moving in the direction of peace and stability.'

CHAPTER NINE

High Hopes and Sinking Feelings

'When the IRA says their strategies and disciplines will not be inconsistent with the Good Friday Agreement, does that mean an end to all activities inconsistent with the Good Friday Agreement, including targeting, procurement of weapons, so-called punishment beatings and so forth?'

British Prime Minister Tony Blair, 23 April 2003

'The IRA leadership is determined that there will be no activities which will undermine in any way the peace process and the Good Friday Agreement.'

Sinn Fein president Gerry Adams, 30 April 2003

'This is the IRA's endgame. That statement contains new policy, new thinking and a new strategy. This is earth-moving stuff.'

Republican source, 7 May 2003

9 APRIL 2003: In Windsor House, the tallest building in Belfast, the two men waiting for the IRA had high hopes for the peace process. For weeks, the British and Irish governments, the republicans, the nationalists and the unionists had been talking about 'acts of completion'. The power-sharing Executive at Stormont had been suspended since the previous October – suspended in the fall-out over allegations of all sorts of IRA activity in Colombia, inside the Special Branch office at Castlereagh and inside the Northern Ireland Office at Castle Buildings. But these latest negotiations were about a new beginning, about the full implementation of the Good Friday Agreement, about an end to the IRA, about restoring power-sharing and about what Tony Blair called 'acts of completion'.

His chief of staff, Jonathan Powell, and the secretary general of the department of justice in Dublin, Tim Dalton, were now waiting inside Windsor House in Bedford Street for Gerry Adams and Martin McGuinness to deliver the IRA's latest peace offering.

In 24 hours' time, Blair and the Irish Taoiseach Bertie Ahern were due at Hillsborough Castle to unveil their Joint Declaration. It was a declaration that would signal significant change, including a radical reduction in troop numbers in Northern Ireland and the closure and demolition of many army bases, notably the controversial watchtowers in South Armagh. This demilitarisation plan would be spread over two years with a completion date in April 2005. It was so radical, indeed, that Ian Paisley Jnr called it 'Brits Out'.

There were also plans to deal with the controversial issue of paramilitary suspects still on the run. Their cases would be heard by a Special Judicial Tribunal. Suspects, who would not have to be present at the hearing, would be released on licence, but no one would go to jail. This was probably the piece of this deal that the unionists hated most. It would be dealt with in a separate paper from the Joint Declaration, but, whatever way it was dressed up, it was all part of the same package.

There were plans, too, to transfer policing and justice powers to Northern Ireland politicians. The fine detail of this still had to be worked out, but in the unionist mind it opened up the possibility and the fear, however far down the road, of a Sinn Fein minister having control of one of these departments. If Martin McGuinness as Education Minister had sent a shiver down the unionist spine, what would this do?

The deal was interlocking. It depended on acts of completion from all sides and the one big piece of the jigsaw still missing was the detail of the IRA's contribution. That is what brought Powell and Dalton to Belfast for a meeting with Adams and McGuinness. The unionists had set the bar high – some had demanded IRA disbandment and public decommissioning, things the IRA had long ago dismissed as 'unrealistic and unrealisable'.

Ulster Unionist MP Jeffrey Donaldson:

> For the Republican Movement the bar has become higher, and it has become higher not out of some perverse desire on the part of unionists to make republicans jump higher. It's because of their actions and the damage they've done to unionist confidence and trust, and this piece-by-piece approach to the process. Because of the lack of movement, because of the lack of progress on the arms issue and on ending all paramilitary activity, inevitably the longer time goes on, the greater is the requirement that is needed to build that trust again, because the trust gets lower and lower each time a Castlereagh, a Colombia, a Florida, a 'Stormontgate' happens. It is those things that make the bar higher.

Normally in negotiations in this process the IRA's offer comes last, and usually the fine detail is withheld until publicly announced by P. O'Neill. Indeed, it was the Taoiseach who described this as the business of the '13th hour', but in this specific negotiation – in these talks on acts of completion – the governments needed to know what they could expect before Blair and Ahern disclosed the detail of their blueprint at Hillsborough. It was all last minute – the stuff of the high wire. A British Government source told me: 'This time, with so much riding on it, they had to see something.'

What Powell and Dalton were shown in that 9 April meeting in the offices of the British–Irish Joint Secretariat led to the postponement of the Blair–Ahern summit. An Irish source told me:

> It was our belief and understanding, and also the British belief and understanding, that Adams and McGuinness were going for broke, and we believed them and we never doubted their bona fides. The offer that came in was considerably lower than what they had implied . . . The first formal offer was to Powell and Dalton. That came in considerably under the bar, because we thought they would spell out a definitive end to paramilitarism.

This meeting came just 24 hours after a Blair–Bush Iraq war summit at Hillsborough. This backdrop and build-up had raised the hopes of a breakthrough, but now there was a sinking feeling and a general sense of let-down.

The 9 April meeting involving Powell, Dalton, Adams and McGuinness was not something widely known about at the time, but on 10 April, as news leaked out of plans to postpone the Blair and Ahern visit, there was speculation about an IRA offer that had not measured up to the expectations of the governments. An Irish source told me: 'We felt that words and promises, however well meaning, without some sort of definitive delivery point on it, wasn't going to work.'

The Joint Declaration had not yet been published, but much of its detail had been leaked and unionists were being unsettled by what was emerging. The governments hoped that what the IRA would deliver would cushion that blow, and the test for the IRA was set in paragraph 13 of the declaration:

> Paramilitarism and sectarian violence, therefore, must be brought to an end, from whichever part of the community they come. We need to see an immediate, full and permanent cessation of all paramilitary activity, including military

attacks, training, targeting, intelligence gathering, acquisition or development of arms or weapons, other preparations for terrorist campaigns, punishment beatings and attacks and involvement in riots. Moreover, the practice of exiling must come to an end and the exiled must feel free to return in safety. Similarly, sectarian attacks and intimidation directed at vulnerable communities must cease.

The acts of completion set out in the Joint Declaration were all going to take time to achieve. They were set in a context and in a process, and the IRA's response was always going to be similar. It was never going to read out the list of activities detailed in paragraph 13 of the Joint Declaration and as for the unionist demands for instant disbandment and public decommissioning, these are the things of magic-wand politics. In the reality of Northern Ireland, and in a process of conflict resolution, they were not going to happen. So, in these negotiations, which had begun in earnest towards the end of 2002, either the IRA had misread the governments and the unionists, or they had misread the IRA. In an interview in May 2003, Gerry Adams said:

> When we eventually got talking to the British Government, we said to them, we are prepared to go to the IRA, [but] we're not going near the IRA until you have given us time-framed implementation programmes for the full implementation of the agreement and one or two issues which fall, I suppose, in the spirit of the agreement, but fall outside the letter of the agreement, and what we'll do is look for an advanced IRA statement, which deals with its present or current disposition, which gives its view of the cessation – the status of the cessation – which talks about its future intentions, and also we'll see if we can do something around the arms issue. We will, in all of that, try to get the most advanced language possible.

Describing the role that he and Martin McGuinness played in these lengthy negotiations, Adams said:

> We told them if there was conditionality, if there were qualified, protracted statements from the British or the unionists, they could expect the same from the IRA – that the best way to get the most advanced movement from the IRA was to have the most advanced movement from the British and the unionists, and that, after all, what we were talking

about was the same deal which had been done five years
previously on Good Friday, that what they were looking for
was new stuff from the IRA, whereas what we were looking
for from the British and the unionists was for them to knuckle
down to do what they were supposed to be doing.

A source told me that 'simultaneously' or 'shortly after' the Powell,
Dalton, Adams and McGuinness meeting on 9 April the senior
Ulster Unionist negotiator, Sir Reg Empey, was taken through the
IRA offer: 'Empey didn't think it was worth showing to Trimble and,
frankly, nor did the governments,' the source told me.

Whether anyone else thought it worthwhile or not, soon
afterwards Adams did take Trimble through it. The Sinn Fein
president was furious that details of the 9 April offer were leaked and
so publicly dismissed by the governments, and the IRA would later
describe what was passed to Powell and Dalton as 'concepts and
draft elements'. Others believed it was something more – a
statement which, according to one source, had 'a beginning, middle
and end'. That source said there was then 'a frantic attempt to try to
improve it from a pretty low base'.

During this period, the IRA was speaking directly to the de
Chastelain commission and making preparations to put more of its
arms beyond use if Trimble and the Ulster Unionists bought into a
deal. Adams said:

> They [the unionists] weren't moving on the issues that they
> would have influence on and were therefore delaying IRA
> movement, and us actually bringing the statement forward
> [on 9 April] was an attempt to cut that knot . . . and, I also
> have to say, that points put by both the unionists and the
> British Government were reflected back to the IRA and are
> in the IRA statement [of 13 April].

That date, 13 April, was the next big day in this process of trying to
get a deal, and in his constituency office at Drumcondra in Dublin,
the Taoiseach Bertie Ahern, his Foreign Minister Brian Cowen,
Powell and Dalton waited and waited for Adams and McGuinness.

'They had pre-agreed with the two governments to meet on
Sunday afternoon with the Taoiseach and Jonathan Powell,' a source
told me – a source who believes that Dublin was chosen because that
weekend Adams and McGuinness had crossed the border to meet
with the IRA.

I knew that something was happening, not because I have a crystal ball, but because of a phone conversation with a republican contact that morning. In the course of a chat, he asked me if I had any plans and suggested that if I had then I should cancel them. It meant no golf that Sunday – or what in my case passes for golf – and it meant that I held onto the fiver that I usually pay out in defeat to my friend and neighbour, Colman Lynch. So, in Dublin, Ahern and Powell waited; the Secretary of State Paul Murphy and George W. Bush's special envoy, Richard Haass, waited at Hillsborough; and I waited at the office. By lunchtime that Sunday the IRA's spokesman had advised me that he would probably be in contact within a couple of hours, but the wait was much, much longer.

We eventually met at around a quarter to seven that Sunday evening and he passed me an envelope from across the table. He asked me to remove the statement inside and to pass the envelope back. This procedure is intended to ensure that his fingerprints are not left on the IRA statement. We then spoke briefly and I left with the statement, which was embargoed until eight. This was not the full text that Adams and McGuinness would pass to Ahern and Powell in Dublin, but a more general outline of the issues it would cover.

> IRA STATEMENT PASSED TO AUTHOR, BELFAST,
> 13 APRIL 2003:
> Following approaches from others, the leadership of the IRA undertook to draw up a statement setting out our views on recent developments in the peace process. We did so because of our commitment to this process and our desire to see it succeed.
>> In this context we decided to give our attitude on:
>> - the current disposition of Oglaigh na hEireann and the status of our cessation;
>> - our future intentions;
>> - our attitude to a re-engagement with the IICD and engagement in a process of putting arms beyond use;
>> - a third act of putting arms beyond use to be verified under the agreed scheme.
> We shared concepts and draft elements on these matters with others and now, following an internal consultation, we have closed on a statement which will be passed to the two governments. We stand ready to issue it in due course.

Later that night, London and Dublin confirmed they had the statement and the following morning Tony Blair's official spokesman said the two governments were now seeking clarification from the IRA.

Their questions were faxed to the Sinn Fein negotiators and this previously unpublished text can now be revealed.

MESSAGE FROM BOTH GOVERNMENTS, 14 APRIL 2003:

We welcome the many positive aspects of the IRA statement. There has been obvious progress and the statement shows a clear desire to make the peace process work. You are aware from the extensive discussions that have taken place of the need, on the part of the two governments, for clarity on certain issues and of the very valid reasons for this. In the spirit, therefore, of a genuine attempt by the two governments to advance matters at this point, we have three questions of clarification on it:

QUESTION 1: Paragraph eight of the IRA statement states that:

'The full and irreversible implementation of the agreement and other commitments will provide a context in which the IRA can proceed to definitively set aside arms to further our political objectives.'

Paragraph eleven states that:

'The IRA leadership reiterates our commitment to resolving the issue of arms. The commitments from the two governments, including the ending of the suspension of the political institutions, and the firm pledge by the leader of the Ulster Unionist Party that he will actively support the sustained working of the political institutions and other elements of the Good Friday Agreement, enables us to do this.'

Do these two paragraphs, taken together, mean that if the two governments and all parties fulfil the commitments referred to, that this will provide the basis for definitively ending the conflict?

QUESTION 2: Paragraph seven of the IRA statement states that:

'We are resolved to see the complete and final closure of this conflict. The IRA leadership is determined to ensure that our activities, disciplines and strategies will be consistent with this.'

Activities of the kind described in paragraph 13 of the Joint Declaration (such as targeting, punishment beatings etc.) are inconsistent with 'complete and final closure of the conflict'.

Does paragraph seven therefore mean that if activities of the kind described in paragraph 13 of the Joint Declaration were to occur, that this would be inconsistent with the IRA leadership position?

QUESTION 3: Does paragraph 12 of the IRA statement mean that the IRA will agree to the implementation of a process that completely puts arms beyond use at the earliest opportunity?

This previously unpublished message from the two governments does not specify that the clarification that was being sought had to be provided by the IRA and in the end it would be Adams who would do the explaining and the public speaking.

On the phone at just after six on that evening of 14 April the IRA's spokesman told me the organisation had 'concluded' on its statement and according to another republican source it meant just that: 'The IRA wasn't then going to get into the business of publicly re-negotiating its position – its position was its position.'

At first, there was an angry response to the request for clarification and Gerry Adams repeated privately what he had already said publicly: 'I find it incredible that you've not acted on the basis of this unprecedented intervention [by the IRA].'

By now, republicans were getting hot under the collar and those who were not bound by the diplomatic language of the negotiations were speaking their minds: 'If it's going to take the Brits two or three years to dismantle their bases, why does the IRA have to deliver within two or three days . . . what they are about is trying to screw the IRA.' The republican told me the British were not getting 'the war is over' and they were not getting 'finality'.

'The source of the mess is that the two governments thought they were going to get more out of the republicans than what is on offer,' my contact told me. He said if the planned May elections were postponed, then you would have 'a boat with no oars'.

From the high hopes before that 9 April meeting in Belfast's tallest building, there was now that sinking feeling that I mentioned earlier. In the angry corners of the republican community this was the mood that Adams and McGuinness found themselves having to manage. They were very aware that their people were angry. Adams spoke to me of 'high blood pressure', of people 'shouting at the TV' and, in terms of the attitude towards the British and the unionists, he was being told 'give them nothing'.

In an interview for this book he told me:

> It is important that as we try to advance a process, that we don't allow vacuums to arise. It's important that others can't come and steal the IRA clothes. If it comes down to it, are you better with an IRA which is on cessation for eight or nine

years, which has a leadership which is clearly and obviously trying to help the process. If anybody looks at it with unblinkered eyes they'll see – whether they like the end product or not – there is clearly an effort here to move it on . . . Could you imagine such a statement coming to Brian Faulkner in the 1970s? Can you imagine the leader of unionism being told at that time by the leader of Sinn Fein, by the way there's people standing by with gear for you to put beyond use? . . . I was told, on the record, that if David Trimble could live with this, that the British Government could live with it . . . and my view is that the Irish Government recognised, absolutely, the significance of the statement [of 13 April]. I think they had a worry of whether David Trimble would come on board.

Those who are hoping that Adams trips up, and those who are waiting to steal the IRA's clothes, are the republican dissidents who play in the vacuums of the peace process and who are seen at their most active when that process is at its most fragile and frail. From the sidelines they have shouted 'sell-out' and they have shown in their activities the threat they still pose. As I mentioned earlier, what happened in Omagh forced the dissidents into hiding, but they reurned and remain a dangerous enemy of the peace. Their capability and potential is seen in a range of actions – in the murder of David Caldwell, a civilian worker killed in an explosion at a Territorial Army centre in Derry in August 2002, in the bombings in Britain the previous year, including an attack on the BBC, and in the continuous targeting of the security forces in Northern Ireland. But the dissidents have been infiltrated and in at least one of their high-profile attacks their bomb had been tampered with and its explosive replaced with Plasticine. The Army still blew it up and made it look real, and politicians and uniformed police officers – not knowing what had happened – condemned the attack, but the bomb was a dummy and it posed no danger.

The dissidents, despite the threat they pose, have not been able to mount a serious challenge to Adams and McGuinness, who remain the undisputed leaders of modern-day republicanism. But that is not to say that, within their own ranks, they are above criticism. During these latest negotiations – in the talks on acts of completion – the view was expressed that Adams and the IRA had given too much to the British and the unionists. Indeed, Adams told me that at one internal meeting:

A young woman, a relative of a volunteer who was killed, asked, 'Is this surrender?'
    From one point of view, I think quite a lot of republicans

felt that we and I – for that matter, the IRA – went too far
. . . particularly, probably, felt that I went too far.

This was because, in the absence of IRA clarification of its 13 April
statement, Adams was given the role of public explanation –
something he told me had been suggested to him by Ambassador
Richard Haass. Adams said Haass knew there would be no more
'sweeteners' with the IRA statement and had suggested that 'words'
from the Sinn Fein president would be useful. What Adams didn't
know at this time was that Blair was going to paraphrase publicly the
questions of clarification the governments were seeking answers to.
Blair acted at a Downing Street news conference on 23 April –
something the Prime Minister did without prior notice, and at a
time when the Sinn Fein leader and his senior aide, Richard
McAuley, were on a break. Adams had been bounced by this
development: 'In fact, I said to them, you shouldn't ask questions
unless you know the answers . . . my view was that it got personal,
which is always a dangerous thing to do with any of this stuff.'

Inside Sinn Fein there is a 'core group' – a small committee which
has the job of 'monitoring, assessing and directing negotiations'. This
is Adams' 'kitchen cabinet', which includes public figures such as
McGuinness, Gerry Kelly and Bairbre de Brun, and others not so well
known on the public stage but who have key roles within this group.
Richard McAuley, Ted Howell, Aidan McAteer, Siobhan O'Hanlon
and Leo Green are part of the negotiating 'cabinet', and there are
'occasional' roles for senior party figures such as Pat Doherty, Mitchel
McLaughlin, Alex Maskey, Conor Murphy, Michelle Gildernew,
Chrissie McAuley, Séanna Walsh and Dawn Doyle. Walsh, as I
mentioned in an earlier chapter, was a close friend of Bobby Sands and
one of the first IRA prisoners to be freed as part of the Good Friday
Agreement; Doyle is the party's Dublin-based director of
communications.

This 'core group' is the Sinn Fein engine in negotiations and it
was this committee that formulated the party's response – the Adams
response – to the request for a public explanation of the IRA's 13
April statement. It is the very role that Adams had avoided for years.
As Richard McAuley told me:

> Adams has consistently refused over many years to act as a
> proxy spokesperson for the IRA. He has said so publicly and
> bluntly many times. However, on this occasion, it was
> suggested to Gerry by Ambassador Haass, and also by the
> Irish Government, that it would be helpful to the effort to
> construct a deal if he were to provide a commentary or

explanation of the IRA's position. This was accepted by the three governments, but he was reluctant to do it.

However reluctantly, Adams stepped onto the stage on Sunday, 27 April – a Stormont stage on which he had the IRA veterans Joe Cahill and Martin Meehan for company. Martin McGuinness and Bairbre de Brun, who had been ministers in the power-sharing Executive, were also there, and so too were the 1980 hunger striker Raymond McCartney and the senior Belfast republican Gerry Kelly. Howell, McAteer and McAuley sat and stood at the back of Stormont's Long Gallery and listened as Adams spoke.

It was a speech that will not have surprised the governments. The Sinn Fein president had been to Hillsborough that morning to take the Secretary of State Paul Murphy through it and he had also been in touch with Dublin. Its key paragraphs read:

> The IRA statement is a statement of completely peaceful intent. Its logic is that there should be no activities inconsistent with this . . .
>
> Secondly, the IRA has clearly stated its willingness to proceed with the implementation of a process to put arms beyond use at the earliest opportunity . . .
>
> Obviously this is not about putting some arms beyond use. It is about all arms . . .
>
> And thirdly, if the two governments and all the parties fulfil their commitments, this will provide the basis for the complete and final closure of the conflict.

In London and Dublin, the governments believed that two of their three questions had now been answered, but in the first of the paragraphs I quoted from the Adams speech, they wanted the word 'should' replaced with 'will'. In other words, they wanted that paragraph to read: 'The IRA statement is a statement of completely peaceful intent. Its logic is that there will be no activities inconsistent with this.'

By now republicans were well and truly fed up with this word-play and they were coming to the view that no matter what the IRA offered, and no matter what Adams said by way of explanation, that Trimble wasn't going to move. Earlier, I quoted Adams as saying that he had been told by the British Government that if Trimble could live with the IRA statement, so too could they. But the Sinn Fein leader knew that the flip side of that was that if Trimble refused to buy in, then the IRA initiative would not be good enough for London or Dublin: 'If you give unionists a veto, they'll use it. Why wouldn't they? This guy [Trimble] and his party are mesmerised by the prospect of the DUP coming at them.' That said, Adams accepts that Trimble has 'deeper motivations' that go beyond electoral concerns: 'He is a unionist, he does want the Union maintained. He does want to see the influence of unionism maintained and strengthened. So, it isn't just about an electoral contest.'

But that election was playing on unionist minds and all the words they had so far heard from Adams and the IRA had had little or no impact. As Jeffrey Donaldson commented:

> What had to happen needed to be so significant that the people would say, well, that's it, the war is over, even if the IRA didn't say it, that had to be the impact that the IRA's words and actions would have on the unionist community. Castlereagh, Colombia, Florida, Stormontgate all contributed towards undermining any trust that there was on the unionist side and left David Trimble in an impossible position insofar as he knew by September 2002 that the UUP's continued participation in the Executive with Sinn Fein was becoming untenable. Stormontgate finished it. What the IRA offered in words was, I think, hedged; it was conditional, it talked about a context in the future, and it fell well short of what I – as an Ulster Unionist with a sceptical perspective on this process – would need to go out and say, yeah, this time, it's for real.

On Wednesday, 30 April, Adams gave the word-game one last try, but he could not move Trimble and this long phase of negotiations failed to achieve its acts of completion. At Sinn Fein's offices on the Falls Road, Adams changed the 'should' to 'will' and at a lunchtime news conference he read out the following sentence: 'The IRA leadership is determined that there will be no activities which will undermine in any way the peace process and the Good Friday Agreement.'

It now seemed that all three questions, raised those 16 days earlier when the governments first sought clarification of the IRA statement, had been answered – or had they? Within minutes of the Adams news conference, Downing Street contacted my BBC colleague Mark Devenport and posed another question. Did this mean an end to punishment beatings, exiling, arms procurement and development, targeting and involvement in riots? It was back to paragraph 13 of the Joint Declaration and to the list of specific activities that the governments knew was not going to be read out by the IRA. Adams ended the word-game and in an angry tone he asked the two governments what part of 'no activities' did they not understand?

'It was being reduced to words, but it wasn't about words. It was never about words,' Adams told me.

> The unionists know the state of play within republicanism, the British know the state of play within republicanism, the Irish Government knows the state of play within republicanism, and either we in the Sinn Fein leadership have credibility or we don't . . . This was never about words, never about republican intentions, it was always about a process of change. There was always a package there that was deliverable in a good faith negotiation if there was a willingness on the other side to drive it on. It was doable – totally doable.

Adams is obviously speaking from a republican perspective, but the credibility of the republican leadership had been undermined by all of the allegations around Colombia, Castlereagh and Castle Buildings.

Yes, it is true, that the IRA has not been involved in sectarian murder while on ceasefire, that it has not killed inside the loyalist, unionist, Protestant community, and that it has not murdered members of the security forces during its 'cessation of military operations'. But, almost ten years on from that original ceasefire of 1994, the IRA has been far too obvious and the allegations of intelligence gathering and the claims of what it was up to in Colombia spooked the unionists and spilled over into this negotiation. Its ceasefire has been much more disciplined than some of those on the loyalist side, but the unionists need something more, and that something more was not on offer in these acts of completion talks. Who knows if it will be available in the future?

Jeffrey Donaldson believes:

> Even what Gerry Adams said made it clear that what they were doing was tactical; it was designed to help David Trimble sell a package to the Ulster Unionist Council. It wasn't a strategic move it was a tactical move, and it wasn't about saying the armed struggle is over, it is no longer legitimate, it wasn't about saying the war is over. So, the IRA's words and their potential actions were going to fall far short of what would have been required for unionists.

Within weeks of the Joint Declaration, Donaldson moved to have the document rejected by the Ulster Unionist Council and only narrowly failed. It was another indication of the divisions within unionism and further evidence that Trimble's troubles were far from over.

As the acts of completion negotiation came to a close, unionists and republicans would argue over the worth of the IRA statement, but this was a significant text – significant because it provides a road map and shows the route to the IRA's end game. This time the negotiations may have failed and there may well be big questions now being asked about the future of the Good Friday Agreement, about the fragmented state of unionism and loyalism – questions, too, about David Trimble's leadership and about the fact that, as these talks hit the wall, there was another postponement of planned elections in Northern Ireland. But there are also positives to take out of these latest negotiations. Gerry Adams may well argue that the talks ended in a 'mess', but he will also know that he and Martin McGuinness moved the IRA and left something significant to build on in the next round of discussions. As part of the IRA's end game there will be an Army Convention at the point of the full implementation of the Good Friday Agreement and when the commitments contained in the Joint Declaration are delivered. The IRA still wants a United Ireland, but it has now set a context in which it seems it would be prepared to pursue that goal through political rather than armed struggle. There has been a significant shift in the IRA's position, and it has moved away from the rhetoric and the shouts of 'not a bullet – not an ounce' and 'Brits Out'. That said, each time the politics of this process fail, the existence of the IRA is prolonged and the day of its potential end is pushed further away. As the governments and the parties now look ahead to what happens next, there is some advice from Adams – his last word on this most recent negotiation.

> I said to the Irish Government and I said to the unionists, protect and defend what we have, don't let it be frittered away, that's what you've got, don't ridicule it, protect it, defend it, because if we are coming back to these issues, that's what you have.

Epilogue

THE 'PROVOS'

They haven't gone away you know, they haven't disbanded and they haven't decommissioned in public. The IRA is still out there, but it's a very different organisation from the IRA of old – the IRA we knew before the ceasefires of 1994 and 1997. We no longer hear its gunfire and we no longer hear its bombs, but its presence, all these years into this peace process, is what the unionists can no longer cope with. But what the latest political negotiation told us was that the IRA will not be forced out of existence. It has travelled through this process at its own pace and on its own terms – and it will only leave the stage when it thinks the time is right. Unionism is nervous, it's fragmented and at times Trimble looks extremely vulnerable and extremely weak. Republicanism is quite the opposite. Adams and McGuinness are confident political leaders, Sinn Fein is growing in electoral strength on both sides of the Irish border, and the republican dissidents have not been able to steal the IRA clothes. That is not to say that the dissidents don't pose a threat. They do, and there has been recent evidence to underline this. Republicans – including the IRA – have been able to adapt to the changing politics and to this process of peace. This has been made easier because of Sinn Fein's electoral success – not just in the north, but also in the Republic, where it now has five seats in the Irish parliament. Peace making – peace building – in a place which has seen conflict for 30 years and more was always going to take time, and Adams and McGuinness appear to have the patience for the process. We no longer hear the IRA's drums of war.

THE 'PRODS'

They are still killing each other – inside the UDA and inside loyalism. Adair is in jail and John White is in hiding, but inside this community the feuding continues. The largest of the paramilitary organisations – the UDA – is supposedly on ceasefire, but in May 2003 it murdered one of Adair's closest associates – his military commander Alan McCullough. This was revenge for the killing of John 'Grugg' Gregg, and a warning to Adair's men to stay out of the Shankill and to stay out of Northern Ireland. Within days, two of the most senior figures in the UDA leadership – William 'Mo' Courtney and Ihab Shoukri – the brother of Andre – had been charged with the McCullough murder, charges they deny.

Also in May, a senior figure in the Red Hand Commando, Jim Johnston, was shot dead by the LVF. Eight months earlier, the Commando group had killed Stephen Warnock – a leader in the LVF, and the Johnston murder was payback. This is a place of long memories – a place in which one killing inevitably leads to another.

The loyalism of 2003 is so different from what we saw in 1994. It is missing the voices of Gary McMichael and David Adams – missing the combined decision making of that period. While David Ervine and Billy Hutchinson have held on to their positions, the rest of political loyalism is struggling as paramilitary figures such as Johnny Adair and others in the UDA leadership whose only interest is self-interest have taken centre stage. Clearly they don't want to be part of the peace process – and that is a political reality that needs to be recognised sooner rather than later. The longer the governments and the politicians wait, the more damage these people are doing – mainly inside their own communities – communities which have been abandoned and left to the control of the loyalist godfathers.

THE 'PEELERS'

Policing in Northern Ireland now has a new voice – the voice of its Chief Constable Hugh Orde. It's a voice that is being used to encourage republicans to sign up to the new policing arrangements; a voice that says Sinn Fein should be on the new Policing Board and should be doing its bit to get young nationalists and republicans to join the police service. More Catholics are coming forward and more change is in the pipeline – including changes to the Special Branch. But Sinn Fein has not yet endorsed the new policing arrangements, although it appears to be moving ever closer to doing so.

Orde is not afraid to speak his mind and to do so on even the most sensitive and controversial of issues. More than half the deaths of the Troubles remain unsolved – no one has been brought to justice. But Orde has presented the Northern Ireland public with a choice – a choice between investigating the past or policing the present. He believes that some sort of truth and reconciliation process may be needed in Northern Ireland – that at some point all sides may have to come to a table of explanation and say their piece. It is a controversial suggestion, and when he made it in June, as well as opening up the debate again, he opened himself to criticism from those who believe that closure can only be achieved when the guilty are convicted.

In the course of this peace process much progress has been made, but many difficult issues have yet to be settled and Orde touched on one of them – and touched a raw nerve – when he spoke in June. The 'Long War' may well be over, but it has left behind many painful memories – and that hurt has yet to be healed.

Appendix: IRA Statements

STATEMENT PASSED TO THE TWO GOVERNMENTS, SUNDAY, 13 APRIL 2003, BY THE IRISH REPUBLICAN ARMY

The leadership of Oglaigh na hEireann takes this opportunity to give our view of the current phase of the peace process. In particular we want to address unionist concerns.

The political responsibility for advancing the current situation rests with the two governments, especially the British Government, and the leaderships of the political parties.

Accordingly the IRA leadership have assessed commitments from the two governments and the UUP.

The IRA has a genuine interest in building an enduring political process because we want to see the removal of the causes of conflict in our country. Although the Irish Republican Army is not a party to the Good Friday Agreement we are disappointed that the agreement has not been implemented.

We are disappointed also that the commitments in the Joint Declaration are conditional and protracted. Despite this, we want to give them a fair wind.

Oglaigh na hEireann supports the peace process. We want it to work. We affirm that our cessation is intact.

We are resolved to see the complete and final closure of this conflict. The IRA leadership is determined to ensure that our activities, disciplines and strategies will be consistent with this.

Furthermore, the full and irreversible implementation of the agreement and other commitments will provide a context in which the IRA can proceed to definitively set aside arms to further our political objectives. When there is such a context, this decision can be taken only by a General Army Convention representing all volunteers.

We want to enhance the climate at all levels of society so that unionists and loyalists, nationalists and republicans, free from threats to their rights and safety, can engage together in community, political and other areas of co-operation and work.

The IRA poses no threat to the unionist people or to the peace process.

The IRA leadership reiterates our commitment to resolving the issue of arms. The commitments from the two governments, including the ending of the suspension of the political institutions, and the firm pledge by the leader of the Ulster Unionist Party that he will actively support the sustained working of the political institutions and other elements of the Good Friday Agreement, enable us to do this.

We have authorised our representative to meet with the IICD with a view to proceeding with the implementation of a process to put arms beyond use at the earliest opportunity.

We have also authorised a third act of putting arms beyond use.

This will be verified under the agreed scheme.

These initiatives are part of our ongoing contribution to the collective endeavour. The commitments made by the two governments and the UUP are a necessary part of this.

We support genuine efforts to build a just and peaceful future for all the people of this island. This is a collective task for all sections of society. Unionist political leaders have a special contribution to make.

We are Irish republicans. Our objective is a united Ireland. We are not unionists or British and no one should expect us to set aside our political objectives or our republicanism.

We do not claim to fully understand unionist perceptions. But we are prepared to listen and to learn. And we are committed to playing our part in creating the conditions in which unionists, nationalists and republicans can live together peacefully.

Building the collective trust to achieve this is a huge challenge for everyone. Given the experience of nationalists and republicans during decades of conflict and before, this is a particular challenge for us. It is also a challenge for unionists and the British government.

Much hurt has been inflicted by British Government policy, by successive British governments and by the old unionist regime. Great pain has been caused by the British Army, the RUC and Loyalist paramilitaries. Irish republicans and nationalists have a proud and honourable record of resistance against these forces. We know unionists do not see it like that.

We are also conscious that non-combatants were killed and injured as a consequence of some of our actions. We offer our sincere apologies and condolences to their families and friends.

The IRA is committed to supporting every effort to make conflict a thing of the past. To this end the IRA leadership has previously authorised a series of unprecedented initiatives to enhance the search for a lasting peace.

On occasions these have been undervalued or dismissed. Despite this we are persisting in our endeavours. The initiatives outlined in this statement involve further substantive and additional contributions by the IRA.

Both governments – and unionists and republicans alike – have now an opportunity which cannot and should not be wasted.

P. O'Neill, Irish Republican Publicity Bureau

IRA BRIEFING NOTE, RELEASED 6 MAY 2003

This was a major initiative by the IRA. Despite the obvious conditionality of the Joint Declaration, it was a comprehensive statement dealing with a wide range of issues. These included:

- The current disposition of Oglaigh na hEireann and the status of our cessation.
- Our future intentions.
- Our attitude to re-engagement with the IICD and engagement in a process of putting arms beyond use.
- A third act of putting arms beyond use to be verified under the agreed scheme. Addressing unionist concerns.
- An apology to the families and friends of non-combatants killed as a consequence of our actions.
- Re-affirmation of our republican objectives.

All of this represents further substantive and additional contributions by the IRA to the peace process.

Para 6 makes clear our support for the peace process. We want it to work and our cessation remains intact.

Para 7 expresses our desire to see the complete and final closure of this conflict. It also sets out clearly our determination to ensure that our activities, disciplines and strategies will be consistent with this.

Para 8 spells out our view that the full and irreversible implementation of the GFA and other commitments can provide a context for definitively setting aside arms to further our political objectives. This would involve a GAC.

Para 22 expresses our commitment to supporting every effort to make conflict a thing of the past.

Para 12 and para 13 deal with the re-engagement with the IICD, the implementation of a process to put arms beyond use at the earliest opportunity and the authorisation of a third act.

Para 9 expresses our desire to enhance the climate in society in which everyone can live free from threats to their rights and safety.

We expressly say there is no threat to the unionist people or the peace process from the IRA. And we go further and accept that we do not fully understand unionist perceptions and are prepared to listen and learn.

And once again we express our apology to the families and friends of non-combatants killed by us.

STATEMENT BY THE IRISH REPUBLICAN ARMY, 6 MAY 2003

The IRA leadership is committed to making the peace process work.

That is why we called our cessation.

That is why we have maintained it.

That is why we have taken a series of significant initiatives.

That is why at the beginning of April we shared concepts and drafts with others. While that process was ongoing these concepts and drafts were mischievously leaked and misrepresented by the two governments. This was an abuse of trust.

Despite this, on Sunday, 13 April, the IRA leadership closed on a statement setting out our view on recent developments in the peace process, and on:

–the current disposition of Oglaigh na hEireann and the status of our cessation;
–our future intentions;
–our attitude to re-engagement with the IICD and engagement in a process of putting arms beyond use;
–a third act of putting arms beyond use to be verified under the agreed scheme;
–a willingness to address unionist concerns;
–an apology to the families and friends of non-combatants killed as a consequence of our actions.

This statement, which contained significant proposals to move the process forward, was given to the two governments on 13 April. They described it as positive, welcomed the obvious progress and said that the statement showed a clear desire to make the peace process work.

On 23 April, the British Prime Minister in a clear breach of protocol publicly misquoted aspects of our statement and went on to pose three questions. This and the subsequent word games have caused justifiable anger and annoyance.

Despite this the president of Sinn Fein responded in a clear and unambiguous way. His answers accurately reflected our position.

There is no lack of clarity. Our statement and the commitments contained in it was dependent on agreement involving the two governments, the UUP and Sinn Fein.

With regard to putting arms beyond use our representative met, several times, with the IICD. In order, in particular, to facilitate the UUP and to enhance the process to achieve agreement we made preparations for a quantity of munitions to be put beyond use.

In the event of agreement we were prepared to act immediately and our preparations were at an advanced stage.

Regrettably the two governments and the UUP rejected our statement and our initiatives.

Our 13 April statement has now been overtaken by events. We are placing it on the public record so that people can judge for themselves the significance of our proposed initiatives to advance the peace process.

P. O'Neill, Irish Republican Publicity Bureau

List of Abbreviations

CLMC: Combined Loyalist Military Command
DUP: Democratic Unionist Party
IICD: Independent International Commission on Decommissioning
INLA: Irish National Liberation Army
IRA: Irish Republican Army
LVF: Loyalist Volunteer Force
NIO: Northern Ireland Office
OTRs: Prisoners on the run
PIRA: Provisional Irish Republican Army
PSNI: Police Service of Northern Ireland
PUP: Progressive Unionist Party
RHC: Red Hand Commando
RHD: Red Hand Defenders
RIRA: 'Real' IRA
RUC: Royal Ulster Constabulary
SDLP: Social Democratic and Labour Party
UDA: Ulster Defence Association
UDP: Ulster Democratic Party
UFF: Ulster Freedom Fighters
UPRG: Ulster Political Research Group
UUP: Ulster Unionist Party
UVF: Ulster Volunteer Force

Index